BARGAIN HUNTERS' LONDON

Andrew Kershman

BARGAIN HUNTERS' LONDON

Written by Andrew Kershman
Additional research and writing by
Catherine Belonogoff and Susan Grossman
Cover photographs by Metro
Photography by Andrew Kershman
Edited by Abigail Willis
Maps by Lesley Gilmour
Design by Metro

Published in 2003 by
Metro Publications
PO Box 6336
London
N1 6PY

Printed and bound in India by Thomson Press Ltd

British Library Cataloguing in Publication Data.
A catalogue record for this book is available from the British Library.

ISBN 1 902910 15 X

Past Caring £20.00

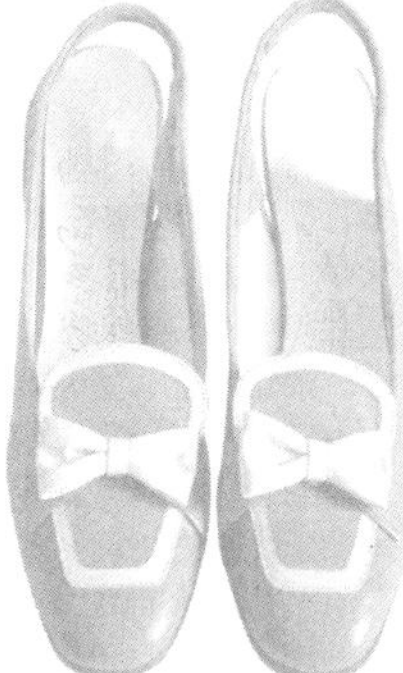

Beyond Retro £6.00

Susse Anderson £52.00
(RRP £75.00)

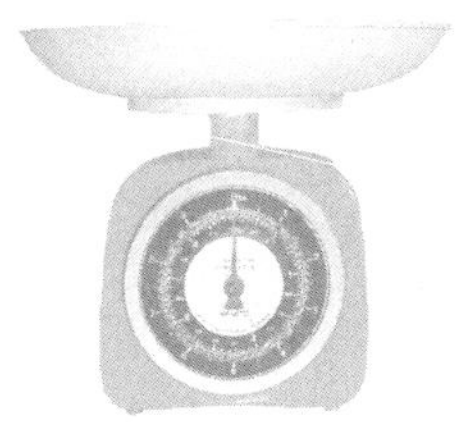

Brick Lane Market £3.00

ACKNOWLEDGEMENTS

It has been a huge and ongoing task updating the book, and I have been assisted in this by a small team of researchers whose dedication has proved invaluable in getting the job done. My thanks to Catherine Belonogoff and Susan Grossman for their help researching and writing this new edition. My colleagues at Metro, Susi Koch and Lesley Gilmour, have both been very supportive and have done an excellent job of creating the maps and making sure the book is well laid-out and organised. Thanks also go to my long standing editor, Abigail Willis, who has had the difficult task of translating my often confused text into readable English. Lastly I wish to express my gratitude to the many shop keepers who took time out to help me in my research, and to the many readers that have written with encouraging words and often useful suggestions for this new edition.

Salvation Army Charity Shop

CONTENTS

Designer Sale UK

INTRODUCTION

When this book was first published it was something of a leap in the dark as no similar publication existed at the time. Seven years later and having now completed the third edition, I am happy to report that Bargain Hunters' London has found a ready niche in the market as well as an enthusiastic readership.

For this third edition, the structure of the book remains the same but we have added sections on Architectural Salvage Yards and Furniture and greatly expanded the sections on Bikes and Photography – all great bargain hunting territories. A further improvement has been the addition of maps for Tottenham Court Road, and the Brick Lane area which in recent years has seen an explosion in the number of cheap and interesting shops on its streets.

People tend to fall into one of two camps when shopping; those who enjoy the experience and really like to rummage for bargains in unusual places and those who consider shopping a necessary chore. Bargain Hunters' London is designed to appeal to both groups. People who revel in the experience will probably be drawn to sections like Classic and Retro Clothing, Charity Shops, Markets and Car Boot Sales and they can pore over the maps which will allow them to plan a day's shopping. Those who hate even the thought of a shopping trip can simply use the index to find what they are looking for and will often be able to determine the cheapest price over the phone with the minimum of fuss.

Whichever camp you fall into this book will reward the enthusiastic reader or the casual user alike with lots of savings on anything from second-hand clothing to top quality curtains and even package holidays. The book is primarily about getting great value, but it is also written for those in search of original and quirky things and who appreciate the pleasure of shopping in independent shops with a unique atmosphere. Chain stores are often good value and many of the best are included here, but my main focus is on the small shops you can only find in London and this book will undoubtedly provide the reader with lots of new places to explore.

It has been great fun researching the new edition of this book and very gratifying to have received such positive feedback from shops who have had visitors brandishing the book. Letters from readers recommending new outlets were also very welcome and I have incorporated some of these shops in this new edition: keep those letters coming and happy bargain hunting!

Andrew Kershman
Hackney
e-mail: metro@dircon.co.uk

Clothing

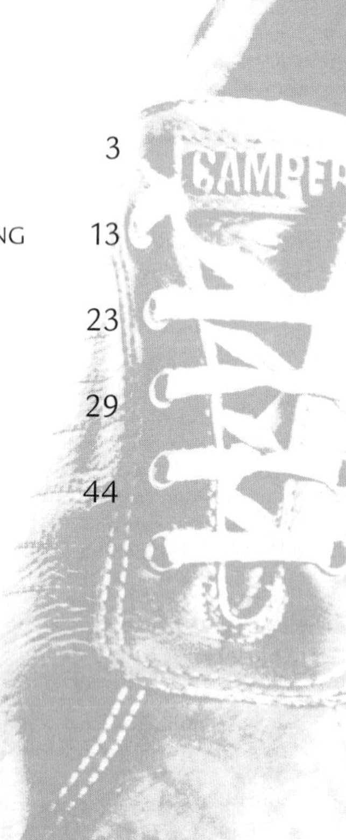

BASIC CLOTHING

Basic clothing is a catch-all phrase we have used to describe any clothing that does not carry a designer label and is not a classic or retro garment – in other words, everyday essentials like T-shirts, jeans and underwear. London is a great place to shop for this kind of casual clothing as it still has a fairly vibrant rag trade and clever designer copies from Eastern Europe and the Far East regularly feature in London shops, many of which are reviewed here. This book is generally very much in favour of small independent outlets, but in this chapter it has to be conceded that there are many High Street names that offer great value and the best of these are featured here too.

CENTRAL

Central Park

West One Shopping Centre
381 Oxford Street, W1
Tel: 020 7495 5097
Tube: Bond Street
Bus: 7. 8, 10, 25, 55, 73, 98, 176, 390
Open: Mon-Sat 9.30am-6pm, Sun 11am-5pm

Racks of rapidly changing women's clothing priced from £5 to £30. Bulk buying ensures massive discounts on both this season's and last season's fashions. They also sell bags and swimwear. *Also at: Muswell Hill, N10 (see North), and Ealing, W5 (see West)*

Discount Dressing

58 Baker Street, W1
Tel: 020 7486 7230
Tube: Baker Street
Bus: 2. 13, 30, 74, 82, 113, 139, 189, 274
Open: Daily 10am-6pm

This established chain of outlets has a professional team of buyers sourcing quality women's labels from manufacturers in France, Italy and Germany and sells direct to the public in the UK for up to 80% discount on the usual retail price. One of the most impressive aspects of shopping here is the range of sizes available (6-24), so people of all shapes and sizes will find something of interest. The rails contain all kinds of garments from casual to evening wear. 10% discount on production of this book.
Also at: 16 Sussex Ring, Woodside Park, Finchley N12, Tel: 020 8343 8343
The Galleria Outlet Centre, Hatfield, Hertfordshire, Tel: 01707 259 925

Factory Direct
17 Strutton Ground, SW1
Tel: 020 7799 2651
Tube: St. James's Park
Bus: 11, 24, 211, 148
Open: Mon-Fri 10am-6pm, Sat 11am-5pm
Small shop in a cobbled mews given over to a weekday market, opposite New Scotland Yard. They sell women's clothes direct from the factories that supply River Island, Karen Millen, French Connection, Top Shop, Miss Selfridge and the like. Labels are cut out but the stock is this season's. On offer when we visited were combat trousers for £11.99, linen trousers for £14.99 and all sorts of other bargains. Most prices were a good deal cheaper than in the High Street.

Om Shanti Om Ltd
6 Gees Court, St Christopher's Place, W1
Tel: 020 7409 7272
Tube: Bond Street
Bus: 3, 8, 25, 55, 176
Open: Mon-Sat 10am-7pm, Sun 11am-5pm
Clearance stock from Fenn Wright Mason from £15-£100. Other labels from £7-£40, including Lotus Leaf, their own brand.
Also at: Holloway Road N7 & Ballards Lane, Finchley N3 *(see North)*

Pink Soda
22 Eastcastle Street, W1
Tel: 020 7636 9001
Tube: Oxford Circus
Bus: 7, 8, 10, 25, 55, 73, 88, 98, 113, 137, 176, 390, 453
Open: Mon-Fri 10am-4pm
In the heart of what was once London's Rag Trade, a tiny wholesale shop with a fast turnover of trendy tops, skirts, accessories and whatever happens to be currently 'in'. They also have concessions in nearby Top Shop and Selfridges.

Stockhouse (UK) Ltd
310 High Holburn, WC1
Tel: 020 7430 1996
Tube: Chancery Lane
Bus: 8, 25, 242, 521
Open: Mon-Fri 9.30am-6pm
Women's clothing at discount prices with garments brought direct from the factories of manufacturers such as Wallis, Principles and Autonomy. Suits can be found from £35, trousers from £15, and bags from £5.

Beller's

Uniqlo
163-169 Brompton Road, SW3
Tel: 020 7584 8608
Tube: Knightsbridge
Bus: C1, 14, 74, 414
Open: Mon, Tues, Sat 10am-7pm, Wed, Thurs 10am-8pm, Sun 12-6pm
Japanese retail phenomenon meets British shopping. Basic, casual quality clothing at low prices for men, women and children. Good for outer-wear as well as tops and trousers and accessories.
Branches at: 84-86 Regent Street, W1 Tel: 020 7434 9688; 1 Lower George Street, Richmond TW9 Tel: 020 8948 7931; 51 The Broadway, Wimbledon SW19 Tel: 020 8944 8836

North

Beller's

193 Upper Street, N1
Tel: 020 7226 2322
Tube: Angel/Highbury & Islington
Bus: 4, 19, 30, 43
Open: Mon-Sat 9am-6pm (Thurs 9am-1pm)
This is the oldest shop in Islington and makes a pleasant change from the gift shops and cafés that predominate on Upper Street. Allan Shaw has been selling underwear and corsets to locals for the last 50 years and neither the shop nor the stock has changed much. It's a great place to get natural fibre underwear, lingerie, towels and some bedding. Long live double gussetted thermal long-johns, long live Beller's.

Central Park
152 Muswell Hill Broadway, N10
Tel: 020 8883 9122
Tube: Highgate
Bus: 43, 102, 134, 144, 234, 299, W7
Open: Mon-Sat 9.30am-6pm, Sun 11am-5pm
See main entry on page 9

Golds Factory Outlet
110-114 Golders Green Road, NW11 9
Tel: 020 8905 5721
Tube: Golders Green
Bus: 13, 82, 83, 183, 210, 245, 260, 268, 328
Open: Sun-Fri 10am-6pm
Rails and rails of cut-price men's suits. Top quality designs and fabrics at greatly reduced prices and a bargain suit rail offering 2 for £150, trousers from £15, and cashmere coats for £99. Attentive staff ensure you don't leave empty handed and the shop next door sells discounted shoes and boots for both men and women.

Factory Outlet
805 High Road, North Finchley, N12 8
Tel: 020 8445 2737
Tube: Woodside Park
Bus: 82, 125, 134, 221, 260, 263, 383
Open: Mon-Sat 9.30am-6pm
Women's street fashion with 'extras' and overstock from Gap, Topshop, French Connection and other High Street names with tops from £5, trousers from £10. The stock is always up-to-date in terms of style and colour and is aimed at the young and fashion conscious. A great place to get stylish street fashion on a budget. Also jogging gear.
Also at: 26 Topsfield Parade, Crouch End N8, Tel: 020 8341 9598

Fatto in Italia
16a Pratt Street, NW1
Tube: Camden Town, Mornington Crescent
Bus: 24, 29, 31, 46, 88, 134, 168, 214, 253, C2
Open: Mon-Sat 10.30am-7pm
Tiny shop offering good discounts (up to 40%) off Italian labels, including Dolce & Gabbana and Versace for men and women. The Italian owner regularly brings back what he can find in the way of bargains from Italy and stock changes rapidly. They also sell accessories.

FWM

474 Holloway Road, N7
Tel: 020 7263 8483
Tube: Holloway Road
Bus: 43, 153, 271, 277, 279
Open: Mon-Sat 9am-5pm

Recently opened outlet selling clearance stock from Fenn Wright and Mason. If you like the brand you will find this store well worth going out of your way for with jackets, trousers and suits from £15-£50.

Laurence Corner

62-64 Hampstead Road, NW1
Tel: 020 7813 1010
Tube: Warren Street
Bus: 24, 27, 29, 88, 134
Open: Mon-Sat 9.30am-6pm

This unassuming shop near the Euston Road has been selling ex-military and industrial clothing since 1953. Some years it comes into fashion and they're bombarded by fashion pundits wanting a 'retro' or 'combat' look, but mostly it's just a practical place to go if you're after the sort of gear that keeps soldiers and policemen warm. When we called in they had combat trousers from £20, green jackets at £24.75, sailors' hats for £9.88 and pure wool peaked caps for £10.95. There's also a bargain bucket to rummage in at £1.23 precisely! Lots of belts and bags. A fancy dress hire department upstairs offers period costume and possibly the best military uniform collection in the country (£45 for a week's hire).

Le Pop 2

83 Golders Green Road, NW11
Tel: 020 8455 1065
Tube: Golders Green
Bus: 13, 82, 83, 183, 210, 226, 240, 245, 260, 268, 328
Open: Mon-Sat 9am-7pm, Sun 10am-7pm

Trendy fashion items at rock-bottom prices. Le Pop 2 has a fast turnover of manufacturers' over-production and ends of lines at prices at least 50% less than any chain store. Brand-new, up-to-the-minute styles, with practically nothing over £10. DKNY t-shirts sell for £5, tracksuits and jeans £10, combat trousers £5, silk shirts £5, leather bags £5, shoes £5-£20, look-a-like Rolexes £5, and copy perfumes £3. There is new stock daily, plus a money back policy for returns within 7 days.
Also at: 459 High Road, Wembley HA9, Tel: 020 8900 9518

Lotus Leaf

480 Holloway Road, N7
Tel: 020 7272 8073
Tube: Holloway Road
Bus: 43, 153, 271
Open: Mon-Sat 9.30am-6pm, Sun 11am-5pm

Posh women's frocks and suits for weddings and christenings with all stock under £100. Fenn Wright Mason samples, and discounted prices on labels like Ralph Lauren, Progressive and Resources. They also have their own label, Lotus Leaf and offer reasonably priced linens.

Also at: 146 Crouch Hill, N8 Tel: 020 8348 7038

Matalan

See main entry on page 214

Monica

37-41 South End Road, NW3
Tel: 020 7794 3737
Tube: Belsize Park
Bus: 24, 46, 168, C11, 268
Open: Mon-Sat 10am-6pm, Sun 12noon-5pm

This twenty year old shop near Hampstead Heath is a bit of a local secret. Monica sells smart casual clothing mostly in linens, cottons and 100% raw silk. Everything is reasonably priced with linen separates at £38, silk cardigans from £25, and beaded sandals for £21.

Next to Choice

(9)

67 Golders Green Road, NW11
Tel: 020 8458 8247
Tube: Golders Green
Bus: 13, 82, 83, 183, 210, 226, 240, 245, 260, 268, 328
Open: Mon-Sat 9am-6pm, Sun 11am-5pm

End of season Next stock from shops and the Directory sold at half-price, with new stock arriving daily. Clothes and footwear for men, women and children.

Also at: Choice, Ealing Broadway, W5 (see West)

Om Shanti Om Ltd

470 Holloway Road, N7
Tel: 020 7561 1114
Tube: Holloway Road
Bus: 43, 153, 271
Open: Mon-Sat 9.30am-6pm

Outlet for clearance stock from various manufacturers at very cheap prices. Most clothes £10 or under with suits from £20-£30.
Branches at: St. Christophers Place W1 (see page 4) and 20 Ballards Lane, Finchley N3, Tel: 020 8371 9962

WEST

Atlantic

7

260 North End Road, SW6
Tel: 020 7381 5566
Tube: Fulham Broadway
Bus: 28, 74, 190, 391
Open: Mon-Sat 9am-6pm, Sun 11am-5pm
This chain of stores offers fashionable clothing, bought in bulk and sold at very low prices to assure a fast turnover. Trousers, tops and jackets from £10 and plenty to choose from at under £20. Well worth a visit for those looking for High Street fashion on a budget.
Branches all over London, including:
174 Kilburn High Road NW6; 32 High Road, Wood Green N22; 47 High Street, East Ham E6; 26 Rye Lane, Peckham SE15; 15 North Square, Lewisham SE13; 32 King's Mall, Hammersmith W6

Central Park

67 The Mall, W5
Tel: 020 8567 2250
Tube: Ealing Broadway
Bus: 83, 112, 207, 607, E11, E2, E8
Open: Mon-Sat 10am-7pm; Sun 11am-5pm
'Own-label' budget versions of top fashion at rock-bottom prices courtesy of production lines in the Far East and Eastern Europe. Knitwear, linen, jackets, jeans and whatever else is selling in the High Street, all priced at £10 or £15.
Branches at: Bond Street Tube Station, 9 Ealing Broadway W5, 152 Muswell Hill Broadway N10 and 10 London Road, Enfield, EN2

L.A.

11 Turnham Green Terrace, W4
Tel: 020 8995 4609
Tube: Turnham Green
Bus: E3, 27, 94, 190, 237, 267, 272, 391, 440,
Open: Mon-Sat 10am-6pm, Sun 11am-5pm
A great shop, popular with local men looking for good value casual clothing (lots of French Connection and other High Street labels). They also sell end of lines with tops starting from £10 and trousers from £20.

MK One
28 Queensway, W2
Tel: 020 7229 2847
Tube: Bayswater
Bus: 7, 12, 23, 27, 70, 94,
Open: Daily 10am-10pm
Up to date fashion for women at the lowest possible prices from £5 to £25 for tops, trousers and jackets. The stock is fast changing stock and some branches have accessories and sell smaller sizes (6-14) in their Sophie Teenwear range.
Also at: 192 Uxbridge Road, Shepherds Bush W12, 20 The Broadway, W. Ealing W13, 420 Brixton Road SW9, 468 Holloway Road N7

Choice
Unit 11, Arcadia Centre, Ealing Broadway, W5
Tel: 020 8567 2747
Tube: Ealing Broadway
Bus: 83, 112, 207, 607, E11, E2, E8
Open: Mon-Sat 9.30am-6pm (Thurs till 7pm), Sun 11am-5pm
End of season Next stock from Next Stores and Next Directory sold at half the usual price. Stock includes fashion, footwear and accessories for women, men and children. New stock arrives daily.

Primark
1 King's Mall, King Street, W6
Tel: 020 8748 7119
Tube: Hammersmith
Bus: 27, 190, 267, 391, H91
Open: Mon-Sat 9am-6pm, Sun 11am-5pm
One of the newest and largest branches of this retail chain of stores that started life in Ireland to provide good quality, good value clothing for men, women, children and babies. Attractive street cred clothes and lingerie at incredibly low prices: basic trousers and jeans (£8), lacy bras (£5), sweatshirts (£5). Also swimwear, shoes and bags. Some named brands like Umbro and Puma.
Other branches at: East Ham E6, Hackney E8, Kilburn NW6, Leytonstone E11, Peckham SE15, Wandsworth SW18, Woolwich SE18

SOUTH

331

331 Garrett Lane, SW18
Tel: 020 8870 6638
Rail: Earlsfield
Bus: 44, 77, 270
Open: Mon-Sat 11am-7pm, closed Wed

331 sell quality leather jackets, coats and trousers to their own designs. New leather jackets start from £95, new leather trousers from £75 and full-length leather and buckskin coats from £180. Fully padded bikers gear costs £200. They also offer great value vintage and recycled leathers and sheepskins and a good stock of Hawaiian shirts based on original 1940s designs. 331 have a bespoke, repair and alterations service. On Saturday and Sunday they run a stall in Camden Lock Market.

EAST

Benny Dee (City) Ltd

74-80 Middlesex Street, Liverpool Street, E1
Tel: 020 7377 9067
Tube: Liverpool Street / Aldgate
Bus: 42, 67, 78, 100, 344
Open: Mon-Fri 9.30am-5.30pm, Sun 10am-4pm
Also at Walthamstow High Street, E17

This no frills shop sells clothing and underwear for women with a more limited stock for men and children kept in the basement. Among the good deals were women's leather boots for only £9.99, T-shirts reduced to 99p and well-made women's cotton/lycra mix slacks for only £6.99. They have a particularly vast stock of women's lingerie ranging from the everyday to the kinky. In the basement could be found a three-pack of men's cotton underpants for only £2.99 and baby grows for 99p. There are no facilities for trying things on in the shops themselves. If they don't fit you have to bring the goods back within two weeks with a receipt if you want a refund.

Other shops with the same name and with similar stock but different (family) owners at:
110-114 Kilburn High Road NW6, Tel: 020 7624 2995 and at Wood Green N22, Tel: 020 8881 8101

Brute Menswear Clearance
73 Wentworth Street, E1
Tube: Aldgate East/Liverpool Street
Bus: 42, 67, 78, 100, 344
Open: Mon-Fri 9.30am-6pm, Sun 9am-3pm
This outlet is good for fashionable men's tops and also has a more limited selection of trousers. There are lots of tops for £10 or less with a few items reduced to clear for only a fiver. The designs and colours are more suited to the younger generation, but if you are young or young at heart this is a useful place to stock up on casual wear.

Mordex

222 Brick Lane, E1
Tel: 020 7729 7550
Tube: Aldgate East
Bus: 8, 35, 47, 67, 78, 253
Open: Mon-Fri 10am-6pm, Sun 10am-3pm
Another good outlet along Brick Lane offering great value leathers at considerable discounts to members of the pubic. A basic leather box jacket can be found here for £90-£130. They also stock a range of other leather garments including leather trousers for £90.

New Look (London) Ltd
226 Brick Lane, E1
Tel: 020 7739 8844
Tube: Aldgate East
Bus: 8, 35, 47, 67, 78, 253
Open: Mon-Fri 10.15am-6pm, Sat 10am-5pm, Sun 9am-5pm
This leatherwear importers offers a friendly welcome to members of the public and has plenty of great value leather jackets for as little as £59.99. Three quarter length leather jackets were reduced from £160 to £120 on a recent visit, and staff are willing to barter on most items.

Truth Trading Ltd

151 Brick Lane, E1
Tel: 020 7729 0825
Tube: Aldgate East/Shoreditch
Bus: 8, 35, 47, 67, 78, 253
Open: Daily 10.30am-6pm
This is a no-nonsense wholesale outlet that specialises in all kinds of leather jackets and is prepared to sell to members of the public directly. There are lots of leathers to choose from with short boxy leather jackets starting from £30. Their main line is fashionable Tuscan sheepskin coats with fur lining, the full-length version of which sells for £1,200 in West End stores, but can be bought here for only £450.

Classic & Retro Clothing

Beyond Retro

Central

Blackout II
51 Endell Street, London, WC2
Tel: 020 7240 5006
Website: www.blackout2.com
Tube: Covent Garden
Bus: 19, 24, 29, 38, 176
Open: Mon-Fri 11am-7pm, Sat 11.30am-6.30pm
This cramped little shop specialising in the 1930s and 1940s is where stylish men and women go to find charming partywear and elegant day clothes. Downstairs in the basement, 1940s day dresses go for £20 to £30. A wool camelhair coat from the 1950s that would look at home in the High Street today cost just £69. Besides all the wonderful clothes (a lot of which are imported from the United States), there is a good stock of shoes, handbags, clip-on earrings, necklaces made from exotically coloured plastics and chic, oversized sunglasses.

Cenci

31 Monmouth Street, WC2
Tel: 020 7836 1400
Tube: Covent Garden
Bus: 14, 19, 24, 29, 38, 176
Open: Mon-Sat 11am-6pm

The whole family can get kitted out here in retro Italian style. Men will find handsome suits from £75 with old-fashioned hats to match from £30. Downstairs women's dresses and children's clothes vie for space. Women's cotton shorts cost £14 and there are plenty of two-toned, modish dresses and even retro, one-piece swimsuits. An excellent place to relive or discover the 50s and 60s.

Also at: 4 Nettleford Place SE27, Tel: 020 8766 8564

Pop Boutique

6 Monmouth Street, WC2
Tel: 020 7497 5262
Tube: Covent Garden
Bus: 14, 19, 24, 29, 38, 176
Open: Mon-Sat 11am-7pm, Sun 12am-5pm

This great little shop in Covent Garden is a magnet for the fashionable in search of good value retro clothing. The turnover of clothes is fast and furious and the garments are well chosen, often very unusual and usually originating from the 60s or 70s – although they do have a small selection of clothes from the 1950s. Among the good deals were cords for £22, a great selection of short sleeve shirts for £12 and classic denim jackets for £45. As well as clothing the shop has a small selection of nick-nacks from the 1970s including on a recent visit, colourful retro ashtrays and that funny musical instrument promoted by Ralf Harris. This shop is popular with Japanese tourists, but it is also possible to spot the occasional pop star rummaging for unusual garments.

Radio Days

87 Lower Marsh, SE1
Tel: 020 7928 0800
Tube: Waterloo
Bus: 12, 53, 76, 159, 211, 341, 381
Open: Mon-Sat 9.30am-6pm

Upon entering this atmospheric shop, customers are greeted by items for the home from the 1920s to the 1960s, everything from a shiny black old-fashioned refrigerator to a myriad of smoking and drinking paraphernalia. They also stock vintage radios, magazines, kitschy artwork and antique underwear in its original packaging. A 1950s white lace wedding dress in excellent condition cost £125, while racks and racks of men's suits carried prices from £55 to £75. The sale rack slashes prices by half.

Worn Out West
14-16 Mercer Street, WC2
Tel: 020 7379 5334
Tube: Covent Garden
Bus: 14, 19, 24, 29, 38, 176
Open: Mon-Sat 11.30am-7pm
Split between two shops on one of Covent Garden's deserted back alleys, Worn Out West caters to both men and women with new and used retro clothing. Upmarket High Street labels are much in evidence with a stripey Joseph sundress costing £20 and a grey embroidered Karen Millen silk sweater priced at just £15. Men's Hawaiian shirts cost from £12 and combat jackets go for £25, while shoes such as Nike trainers or Office mules cost from £25. The stock is arranged in an orderly fashion and the staff let customers get on with browsing without interfering.

What The Butler Wore
131 Lower Marsh, SE1
Tel: 020 7261 1353
Tube: Waterloo
Bus: 12, 53, 76, 159, 211, 341, 381
Open: Mon-Sat 10.30am-6pm
This funky little shop brings Swinging London to life much better than Austin Powers ever could. Authentic 1950s, 1960s and 1970s clothes (all helpfully labelled) fill the racks and, to complement the clothes, the shop's vibe is totally in tune with the past – right down to the dummies and the hip staff dressed in 60s gear. Impressive original tops from Biba and Mary Quant start at £10; men can find slim-line 60s suits from £25. The record department downstairs houses the swinging tunes to accompany the swinging duds.

NORTH

Delta of Venus
151 Drummond Street, NW1
Tel: 020 7387 3037
Tube: Euston/Warren Street
Bus: 18, 24, 27, 29, 30, 88, 134
Open: Mon-Fri 11am-7pm, Sat 11am-6pm
Off the well-beaten path of nearby Tottenham Court Road, Delta of Venus is a shrine to 60s and 70s pop culture. The attention to detail and excellent well-ordered displays make for good browsing and pleasurable purchasing. Shoppers might spend a fiver on a vintage t-shirt or a tenner on a busy, multicoloured 60s blouse. A must for lovers of the 1960s.

Ember
Arch 59, The Stables, Camden, NW1
Tel: 020 8578 0346
Tube: Camden Town
Bus: 24, 27, 31, 168, 214
Open: Mon-Fri 12.30pm-6pm, Sat, Sun 10am-6pm
Relocated from Portobello, Ember sells retro clothes and the biggest bargains are to be found in its capacious basement. Look out for funky 70s shirts as well as more classic items like suits.

Henry & Daughter
17-18 Camden Lock Place, Middle Yard, Chalk Farm Road, NW1
Tel: 020 7284 3302
Tube: Chalk Farm
Bus: 24, 27, 31, 168
Open: Tues-Sun 10am-6pm
Tucked away on the first floor of Camden Lock, Henry & Daughter stocks classic and vintage clothing with leather jackets starting from just £35 and excellent vintage dresses for £25. As a sister business, they also make made-to-measure wedding dresses with prices starting at £550.

Modern Age Vintage Clothing

65 Chalk Farm Road, NW1
Tel: 020 7482 3787
Website: www.modern-age.co.uk
Tube: Chalk Farm
Bus: 24, 27, 31, 168
Open: Mon-Sat 10am-6pm

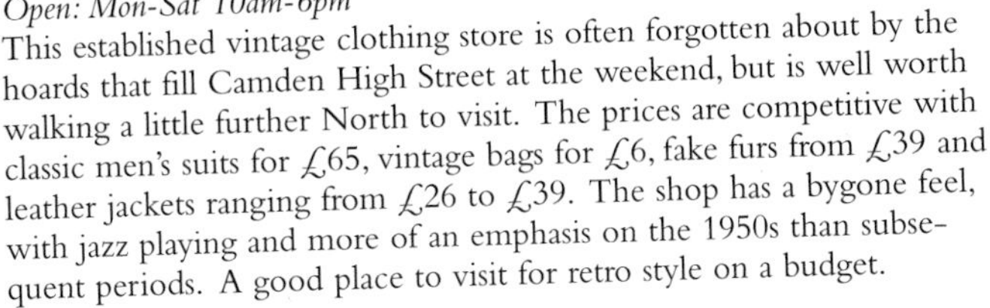

This established vintage clothing store is often forgotten about by the hoards that fill Camden High Street at the weekend, but is well worth walking a little further North to visit. The prices are competitive with classic men's suits for £65, vintage bags for £6, fake furs from £39 and leather jackets ranging from £26 to £39. The shop has a bygone feel, with jazz playing and more of an emphasis on the 1950s than subsequent periods. A good place to visit for retro style on a budget.

Ribbons & Taylor

157 Stoke Newington Church Street, N16
Tel: 020 7254 4735
Rail: Stoke Newington
Bus: 67, 73, 106, 149, 243, 318
Open: Tues-Sat 11am-6pm

This well-established retro clothing store always looks good with a carefully arranged window display and neatly organised, clearly priced stock. Among the bargains were funky men's shirts for £8-£15, jeans from £16 and lots of leather jackets to choose from for £20-£32. They have also expanded the range of women's retro shoes for £15-£20, and have a great selection of reasonably priced chunky new jewellery. Ribbons & Taylor caters primarily for women, but there is enough here to detain the male of the species for a while. For committed bargain hunters there are usually a few discount rails with garments reduced to clear.

Rokit

225 Camden High Street, NW1
Tel: 020 7267 3046
Tube: Camden Town
Bus: 24, 27, 29, 31, 88, 168, 214
Open: Mon-Fri 10am-6.30pm, Sat-Sun 10am-7pm

This Camden institution is deceptively large with a sizeable ground floor and a smaller first floor well stocked with retro and second-hand clothing. Although generally expensive, its high turnover of goods means that anything that doesn't sell is marked down. It's worth having a sniff around, you might unearth a bargain.

Also at: 101-107 Brick Lane E1, Tel: 020 7375 3864

162
162 Holloway Road, N7
Tel: 020 7700 2354
Tube: Holloway Road
Bus: 17, 43, 271, 277
Open: Mon-Sat 10am-6pm, Sun 11am-6pm
This deceptively large shop has a keen following among the student population of North London who are drawn by cheap, retro clothing with lots of discounts. The clothes are imported from thrift stores in the US and are therefore not always washed and ironed as in other fancy retro stores, but they are very cheap. Among the bargains were jeans for £5-£7, denim jackets for £10, classic suits for £20 and leather jackets for £15-£25. As well as being generally very good value they also have lots of discounted rails with all items at half the marked price, and other items on rails and in boxes outside for £1. A great bargain shop.

WEST

Boo's Closet
198 Kensington Park Road, W11 (4)
Tel: 020 7221 3002
Tube: Ladbroke Grove/Notting Hill Gate
Bus: 7, 23, 52, 70
Open: Wed-Sat 10.30am-6pm

Boo's Closet

Pam has been running this well-stocked little shop for years. There are lots of great clothes here from the eccentric to the classic as well as accessories and jewellery. The prices are also very low with belts starting from £2 and handbags from £4.50.

The 1920s-1970s Crazy Clothes Connection

134 Lancaster Road, W11
Tel: 020 7221 3989
Tube: Ladbroke Grove
Bus: 7, 23, 52, 70
Open: Tues-Sat 11am-7pm

A great family-run shop with lots of collectable clothing. The prices are competitive and there are a few rare garments among the rails. The shop also offers a hire service.

Old Hat

66 & 43A Fulham High Street, SW6
Tel: 020 7610 6558
Tube: Putney Bridge
Bus: 39, 85, 93, 265, 270
Open: Mon-Sat 11am-7pm, Sun 1.30pm-7pm

Simply the best gentlemen's vintage clothing shop in London by virtue of its low prices and comprehensive stock. The owner is an expert on men's tailoring and can readily date a suit and even name its maker. Suits cost £30 for an off the peg two-piece going up to £100 for a bespoke three-piece from a Savile Row tailor. There is an excellent selection of shoes, priced £15-£60, and all the details to complete your outfit can be found at good prices. The shop across the road at 43A has formal wear, with evening suits from£70.

TNT

14 Jerdan Place, SW6
Tel: 020 7385 2062
Tube: Fulham Broadway
Bus: 11, 14, 28, 211, 295, 391
Open: Daily 11am-6pm

This shop is a refuge for all kinds of funky clothing from the 60s and 70s. Those who want to dress like Marc Bolan will find original flares for £10-£25, shirts and blouses with huge collars and tight sleeves are £8-£15 and dresses start at £15, going up to £50 for a few rarities. Those of a tougher disposition will find full-length leather coats for £40-£65, while biker jackets are £30-£50. The only major changes to the store in recent years have been the addition of retro jewellery which takes pride of place in a glass cabinet and ranges in price from £5 to £50, and the Sunday opening. A great retro store.

Bertie Wooster
284 Fulham Road, SW10
Tel: 020 7352 5662
Website: www.bertie-wooster.co.uk
Tube: Fulham Broadway
Bus: 14, 211
Open: Mon, Wed, & Fri 10am-6pm, Tues & Thurs 10am-7pm, Sat 10am-5pm

Bertie Wooster is not a bargain clothing shop, but it does carry some second-hand items. The shop's main purpose is to purvey classic gent's tailoring for less than Savile Row (a made-to-measure suit would go for £395). So, if it's quality you're after, drop by to check out their second-hand tweed jackets (£95) and suits (£110-£140 for a two-piece, £125-£155 for a three-piece). New shirts are a bargain at £15-£22 each. All the gentleman's accoutrements from flasks to cufflinks are also sold.

Retro Man & Retro Woman
32 & 34 Pembridge Road, W11
Tel: 020 7598 2233 / 020 7792 1715
Tube: Notting Hill Gate
Bus: 12, 31, 94
Open: Daily 10am-8pm

Part of the chain started by the Record and Tape Exchange on Notting Hill Gate, these shops stock second-hand and new clothing and accessories. The men's shop at number 34 has a bargain basement with items selling for £5. Retro Woman has a good selection of dresses, skirts and jackets at reasonable prices as well as garments to clear for £5. It's all very laidback and groovy, and you might just find that perfect item.

SOUTH

The Emporium
330-332 Creek Road, Greenwich, SE10
Tel: 020 8305 1670
Website: www.emporiumoriginals.com
Rail/DLR: Greenwich
Tube: Island Gardens
Bus: 177, 180, 188, 199, 286, 386
Open: Wed-Sun 10.30am-6pm

The sleek wooden floor and jazz music playing in the background lend the Emporium a classic feel and the clothes follow suit. There are plenty of sophisticated outfits as well as a few things like jeans from £20 and safari shirts at £25. Women can find beautiful 1940s, 1950s, and 1960s suits for £35, coats for £50 and dresses for £20. Drawers of underwear and shoes with the original boxes complete the offerings.

The Observatory
20 Greenwich Church Street, SE10
Tel: 020 8305 1998
Rail/DLR: Greenwich
Bus: 177, 180, 188, 199, 286, 386
Open: Daily 10am-6pm
Looking more like a trendy boutique, the sleek, white Observatory stocks four decades of fashion styles over two floors. To help out the newly hip, the shop has thoughtfully provided giant posters with definitions of the 20th century's major styles from rockers and psychedelics to mods and beats. All the clothes to complete the various looks are on the rails – each item dry cleaned to perfection. Men's suits go for £30 to £80 and 1950s summer dresses cost £20. New kitsch accessories and trendy household goods are also sold.

EAST

Beyond Retro (11)
112 Cheshire Street, E2
Tel: 020 7613 3636
Website: www.beyondretro.com
Tube: Liverpool Street, Bethnal Green or Shoreditch
Bus: 8, 25, 35, 47, 67, 78
Open: Daily 10am-6pm

Beyond Retro is a massive warehouse with an equally impressive range of retro clothing. The space is so large that it has its own lounge area with sofa and coffee table. Pick up a zip-up Addidas tops for £15, or a denim jacket for £6. There are 100's of jeans to choose from for £5-£10, a wide selection of leather goods with jackets for £10-25, unusual sculptured bags for £7, and groovy 70s shirts from £6. There are also rare items like vintage 1950s dresses and an original Levi jacket from the 1930s which takes pride of place on the wall. Although Beyond Retro is a little isolated at the far end of Cheshire Street, even on a quiet Friday afternoon there are about 20 trendies rummaging among its rails. If you are a committed bargain hunter look out for the many discount rails and bargain bins that are always kept well stocked with garments reduced to clear. The Brick Lane area is now developing into something of a magnet for the fashionable with lots of good cafes in the area if you fancy a snack while inspecting your new purchases.

The Laden Showroom
103 Brick Lane, E1
Tel: 020 7247 2431
Website: www.laden.co.uk
Tube: Aldgate East/Liverpool Street
Bus: 8, 25, 35, 47, 67, 78
Open: Mon-Sat 12noon-6pm, Sun 10.30am-6pm

This outlet acts as a showcase for young designers who pay for a concession within the store. Among the rails we found a great Paul Ashley top for £35, as well as a milliner offering a range of fashionable hats from just £18. The vintage clothing concession also turned up some real finds, including a very funky hide coat for £95. If your budget is more limited look out for the many cut-price items and boxes of clothes for even greater discounts.

Rokit
101 & 107 Brick Lane, E1
Tel: 020 7375 3864
Website: www.rokit.com
Tube: Aldgate East/Liverpool Street
Bus: 8, 25, 35, 47, 67, 78
Open: Mon-Fri 10.30am-6.30pm, Sat-Sun 10am-7pm

Rokit are an established part of Camden High Street and have now expanded to these two large outlets on Brick Lane. Always trendy, the shop strives for an industrial look with its stone floors, steel counters and scaffolding rails. The shop sells their own label, customised clothes and a mix of second-hand clothing from Hawaiian shirts for £20-£25, leather belts £6-£8 and jeans for about £20. On a recent visit there was a very funky classic bomber jacket with fur collar for only £20. A welcome addition to Brick Lane and just opposite the excellent café, Coffee @ Brick Lane.

Thea

120 Bethnal Green Road, E2
Tel: 020 7729 8671
Tube: Liverpool Street
Bus: 8, 25, 35, 47, 67, 78
Open: Daily 11am-7pm (times may vary)

This small corner shop is located at the top of Brick Lane and has a good selection of retro clothes including 70s shirts for around £8, a Fred Perry wool top for £10 and a cord jacket for a mere £16. My favourite garment was a bright orange, full-length, 60s dress which looked like something out of "Abigail's Party" – a kitsch bargain at £28.

DESIGNER SALES

If your taste runs to the glamorous and expensive but your wallet doesn't, then the London-based designer sales are for you. Geared mostly towards women's fashion, there are a few for men. In any event, be prepared to wait in long lines to pay, to forgo the luxury of a dressing room and to jostle with the crowds for the best deals. In most cases, you must sign up on a mailing list to find out about the sales. A few charge admission.

Designer Sale UK

CENTRAL

Designer Showroom Sale

53 Wells Street, 5 Bywell Place, London, W1
Tel: 020 7580 5075
Tube: Oxford Circus
Women's Fashion

Importers and wholesalers BLD run end-of-season and sample sales from their showroom four times a year. Find Marina Rinaldi, MaxMara and Passport amongst other labels for women here. Join their mailing list to be kept apprised of sales.

Jasper Conran Showroom

Tel: 020 7717 8440
Men's fashion

This showroom hosts sporadic sales of Jasper Conran men's clothing, both samples and end-of-season stock. There are great bargains to be found here, but it is not well publicised. Give them a call to find out about the next sale and put your name on their mailing list.

Louis Féraud

23 Old Bond Street, W1
Tel: 020 7518 8440
E-mail: feraudsales@btopenworld.com
Women's Fashion

French designs for seriously upmarket style, this showroom hosts end-of-season sales of its women's wear and accessories. If you're interested, e-mail them to join their mailing list.

Oakville

Fifth Floor, 32-36 Great Portland Street, W1
Tel: 020 7580 3686
Women's Fashion

Shop for Fendi and Ungaro at this fashion showroom where shoppers will find women's casual and dressy clothing at well below High Street prices. In order to be invited to preview sales, you need to get your name on the mailing list.

Wahl Fashions
97 New Bond Street, W1
Tel: 020 7499 4000
E-mail: sales@wahlfashions.co.uk
Women's Fashion
Women's designer clothing from Plein Sud, C'est Duo and Beppe Bondi as well as other labels are put on sale twice a year, usually in April and October. Prices are usually 50% less than the retail price. Phone or e-mail to join the mailing list and to find out where the sales are held.

NORTH

David Charles
2-4 Thanes Works,
Thane Villas, N7
Tel: 020 7609 4797
Childrenswear
David Charles holds spring and winter sales of their childrenswear at their showroom in Finsbury Park. The clothes cater for children from 2-16 years old and the prices are well below those found in the High Street. Phone to be put on the mailing list.

The Designer Warehouse Sales
The Worx, 45 Balfe Street, N1
Tel: 020 7704 1064
Website: www.dwslondon.co.uk
Tube: King's Cross
Entrance fee: £2
Open: 12 times a year for three-day sessions, phone for details
Women's and Men's Fashion
Held in a massive photographer's studio twelve times a year over three-day periods (one for each sex), this is the daddy of the London sales. Be ready to paw through racks and racks of high-fashion clothing from makers like Alberta Ferretti, Vivienne Westwood and Mandarina Duck. Local designers are also featured. The place is always busy with fashionable punters sifting through the racks in search of bargains, while funky music is played and staff rush around helping things run smoothly. There are plenty of garments and accessories to be found here to suit every pocket with lots of smaller items for a tenner or less, so no one need leave empty handed. Turn up with enthusiasm, energy and cash to pick up this season's designer labels at about 60% less than retail.

Jacques Vert
Windsmoor House, 83 Lawrence Road, N15
Tel: 020 8800 8022
Website: www.jacques-vert.co.uk
Women's Fashion
For grown-up, ladylike clothes such as boxy jackets and sequinned tops, Jacques Vert's seasonal warehouse sales are good. Labels include Dannimac, Précis Petite and Windsmoor and prices are 50% off regular prices so you could walk out with a skirt for £35 instead of £70. These are not high-fashion clothes, but rather wearable, unpretentious and dignified. Phone Windsmoor on 0845 355 5445 to be put on the mailing list.

WEST

Ghost Ltd
263 Kensal Road, W10
Tel: 020 8960 3121
Website: www.ghost.co.uk
Women's Fashion
Elegant, ethereal, avant-garde fashion is the forte of this local design house. Usually out of reach for bargain hunters, Ghost's floaty dresses, baggy pants and loose tops are put on sale here at the beginning of December. Shop for slight seconds, samples and end-of-season stock all at a discount. Contact them to put your name on their mailing list.

London Fashion Weekend
Duke of York Headquarters, King's Road, SW3
Tel: 0871 222 3214
Entrance fee: £8.50 (book in advance); £12 (at the door)
Men's and Women's Fashion
After the exclusive London Fashion Week, the fashion élite throw open their doors to the public for a weekend of shopping. Find designer clothing and accessories aplenty at seriously reduced prices. Most London designers are here from Jasper Conran to Philip Treacy with plenty of smaller labels represented too. Besides the fashion, there's also the lifestyle – with delicious food, pampering beauty treatments and other little luxuries on offer to help you part with your money. If you've got the energy and the dedication, you can find some unique pieces for lower than regular prices here.

SOUTH

The British Designers Sale

42 York Mansions, Prince of Wales Drive, SW11
Tel: 020 7228 5314
Open: Five times a year for women; twice a year for men
Men's and Women's Fashion
Chelsea Old Town Hall is the venue for this massive gathering. Since this is run by an umbrella organisation, there are many agents selling designer labels at competitive prices. All garments are at least 50% off and some are as much as 80% off the retail price. Despite the name, this long established designer sale offers labels from all over Europe. There are two men's sales in June and December, which are open to all, and five women's sales requiring membership, which costs £32 per year or £5 for entry just on the Saturday.

EAST

Designer Sale UK

The Old Truman Brewery Complex, Brick Lane, E1
Tel: 01273 470 880
Website: www.designersales.co.uk
Open: Five sales per year in February, March-April, May, September and November-December. Each sale lasts four days from Thursday to Sunday with Wednesday reserved for mailing list customers.
Contact name: Ellain Foster
Entrance fee: £2
Men and Women's Fashion
This long-established designer sale has become a regular event on now fashionable Brick Lane in East London. The space used for the sale is large enough to display 100's of rails holding clothing from over 50 designer labels and all at substantial discounts. The atmosphere of the sales is great with lots of attractive, fashionable people, milling between the rails and often emerging with a mountain of clothing in their arms. On a recent visit bargains included an Artemesia summer skirt for £19 (reduced from £59), a well-cut leather jacket from RB for £30 (reduced from £170) and funky Duffer of St George shirts for £26 (reduced from £85). Among the other labels featured were Burro, D&G, Armani and Vivienne Westwood. For those on a limited budget there are always cheaper items such as fashionable T-shirts reduced from £39 to only £10, so no-one need return empty-handed. Phone the office number to get on the mailing list.

Permanent Designer Outlets

Comfort and Joy

109 Essex Road, N1
Tel: 020 7359 3898
Tube: Angel / Highbury & Islington
Bus: 38, 56, 73, 341
Open: Mon-Sat 10.30am-6pm

Comfort and Joy sell their own range of funky, casual womenswear for a very reasonable price. The clothes are exceptionally well-made and have a real attention to detail. Among the garments was an oriental style satin jacket for £45, and an original pair of denim trousers was the same price. The accessories are even better value with a wide choice of bags and rucksacks for £12-£15, and fashionable sunglasses for £9.50 a pair.

Della Finch Designer Sales

75 Wilton Road, SW1
Tel: 020 7233 6385
Tube: Victoria
Bus: 11, 24, 211, 239, C1, C10
Open: Mon-Thurs 10am-5.30pm, Fri-Sat 10am-7pm

Eager shoppers don't have to wait for the annual sales of other outlets since this outlet offers bargains all year round on big labels like Armani, Moschino and Versace. Catering for both men and woman, the huge selection and excellent range of sizes promises something for everyone and even super budget shoppers should find something on the £5 rack. Add your name to the mailing list to be informed of new developments.

Mad Fashion Bitch

87 Goldsmiths Road, E2
Tel: 020 7729 8114
Website: www.madfashionbitch.com
Tube: Old Street
Bus: 26, 48, 55
Open: Sat-Sun 11am-5pm

This groovy little shop sells its own women's fashion label as well as a number of other small independent designers. Colourful blouses made from natural fibres are great value at £45. Another designer intricately customises military shirts that are well worth the £45 asking price. The shop also sells a range of hand knitted children's tops under the label Mad Fashion Titch for the very reasonable price of £5 per top. As well as new designer labels, the shop also has vintage clothing, shoes and accessories and an extensive selection of vintage jewellery from £1-£35. On Sundays Columbia Road Flower Market is 5 minutes walk from here.

DRESS AGENCIES

Dress agencies are brilliant places to find second-hand designer clothing as well as big name bags, shoes and accessories. They are also an excellent way of recouping money for garments that you no longer wear, with agencies usually splitting the sale price 50/50 with sellers. Many agencies only cater for women, but there are a few who carry clothing for men and children, enabling the skillful bargain hunter to pick up stylish deals for the whole family under one roof. Although the stock consists largely of other people's cast-offs this is no indication of their quality as most agencies will not even consider clothes that are more than two years old and the smarter ones will only accept top names. Other agencies are more laid-back and will take High Street labels like Jigsaw, Kookai and Gap. Reviewed within this chapter are over 40 of the Capital's best dress agencies from long established shops like Designs on Her (see page 32) to relative newcomers like Bang, Bang (see page 30). The savings you can make at these shops are considerable and with a bit of effort you can emerge with some top quality designer gear for a fraction of the original price.

Dress for Less

CENTRAL

Bang Bang

(Women's Clothing Exchange)
21 Goodge Street, W1
Tel: 020 7631 4191
Tube: Goodge Street
Bus: 10, 24, 29, 73, 134
Open: Mon-Fri 10am-6.30pm, Sat 11am-6pm

This funky little shop with its furry sofa and scarlet decor is different from most dress agencies, catering as it does for the young and young at heart and offering a good selection of clothing from cheap street fashion to exclusive designer labels. On a recent visit could be found a Relaxed Denim Skirt for a modest £8, a very sexy pair of Gucci high heels for £90 and a Matthew Williamson two-piece suit for £180. The glass counters at the front of the shop display lots of interesting jewellery with rings starting at £5 and brooches from £6. The exchange policy here is also simple and original with cash paid for clothes, or clients allowed to spend double the cash amount in the shop. A definite must for fashionable bargain hunters.

Catwalk

52 Blandford Street, W1
Tel: 020 7935 1052
Tube: Baker Street
Bus: 2, 13, 30, 74, 82, 113, 139, 274, 189
Open: Mon 12.30pm-6pm, Tues-Fri 11.15am-6pm, Sat 11.15am-5pm

This small boutique is packed full of funky gear from the top end of the High Street like Whistles to carefully selected designer labels. Maharishi trousers were £80 (retail at £300), a Marni top was £60, and a Chanel jacket £399 (sells at £1,200). Also Prada shoes and Chanel bags. L'Homme Designer Exchange for men is next door.

Dress for Less

(2)

391 St. John Street, EC1
Tel: 020 7713 5591
Tube: Angel
Bus: 4, 30, 73, 153, 214, 274, 394
Open: Mon-Wed 11.30am-5.30pm, Thurs 11.30am-2pm, Fri 11.30am-6pm, Sat 11.30am-4.30pm

Small, well-organised shop that caters for a youngish clientele of both sexes on the look out for High Street (Jigsaw, Karen Millen, Whistles) and designer (Prada, Chanel, Gucci) labels, bags, hats and accessories. Jimmy Choo shoes and boots. Prices range from £20 to £400.

The Exchange, Belgravia

30 Elizabeth Street, SW1
Tel: 020 7730 3334
Tube: Victoria
Bus: C1, C10, 11, 211, 239,
Open: Mon-Sat 9.30am-5.30pm, Thurs 10am-6pm

Non-profit making dress agency with proceeds donated to National Kidney Research Fund. Designer and High Street labels, hats, handbags and shoes discarded by local ladies. Moderate prices range from £20-£200. Also new 'designer samples' from Italy.

L'Homme Designer Exchange

50 Blandford Street, W1
Tel: 020 7224 3266
Tube: Baker Street
Bus: 2, 13, 30, 74, 82, 113, 139, 189, 274
Open: Mon-Thurs 11am-6pm, Fri 11.30am-6pm, Sat 11am-5pm

A small, well-established boutique with big names in designerwear for men only. Prada, Gucci and Versace mingle on hangers alongside Paul Smith, Jean Paul Gaultier and Armani. While you can pick up trousers and shirts from £15, jackets from £40 and suits from £90 you could also pay £449 for a this season's Gucci suit which would have set you back £1,900 if you'd bought it new. Most of the clothes come off the catwalk, from photo shoots, or from celebrities who get 50% of what their outfits sell for. We found Prada shoes for £90 (were £250), Armani suits for £180 (were £700), and an outrageous Versace sequinned jacket. All clothes are less than two to three years old and are only held for six months.

The Loft

35 Monmouth Street, WC2
Tel: 020 7240 3807
Website: www.the-loft.co.uk
Tube: Covent Garden/Leicester Square
Bus: 19, 24, 29, 38, 176
Open: Mon-Sat 11am-6pm, Sun 1pm-5pm

The owners of this trendy shop selling contemporary designers have good contacts and some clothes come direct from film stylists and photographers. Labels include Comme des Garçons, Prada, Joseph, Vivienne Westwood and many more. Items sell for approximately one third of their original price and recent bargains have included a Marc Jacobs jacket for £125 (original price £650) and a Gucci shirt for £45 (usual price £180). For real bargain hunters they usually have a well stocked £5 rail, with items reduced to clear.

Seventy Four
74 Marylebone Lane, W1
Tel: 020 7486 2901
Tube: Bond Street
Bus: 7, 8, 10, 25, 55, 73, 98, 176
Open: Mon-Sat 10.30am-5pm
Small and well-stocked agency just off Wigmore Street with designer and retro clothes for men and women. Chanel, Prada and Gucci suits and dresses, furs and large stocks of designer bags. Chanel jackets were £250 (retail for £1,200), a Louis Vuitton shoe trunk was £950 (retails for £1,950) and a Chanel bag was £150 (retails for £550).

North

Change of Heart
The Old School,
59c Park Road, N8
Tel: 020 8341 1575
Tube: Finsbury Park/Highgate
Bus: W7
Open: Mon-Sat 10am-6pm, Sun 10am-5pm
Spacious, stylish showroom offering hardly worn, top quality women's designer clothing. Children have their own play area, and weary shoppers or their patient partners are offered a glass of wine and the papers. Very reasonable prices for seriously trendy items: a Dolce & Gabbana basque cost £80 (£350); embroidered and beaded handbags £15 (£45); and an Armani suit £80 (sells at £700). Other labels include Ghost and Miu Mui.

Designs on Her
60 Rosslyn Hill, NW3
Tel: 020 7435 0100
Tube: Hampstead
Bus: 46, 268
Open: Mon-Sat 10am-5.45pm, Sun 12noon-5pm
Long-established agency specialising in contemporary designerwear in top condition. Hot on accessories from current Prada bags to Jimmy Choo shoes. Labels include Gucci, Armani, Missoni and Marc Jacobs. On offer as we went to press was a Dolce & Gabbana black lace dress for £225, a Chloe sweater for £44 and a Gucci leather jacket for £269.

Exclusivo

24 High Street, NW3
Tel: 020 7431 8618
Tube: Hampstead
Bus: 46, 268
Open: Daily 11.30am-6pm

Set among the boutiques and coffee shops of Hampstead Village, this dimly-lit, cramped shop is stuffed with designer labels, bags, boots and accessories. Lots of men's suits (from £60) with Prada, Gucci, Chanel being the names to look for here. Clothes stay for ten weeks and sellers decide for themselves what price they want – the shop then adds its own mark-up. The stock also includes samples of new ranges.

Frock Follies

18 The Grangeway, Grange Park, N21
Tel: 020 8360 3447
Rail: Grange Park
Tube: Southgate
Bus: W9, 329, 125
Open: Tues-Sat 9.30am-5pm

This agency offers all sorts of bargains from M&S tops at under £10 to designer label suits, with a reasonable range of mid-priced garments such as Levi jeans. Their stock evening wear and swimwear samples, accessories and jewellery. Near Enfield town.

Laurel Herman

18a Lambolle Place, NW3
Tel: 020 7586 7925
Tube: Belsize Park/Swiss Cottage
Bus: 46, 168, 268, C11
Open: By appointment only

Discreet business run from a private showroom in a quiet mews. Large collection of hardly worn labels like MaxMara and Donna Karan. Also evening wear and accessories. An Armani trouser suit was £450 (original cost over £900). Free image consultation from MD whose paying clients include large banks and businesses.

Resurrection Recycle Boutique

3a Archway Close, Archway Island, N19
Tel: 020 7263 2600
Tube: Archway   Rail: Upper Holloway
Bus: 17, 43, 134, 210, 263, 271
Open: Mon 1pm-5pm, Tues-Fri 11am-6pm, Sat 11am-5pm

Spacious shop selling designer and vintage clothes as well as samples and graduate designs from the London College of Fashion. You might find anything from a Jigsaw dress for £15 to an Armani suit for £150. Lots of bags and accessories.
Prada shoes from £60.

Seconda Mano

111 Upper Street, N1
Tel: 020 7359 5284
Tube: Angel/Highbury & Islington
Rail: Highbury & Islington
Bus: 4, 19, 30, 43
Open: Mon, Tues 10am-6pm, Wed-Sat 10am-8pm, Sun 12noon-5pm
Funky, contemporary styles for men and women: Prada, Miu Miu, Marc Jacobs, Seven, Evisu, Juicy, Paul Smith, Paul & Joe and Eley Kishimoto with their precocious patterns. Also shoes, bags and sunglasses.

Sheila Warren-Hill

Shepherds Hill, Highgate, N6
Tel: 020 8348 8282
Tube: Highgate/Archway
Bus: 43, 134, 263
Open: by appointment
Personal 'at home' service with open house on Sundays when couture clothes can be tried on over lunch and drinks. Top designer labels (Chanel, Prada, Gucci) are on offer at less than a quarter of their original price. Almost everything is straight off the catwalk or the backs of 'well-known' clients. A Chanel suit 'rejected' after two weeks was on offer for £300 (was £2,000); an Armani skirt that retailed at £600 was on sale for £150. Also accessories and jewellery.

Wellingtons

1 Wellington Place, NW8
Tel: 020 7483 0688
Tube: St. John's Wood
Bus: 46, 13, 82, 113, 187, 274
Open: Mon-Sat 11am-5pm
Mother and daughter run agency just off St. John's Wood High Street with a fast turnover of clothes and accessories at reasonable prices. The range of stock is impressive: leather and suede jackets from £20 to Prada suits for around £400. Lots of Dolce & Gabbana. High Street labels like M&S and Whistles too, a bargain rail for items under £20, and a good selection of shoes and bags. Popular with TV stylists, Wellington offers evening wear at Christmas time.

WEST

Bertie Golightly (UK)

48 Beauchamp Place, SW3
Tel: 020 7584 7270
Tube: Knightsbridge
Bus: 14, 74, C1
Open: Mon-Tues, Thurs-Fri 10am-6pm, Wed 10am-7pm, Sun 12-5pm

An international clientele have been frequenting this very exclusive dress agency near Harrods for over 20 years. Run by ex-stunt woman Roberta Gibbs (already writing her memoirs) the shop on two floors offers top of the range designer labels: Dior, Hermes, and Yves St. Laurent. Chanel suits from £300 to £600; evening dresses for up to £600 – a bargain when you consider they could have originally retailed for around £10,000. Clients have been known to fly in from abroad and buy an outfit for lunch at nearby San Lorenzo's, leaving their own clothes behind to be picked up later. Others regularly call in for a complete outfit for social events like Ascot, and staff will advise on that final fashion accessory that will make the whole thing 'this year' rather than last.

The Corridor

309a King's Road, SW3
Tel: 020 7351 0772
Tube: Sloane Square
Bus: 22, 11, 319, 19, 49, 145, 211
Open: Mon-Sat 10.30am-6pm

The Corridor specialise in nearly new and new designer clothes for women. Their shop's premises may be tiny and narrow (hence the name) but its stock boasts some big fashion names. A Vivienne Westwood suit could be yours for £195, an Escada jacket for £199, Burberry and Mulberry raincoats come in at £90 and a range of shoes and bags complete the picture.

Designer Bargains

29 Kensington Church Street, W8
Tel: 020 7795 6777
Tube: High Street Kensington
Bus: 27, 28, 52, 70, 328
Open: Mon-Sat 10am-6pm

5

Trendy agency that includes It girls, Kate Moss and royalty amongst its buyers and sellers. Top designer labels go for anything between £29 to £999. A great place for bags and shoes (Prada, Jimmy Choo, Gucci and Miu Miu – sometimes unworn). Labels include classics like Dior and Chanel plus Roberto Cavalli, Voyage and Vivienne Westwood.

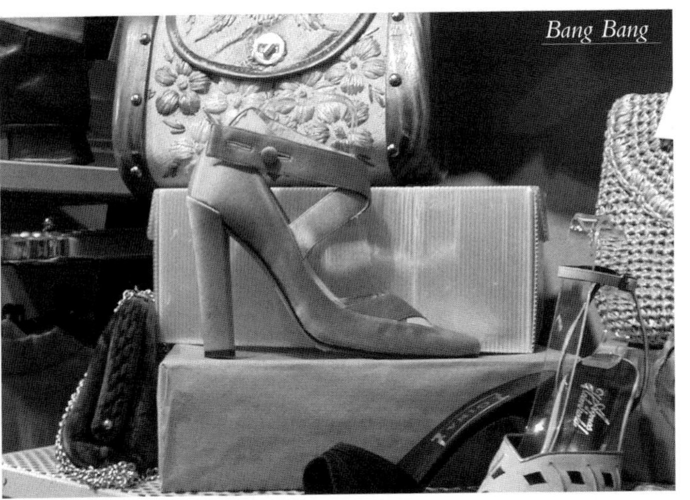

Bang Bang

Dressage
299 New King's Road, SW6
Tel: 020 7736 3696
Tube: Parson's Green
Bus: 22, 39, 85, 93, 265, 270, 424
Open: Mon-Sat 10am-6pm, Sun 11am-5pm

Friendly, good value agency on two floors with lots of bargains. Labels include Jigsaw, Armani and Marc Jacobs, prices from £5-£300. Dressage also hire out evening wear and hats for special occasions and stock accessories and jewellery.

The Dress Box
8 Cheval Place, SW7
Tel: 020 7589 2240
Tube: Knightsbridge/South Kensington
Bus: 14, 74, C1
Open: Mon-Fri 10am-6pm, Sat 10.30am-6pm

One of the oldest dress agencies in town offering the top end of the designer range as well as couture clothes: a Valentino evening dress that retails at around £6,000 was a snip at £700, a Roberto Cavalli gown was £600 (retails at £4,000). The Dress Box also has a vast selection of designer shoes. Next door at No.10, Stelios (same owner), specialises exclusively in Hermes and Chanel as well as leather goods. They have a waiting list for Hermes bags, so get in line and you might just get lucky and snap up a large crocodile Kelly bag for £6,400 (retails at £12,500) before some else gets it! Now that's what we call a bargain.

The Dresser
10 Porchester Place, W2
Tel: 020 7724 7212
Tube: Marble Arch
Bus: 6, 7, 15, 16, 23, 36, 98
Open: Mon-Fri 11am-5.30pm, Sat 11am-5pm
Contemporary designerwear and couture for women and for men (although there's less choice for the latter). A Prada leather two piece suit was being snapped up when we visited for £250 (retails for £2,000 plus) and a Helmut Lang cream coat was £160. Other top notch labels included Prada, Paul Smith and Dolce & Gabbana for men. Also bags and shoes (think Gucci, Prada and the divine Manolo Blahnik.

Dynasty (almost new) Designer Wear
12A Turnham Green Terrace, W4
Tel: 020 8995 3846
Tube: Turnham Green
Bus: E3, 190, 237, 267, 272, 391, 440
Open: Mon-Sat 10.30am-5pm
Tiny designer shop that caters for all budgets. Classic labels include Gucci, Burberry, and Fendi. Escada suits from £199 (£700 new), Prada suits from £275 (£1,000 new). Gucci bags (£99) and Ferragamo (£175). High Street makes like Kookai and Karen Millen, also jewellery, shoes and scarves. Men's stuff next door.

Dynasty (almost new) Menswear
12 Turnham Green Terrace, W4
Tel: 020 8994 4450
Tube: Turnham Green
Bus: E3, 190, 237, 267, 272, 391, 440
Open: Mon-Sat 10.30am-5pm
Rich pickings for the well-dressed bargain hunter. Expect Armani suits from £175, Blazer suits from £79 and natty Thomas Pink shirts from just £18. There are also lots of casual shirts for the dressed-down gent. With prices so low, it's possible to leave this shop looking like a million dollars for less than £100.

Insight

201 Munster Road, SW6
Tel: 020 7385 5501
Tube: Fulham Broadway, Parsons Green
Bus: 14, 74, 211, 220, 424
Open: Times vary – phone in advance

Dress agency in a two storey terraced house, selling designer labels for men and women (Prada, Gucci, Dolce & Gabbana), bags and shoes. Also vintage clothes, antique linen, decorative textiles and costume jewellery at very competitive prices. In addition they offer a hire service.

Salou
6 Cheval Place, SW7
Tel: 020 7581 2380
Tube: Knightsbridge/South Kensington
Bus: 14, 74, C1
Open: Mon-Sat 10am-5pm
One of a row of dress agencies in Cheval Place (across the road from Harrods), Salou offers classics like Prada, Chanel, Gucci (bags from £99); accessories, shoes and jewellery. A Joseph knitted fur jacket was £450 (retails at over £1000) and a Blumarine cashmere two piece £500 (sells at £1,200).

La Scala
39 Elystan Street, SW3
Tel: 020 7589 2784
Tube: South Kensington
Bus: 14, 49, 74, 345
Open: Mon-Sat 10am-5.30pm
Italian labels for women and men including Gucci, Prada and Armani. Contemporary styles at reasonable prices and featuring lots of suede and cashmere. A coat with a fox collar was £250 (retails at £550). Wedding outfits from £80-£350. Accessories, bags and shoes.

Sign of the Times
17 Elystan Street, SW3
Tel: 020 7589 4774
Tube: South Kensington
Bus: 14, 49, 74, 345
Open: Mon-Fri 10am-6pm; Sat 10am-5.30pm
Well-established (26 years) dress agency with a loyal clientele and a quick turnover. We found a bright blue Dolce & Gabbana coat, made famous by Carrie of 'Sex in the City' in her falling over on the catwalk scene, for £295 and Manolo Blahnik sandals for £40. Other labels include Marc Jacobs, Armani, Prada and Miu Miu. Also shoes, hats and scarves.

Stelios
10 Cheval Place, SW7
Tel: 020 7584 4424
(see The Dress Box on page 37)

Tresor

13 Cale Street, SW3
Tel: 020 7349 8829
Tube: Sloane Square/South Kensington
Bus: 11, 19, 22, 211, 219
Open: Tues-Sat 11am-6pm, Mon 2.30pm-6pm

Unique boutique and decorative arts gallery with 19th century paintings hung to 'complement' the clothes, scarves and jewellery. Dior, Yves St. Laurent and other top designers, plus fur coats.

Pandora

16-22 Cheval Place, SW7
Tel: 020 7589 5289
Tube: Knightsbridge/South Kensington
Bus: 11, 19, 22, 137, 211, 319, C1
Open: Mon-Sat 9am-6pm

Established in Sloane Square in 1947, Pandora is the doyenne of dress agencies and, with some 5,000 items in stock, offers a huge choice. Chanel suits sell from £300-£900 (over £3,000 new) but you might also find a Gaultier or Yves St. Laurent T-shirt from £35. If it's accessories you're after, they have Fendi and Gucci bags for £165 (original cost £400) and designer shoes from £47.

SOUTH

The Anerley Frock Exchange

122 Anerley Road, SE20
Tel: 020 8778 2030
Tube: Crystal Palace Rail: Anerley
Bus: 157, 351, 358
Open: Mon-Sat 9am-5pm, Wed 9am-5pm

Large shop in its ninth year, down the road from Crystal Palace. Ladies and children's clothes from Next and Gap to Armani and Versace. Plenty of bargains, with prices starting from a few pounds up to several hundred.

Butterfly Dress Agency

6

3 Lower Richmond Road,
Putney Bridge, SW15
Tel: 020 8788 8304
Tube: Putney Bridge
Bus: 22, 265
Open: Mon-Fri 10am-6pm, Sat 10am-5pm

A friendly shop that's been around for 18 years selling good quality clothes and accessories at fair prices. Top designers plus Monsoon, Jigsaw and other 'better shop' labels. Mums with buggies welcome. Prices from £15 to £250.

Frock Market

6

50 Lower Richmond Road, SW15
Tel: 020 8788 7748
Tube: Putney Bridge
Bus: 14, 22, 39, 74, 85, 93, 265, 424, 485
Open: Mon-Sat 10.30am-6pm

An Aladdin's cave of designer bargains, owned by a painter who chooses clothes as much for their colour and originality as for their designer labels. You might find floaty Ghost separates for £25, Prada bags at £50, Earl Jeans for £30. Also Manolo Blahnik and Jimmy Choo shoes.

Jasmine

65 Abbeville Road, SW4
Tel: 020 8675 9475
Tube: Clapham South or Common
Bus: 155, 255, 355
Open: Mon-Fri 9am-6pm, Sat 10am-6pm

Womenswear and accessories as well as home and garden furnishings. Good value labels from High Street to designer.

The Changing Room
148 Arthur Road, Wimbledon Park, SW19
Tel: 020 8947 1258
Tube: Wimbledon Park
Bus: 156
Open: Mon-Sat 10am-6pm
Small friendly shop selling 'anything decent that's in fashion' for women and children. High Street labels like Gap, M&S and Nicole Farhi as well as Joseph knitwear, Yves St. Laurent and Armani. Prices from £10 to £180. Also bags and shoes.

The Second Look
242 Upper Richmond Road West, SW14
Tel: 020 8878 7233
Rail: Mortlake
Bus: 74, 337
Open: Mon-Sat 10am-6pm
Large agency well-stocked with designer and High Street clothes for women from DKNY and Morgan to Paul Smith and Prada. They only take clothes up to a year old. Also shoes, bags and jewellery. Prices from £10-£200.

Twice as Nice
228 Battersea Park Road, SW11
Tel: 020 7720 2234
Rail: Battersea Park
Bus: 44, 49, 319, 344, 345
Open: Mon-Wed 10.30-6pm, Thurs 10am-8pm, Fri 10.30am-7pm, Sat 10am-5.30pm, Sun 12noon-5pm
Small shop that buys 'anything up to date in good condition', from High Street labels like Jigsaw and Warehouse to designers from Joseph to Prada. They have a waiting list for Gucci and Louis Vuitton handbags.

East

Revival
3 High Street, Wanstead, E11
Tel: 020 8989 8030
Tube: Snaresbrook
Bus: W12, W13, W14
Open: Mon-Sat 9.30am-5pm
This dress agency has a loyal following and a reputation for being tidy and well organised with clear labelling on all garments. Among the bargains on offer are High Street labels for men and women and pricier designer labels from DKNY to Moschino. Fake Jeans were £60, a Prada coat £600. Men's suits from £60. Also bags and shoes.

Lady's
10 High Street, Wanstead, E11
Tel: 020 8989 7530
Tube: Wanstead, Snaresbrook
Bus: 66, 101, 145, 308, W12
Open: Mon-Sat 9.30am-5.30pm
Well-established agency choc-a-bloc with clothes from High Street labels to beaded Gucci skirts (£45). Lots of bargains, all under around £350. Everything from cocktail dresses to bags, shoes and jewellery. They also cater for larger sizes.

Children

There are many dress agencies dealing with kids' clothes the best of which are covered in the Kid's Clothes & Equipment section:
Rainbow (see page 137)
Swallows & Amazons, SW12 (see page 139)

SHOES, BOOTS & BAGS

Shoreditch has been the home of shoemakers as far back as the 19th century, and it still retains that tradition, although the shoes available nowadays are mostly Italian imports. There are a number of wholesale outlets for good quality designer shoes on Shoreditch High Street. The East End shops have high quality shoes at low prices, but you should be prepared for vibrant colours, leather and snakeskin, and lots of golden buckles and sparkly diamante touches. It is possible to find workaday shoes, but easier to find something a little more individual and slightly gaudy.

All "Sex in the City" fans will know about Manolo Blahnik and Jimmy Choo, two of fashion's greatest shoemakers. Usually out of reach for the bargain hunter, in the January sales you might just be able to afford a pair. As for the High Street discount shoe chains like Shoe Express and Shoe Zone, remember that you get what you pay for. These are not top quality shoes marked down, but merely cheap shoes for a fair price that won't last long.

CENTRAL

Discount Shoe Sales

31 Strutton Ground, SW1
Tel: 020 7222 5223
Tube: St. James's Park
Bus: 11, 24, 211, 507
Open: Mon-Fri 9.30am-4.45pm

While you can find cheap (both in quality and price) shoes here, this men's shoe retailer also stocks some high-quality, upmarket leather shoes worth seeking out. Leather-soled shoes whether Oxfords or loafers cost about £65 and would normally retail at about £100. They carry a few work and leisure shoes, but excel in business and dressy shoes.

Office (Sale Shop)

61 St Martin's Lane, WC2
Tel: 020 7497 0390
Tube: Leicester Square
Bus: 24, 29, 176
Open: Mon-Sat 10am-7pm, Sun 12noon-7pm

Office shoes are strictly up-to-the-minute, trend-setting footwear. This sale shop is the repository for their discontinued lines, which are sold at a considerable discount. As styles change so quickly it's possible to find shoes here for £30 that were being sold for £60 in one of their main shops just a few weeks before. It's also a great place to look for sandals in winter.

Shoe Express
72 Oxford Street, W1
Tel: 020 7436 8791
Tube: Oxford Circus
Bus: 7, 8, 10, 25, 55, 73, 98, 176
Open: Mon-Wed & Fri-Sat 10am-7pm, Thurs 10am-8pm, Sun 2pm-6pm
This chain of shoe shops keeps its stock cheap and cheerful. The expertly and cheaply imitated fashion footwear in leather and plastic is satisfactory for a few nights out. Sandals go for £16 and children's trainers for about £10.
Also at: *498 Harrow Road, W9; 437 North End Road, SW6; 103 High Street, SE9, 67 High Street, NW10; 19/21 North Mall, The Green, N9; 103 Eltham High Street, SE9*

NORTH

Clarks Factory Shop
Unit 2, 67-83 Seven Sisters Road, N7
Tel: 020 7281 9364
Tube: Finsbury Park
Bus: 259, 279
Open: Mon-Sat 9.30am-5.30pm, Sun 11am-4.45pm
See description under South London (page 48)

Shoe Centre For Men
88 Stamford Hill, N16
Tel: 020 8806 1602
Rail: Stoke Newington
Bus: 67, 73, 76, 149, 243
Open: Mon-Fri 9.15am-6.30pm, Sun 10.30am-3pm
Good, old-fashioned service is a feature at this unusual shop at the tail end of Stoke Newington. Men will find plenty of classic shoes such as brogues, Oxfords and loafers by decent shoemakers. The slightly imperfect shoes that are sold at £55 instead of the normal price of £100 offer the best bargains.

Laga (1)
88 Camden High Street, NW1
Tel: 020 7383 5872
Tube: Camden Town
Bus: 24, 27, 29, 88, 134, 168, 214, 253
Open: Mon-Sat 10am-6.30pm, Sun 11am-6.30pm,
This unassuming shop on Camden High Street offers great value fashion shoes for men and women and a selection of womens' bags. On a

recent visit they had many items on sale including a pair of trendy Gola suede shoes for £34.99 (reduced from £49), and a pair of smart womens black leather shoes for £29.99 (reduced from £54.99). A great value shoe shop that is always worth a visit if you're in the Camden area.

Kate Kuba Sale Shop
49 Chase Side, N14
Tel: 020 8886 1185
Website: www.katekuba.com
Tube: Southgate/Cockfosters
Bus: 125, 298, 299
Open: Mon-Thurs 9.30am-5.30pm, Fri-Sat 9.30am-6pm
Swanky feet will love the designer labels and Kate Kuba's own posh designs sold here. Fashion's fickleness provides the stock of discontinued lines here at substantial discounts of about 50%.

Sample Handbags

11 Ballards Lane, N3
Tel: 020 8349 4477
Tube: Finchley Central
Bus: 82, 125, 260
Open: Mon-Sat 9am-5.45pm
You will probably find what you need here as they have a large variety of bags from name brands like Fiorelli, Carlton and Delsie. Non-leather handbags go for £8 and a really nice Italian leather handbag could set you back £40. Cheap backpacks for occasional use cost £6.

Shoe Zone
750 High Road Finchley, N12
Tel: 020 8446 4875
Website: www.shoezone.net
Tube: East Finchley
Bus: 125, 263
Open: Mon-Sat 9am-5.30pm
Offering dirt-cheap shoes for the whole family, the Shoe Zone is a chain of discount shoe shops all over the UK. We have listed a few London branches below. If you have kids whose feet grow fast you might consider coming here for cheap shoes: trainers cost £9.99 and sandals £4.99. These shoes are not an investment and probably won't last long. Pick up all the accessories here such as shoe trees and polishes at slightly discounted prices.
Also at: 66 High Street Walthamstow, E17, Tel: 020 8520 1810
11 Arndale Walk, SW18, Tel: 020 8877 1317
124-126 Rushey Green, SE6, Tel: 020 8690 5244

WEST

Manolo Blahnik International Ltd

49-51 Old Church Street, SW3
Tel: 020 7352 3863
Tube: South Kensington
Bus: 14, 49, 70, 74, 345
Open: Mon-Fri 10am-5.30pm, Sat 10.30am-5pm

A designer shoe shop selling handmade shoes at an average of £300 a pair. Twice a year, however, usually around the second week of January and the last week of July, prices are reduced by at least 50% in one of the season's most anticipated sales. With ladies' shoes ranging from flat and classic styles, to more flamboyant, high-heeled creations, these are definitely sales the shoe-loving bargain hunter should keep an eye open for.

Jimmy Choo

169 Draycott Avenue, SW3
Tel: 020 7584 6111
Tube: South Kensington
Bus: 14, 49, 70, 74, 345
Open: Mon, Tues, Thurs-Sat 10am-6pm, Wed 10am-7pm, Sun 1pm-6pm

During the first or second week of January, you can pickup sexy, strappy and high-heeled footwear for 50% off the normal retail price of £200 to £300.

J Mark

90 Fulham Palace Road, W6
Tel: 020 8748 3947
Tube: Hammersmith
Bus: 190, 211, 220, 295
Open: Mon-Sat 9am-6pm

The quaint, old-fashioned shop window displays this tiny shop's goods and stepping into this shop is like stepping back in time. Rubber-soled corduroy slippers and sheepskin booties make up a lot of the stock but there are also plain black and brown men's shoes and no-name brand trainers for £20. Also plimsolls for £7.99 and sequinned mesh slippers dressy enough to wear out of the house for £6.99. Stylish, tan leather desert boots are just £20.

Shaukat Fabrics
168-172 Old Brompton Road, SW5
Tel: 020 7373 8956
Tube: Gloucester Road
Bus: C1, 49
Open: Mon-Sat 10am-6.30pm
A large fabric outlet which also sells a great value range of bags and suitcases. Bargains on a recent visit included quality nylon rucksacks for £9.99, a stylish range of handbags for between £9.99 and £18 and a good quality leather weekend bag for only £18.99. They also sell cotton bedding from their basement and good quality bags and suit cases (see pages 90 and 122).

Sid's
70 Fulham Palace Road, W6
Tel: 020 8748 4697
Tube: Hammersmith
Bus: 190, 211, 220, 295
Open: Mon-Fri 8.30am-5.30pm, Sat 10am-2pm
This key cutting, shoe repair, dry cleaning, trophy and engraving shop also manages to keep a few styles of business/dress Loake men's shoes in stock. They stock seconds with slight defects and these upmarket shoes are sold for half the usual price making a smart pair of well-made lace-up, leather Oxfords just £49.

SOUTH

Clarks Factory Shop
61-63 Rye Lane Peckham, SE15
Tel: 020 7732 2530
Rail: Peckham Rye
Bus: 12, 37, 63, 78, 312, 343, P12
Open: Mon-Sat 9.30am-5pm
Find end-of-line styles or slightly defective footwear here that can't be sold on the High Street. Expect to pay the half the usual price for these reasonably good quality shoes. The two pairs for £25 or three pairs for £30 deals represent good value, but you can also choose from single pairs of shoes that cost between £15 and £30. Find trainers, sandals and dress shoes for kids, women and men.
Branch at:
113-117 Powis Street, Woolwich, SE18 Tel: 020 8854 3163

EAST

There are a number of wholesale outlets for good quality designer shoes on Shoreditch High Street. Many of them, such as Barbarella at no 128, Davina at no 133, Danco at no 134 (tel: 020 7613 5076) and Mary Shoes at no 135, are quite happy to sell on a normal retail basis to customers who walk in off the street.

Barbarella Shoes
128 Shoreditch High Street, E1
Tel: 020 7739 9283
Tube: Liverpool Street/Shoreditch
Bus: 25, 35, 43, 47, 48, 55, 48, 67, 78, 149, 242, 243
Open: Mon-Fri 10am-6pm, Sun 10am-4pm
Despite its name, this shop doesn't trade in futuristic footwear, but stocks a good range of smart shoes for men, women and children at reduced prices. The handmade Italian shoes are a real draw here. Though mainly wholesale, they do offer their knockdown prices to the general public.

Davina
133 Shoreditch High Street, E1
Tel: 020 7739 2811
Tube: Liverpool Street/Shoreditch
Bus: 25, 35, 43, 47, 48, 55, 48, 67, 78, 149, 242, 243
Open: Mon-Fri 9.30am-5.30pm, Sun 10.30am-3pm
The nicest of the Shoreditch High Street lot, Davina is an airy, open shop with modern styles and a helpful staff. Leather sandals go for £14 and a stylish pair of high-heels goes for £35.

Ideal Fashions

88 Brick Lane, E1
Tel: 020 7247 8571
Tube: Aldgate East/Shoreditch
Bus: 8, 25, 67, 253
Open: Mon-Fri 11am-6pm, Sun 11am-3pm
This dilapidated, wee shop sits in the heart of Banglatown. A small but solid selection of basic leather men's and women's shoes is on offer. All-leather brogues go for £25 and strong walking boots are £20.

Shaw Leather Goods
21 Wentworth Street E1
Tel: 020 7247 4057
Tube: Aldgate/Aldgate East
Bus: 25, 67, 253
Open: Daily 9.30am-6.30pm

This store with its ever helpful staff, sells a selection of handbags, travel goods and accessories. Supersize suitcases retail for £24.99, lightweight, compact umbrellas for £2.99 and knock-off designer bags such as clutches or sophisticated red leather handbags go for about £20.

Shoe Club

45 Wentworth Street, E1
Tel: 020 7247 6629
Tube:Aldgate/Aldgate East
Bus: 8, 25, 67, 253
Open: Mon-Fri 9.30am-6pm, Sun 9am-4pm

Grown-up shoes for men and women are for sale at this bustling shop. Hush Puppie style men's shoes available in a range of colours from red to tan are reduced from £45 to £25 and plenty of other shoes are marked with reduced prices. Find embroidered sandals for £15 and really stylish leather court shoes in a variety of styles and colours (all with high heels) for £45.

Sivical Shoes

149 Shoreditch High Street, E1
Tel: 020 7729 8611
Tube: Liverpool Street/Shoreditch
Bus: 25, 35, 43, 47, 48, 55, 67, 78, 149, 242, 243
Open: Mon-Fri 10am-6pm, Sun 10.30am-3.30pm

Mainly a wholesaler, but will sell reasonable quantities to retail customers. Regular deals like three pairs of men's shoes for £50 makes this worth a stop if you are already shopping for shoes on Shoreditch High Street. In general, they have a lot of stock, but it's not attractively presented.

Supersport Shoe Warehouse

102-105 Whitechapel High Street, E1
Tel: 020 7247 5111
Website: www.super-sport.co.uk
Tube: Aldgate/Aldgate East
Bus: 25, 67, 253
Open: Mon-Fri 9.30am-6pm, Sat 10am-5.30pm, Sun 9am-5pm

Supersport is part of a citywide chain so don't expect huge savings, but there are bargains among the discontinued trainers. Prices go as low as £25, but mostly hover around £45 for a pair of trendy Nikes. The whole family is catered for here. They also stock a small selection of men's dress shoes and boots as well as some sports clothes.

Also at: 35 Oxford Street, W1R, Tel: 020 7434 1555
111 Oxford Street W1D, Tel: 020 7439 1082
8-14 Seven Sisters Road, N7, Tel: 020 7700 6999
180-182 Queensway, W2, Tel: 020 7243 2333

187 Camden High Street, NW1, Tel: 020 7267 6622
45 Ealing Broadway, W5, Tel: 020 7561 0888
Kingsmall, 25 King Street, W6, Tel: 020 8563 1197
58 Neal Street, WC2H, Tel: 020 7836 5860
12 Rye Lane, SE15, Tel: 020 7277 6611
11 Wentworth Street, E1, Tel: 020 7247 5037

Tina Shoes
32 Wentworth Street, E1
Tel: 020 7246 5235
Tube: Aldgate/Aldgate East
Bus: 8, 25, 67, 253
Open: Mon-Fri, Sun 9.30am-5.30pm
Italian leather shoes are neatly arranged at this small shop. Elegant women's court shoes cost about £25 and smart sandals go for £15. Men's lace-up leather boots good enough for dressing up cost just £35.

DALSTON

What Shoreditch has in terms of wholesale outlets can be easily matched by Dalston's range of retail shoe shops. There are easily a dozen on Kingsland Road alone, on the busy stretch near Ridley Road Market. Listed below are the cheapest ones:

Gemini Shoes
110 Kingsland High Street, E8
Tel: 020 7254 8264
Bus: 67, 149, 242, 243
Open: Mon-Sat 9.30am-6pm
Shoes, boots and sandals for ladies and gents are on offer here. Rugged boots go for about £25 and sandals are as cheap as £10 for synthetic material and £20 for leather. The sale rack offers good value with many shoes priced at less than £10.

Miss Cardini
122 Kingsland High Street, E8
Tel: 020 7254 1515
Bus: 67, 149, 242, 243
Open: Mon-Sat 11am-5pm
Miss Cardini's specialises in sandals as well as large sizes. However, regular sizes for men and women are plentiful. Prices start at £15 for women and £20 for men. Check out the matching handbags.

ELECTRONICS

COMPUTERS

Buying a computer can be a stressful experience with so many different things to consider and constantly changing technology. The complexity of the task is not helped by pushy sales people, usually very keen to sell you over-priced extended warranties. To avoid being misled it's a good idea to consult computer magazines and get a bit of background information before embarking on your quest. The main decision to make is whether to buy a personal computer (PC) which can be made by a wide range of manufacturers and will almost certainly use Microsoft system software, or to buy an Apple Mac which runs on its own software. The choice is a fundamental one and you should probably ask your computer literate friends about what they use and try out both systems before making your decision. Apple Macs are a little more user-friendly, but the new Microsoft software has progressed in recent years and the differences are now less marked. One advantage of going down the PC route is the availability of PC software and the fact that PCs tend to be significantly cheaper than the equivalent Mac. Whichever choice you make, there are several key specifications you will need to consider when buying a computer:

1) Storage memory is where all the computer's information is stored. It is measured in gigabytes (GB), and current models have between 20 and 40 GB (20 should be enough for domestic use).

2) RAM is the level of active memory used for running a programme and is measured in megabytes (MB). The latest models have between 128 and 256 MB. It is a good idea to get at least 128MB RAM when buying a new machine.

3) The processor is the device that moves everything about within the computer. The more powerful the processor, the faster the computer operates. Processors are measured in gigahertz, and anything over 1GHz should be enough, although Macs tend to have less powerful processors.

4) If you would like to play DVDs on your computer, make sure a DVD player is included in the package.

One final thing to make sure of is the nature of the package you are buying, particularly if you are comparing prices. Does the price include a monitor or is it just the base unit, what software is included and are there graphic or sound cards which will increase the capacity of the computer to run design or music programmes? Below are reviewed some of the best outlets in London to find new and used computer equipment; the shops deal only in PCs unless otherwise stated.

Central

Morgan

64-72 New Oxford Street, WC1
Tel: 020 7255 2115; 0870 120 4920 (mail order)
Website: www.morgancomputers.co.uk
Tube: Tottenham Court Road
Bus: 1, 8, 19, 25, 38, 55, 98, 242
Open: Mon-Wed & Fri 9am-5.30pm, Thurs 9am-7.30pm, Sat 9am-5pm
Morgan sell surplus, end-of-line and obsolete PCs at very low prices and often with a full manufacturer's warranty. Recently they had refurbished, ex-show room LMX PCs, with a Celeron 1.1 processor, 128MB RAM, 20GB hard disk and 15" monitor for only £299.99 (exc VAT), with a 1 year warranty. They offer a next day delivery service for a full PC system for only £25 (exc VAT). A great place to get a budget PC, and they also now sell a limited range of digital cameras.

Micro Anvika

245 Tottenham Court Road, W1
Tel: 020 7467 6000 (all branches)
Website: www.microanvika.com
Tube: Goodge Street/Tottenham Court Road
Bus: 10, 24, 29, 73, 134
Open: Mon-Sat 9.30am-6pm, Sun 11am-5pm
This smart chain of computer stores sells largely Macs and accessories but also a limited range of PCs. They are probably not the cheapest outlet in town, but they are reasonably priced. They have an efficient delivery service and a 6 months interest free credit scheme.
Also at: 6-17 Tottenham Court Road W1, 53-54 Tottenham Court Road, W1 13 Chenies Street, WC1 (Macs only)

North

BJ Computers Ltd

1

259 Eversholt Street, NW1
Tel: 020 7383 3444
Website: www.bjcomputer.co.uk
Tube: Mornington Crescent
Bus: 168, 214, 253
Open: Mon-Fri 9.30am-6.30pm, Sat 10am-6pm
This small business sells made-to-order PCs as well as upgrades, networking and a repairs service. On a recent visit they were offering a bespoke PC with 256MB, 1.8GHZ, a 40GB hard drive, DVD player, modem, network and graphics card for only £289 (exc VAT).

Computer Repair Centre

344 Kilburn High Road, NW6
Tel: 020 7624 2446
Fax: 020 7624 8272
Website: www.crcentre.com
Tube: Kilburn
Bus: 16, 32, 89, 98, 189, 316, 328
Open: Mon-Fri 9.30am-6pm

This outlet has been specialising in the repair and sale of Macs for over 7 years and has a reasonable selection of used equipment from which to choose. Among the good deals recently was an old, but still usable PowerMac 8600/200 with a CD drive for only £99 (exc VAT). They offer a 3-month warranty on all used goods.

Computer Precision Ltd

185 Upper Street, N1
Tel: 020 7359 9797
Tube: Highbury & Islington
Bus: 4, 19, 33, 43
Open: Mon-Fri 9.30am-6pm

This place is busy because they offer very competitive quotes for all kinds of computer accessories and hardware. Although they have a limited stock, they can order most items for next day delivery. They also construct their own brand of PCs starting at only £385 (exc VAT).

Kam Computers

567 Finchley Road, NW3
Tel: 020 7431 1223
Tube: Finchley Road
Bus: 13, 82, 245, 260, 328
Open: Mon-Fri 9.30am-7pm, Sat 10am-6pm

This retailer largely sells new computers, but about 10% of their stock is second-hand equipment. Good deals on a recent visit included a used PC with Pentium II processor, 64MB RAM and a 15" monitor for only £150 with a 3 month warranty.

WEST

Personal Computer Solutions

52 Northfield Avenue, W13
Tel: 020 8567 3800
Website: www.fixmycomputer.co.uk
Tube: Northfields
Bus: E2, E3, 65
Open: Mon-Fri 9am-6pm, Sat 10am-5pm

This small shop has been established for over 10 years, offering their own bespoke PCs, upgrades and repairs. All new goods come with a 1 year guarantee. A good value independent computer outlet.

WaMa Computer Services Ltd

59 Westbourne Park Road, W2
Tel: 020 7727 5892
Tube: Queensway
Bus: 7, 23, 28, 31, 70, 328
Open: Mon-Sat 9am-6pm

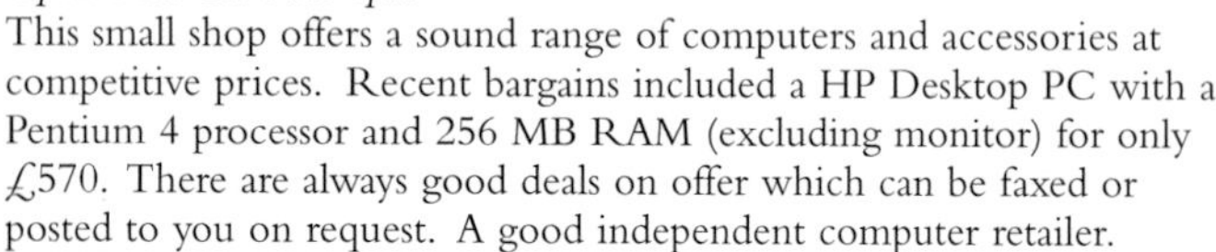

This small shop offers a sound range of computers and accessories at competitive prices. Recent bargains included a HP Desktop PC with a Pentium 4 processor and 256 MB RAM (excluding monitor) for only £570. There are always good deals on offer which can be faxed or posted to you on request. A good independent computer retailer.

SOUTH

Modern Computers

171 Old Kent Road, SE1
Tel: 020 7231 1313
Website: www.moderncomputers.com
Tube: Elephant & Castle
Bus: 21, 53, 63, 172
Open: Mon-Sat 9am-6pm

This is a good value independent computer outlet offering brand-new custom-built and second-hand computers at very competitive prices. Second-hand bargains included a computer with a Pentium 2 processor and 6GB hard drive for only £150, again this is without monitor. Used goods come with a 3 month warranty and new goods are sold with a full manufacturer's warranty. An excellent place to find PC bargains.

The Computer World

Unit 2, 777-8 Old Kent Road, SE15
Tel: 020 7635 8194
Website: www.thecomputerworld.co.uk
Tube: Elephant & Castle
Bus: 21, 53, 63, 172
Open: Mon-Sat 9am-6pm

This chain of computer stores has emerged as a result of Time's take over of its rival Tiny. The new company still offers great value Time PCs with prices starting from £499 (inc VAT), with 256 MB RAM, 40 GB hard disk, CD writer and DVD player. There are 25 branches throughout London, refer to the new website for your nearest branch.

EAST

New Logic Computers
219 Forest Road, E17
Tel: 020 8925 1777
Website: www.newlogic.co.uk
Tube: Blackhorse Road
Bus: 123, 230
Open: Mon-Fri 10.30am-6pm
A large range of all new PCs and accessories. Brand-new base units start at only £249 (inc VAT).

Performance (11)
58 Cheshire Street, E1
Tel: 020 7613 0069
Tube: Shoreditch
Bus: 25, 67, 253
Open: Mon-Fri 8am-4pm, Sat 8am-12noon, Sun 7am-2pm
This shop sells old computers and office equipment at very low prices. Small monitors in working order were only £5, and ancient Dell computers (32 MB RAM and no CD ROM) were a mere £20. If you're looking for a simple word processor without internet access this could be a very cheap option. A great little shop.

Simply Computers
2-3 Forest Works, Forest Road, E17
Tel: 0870 727 4020
Website: www.simply.co.uk
Tube: Blackhorse Road
Bus: 123, 230
Open: Mon-Fri 9am-6.30pm (Thurs 9am-8pm), Sat 9am-5pm, closed Sunday
This large warehouse sells a wide range of PCs, accessories and software on line or via their order line. There are plans for a retail outlet on site, but at the time of going to press this was still to be established. The prices are low with their own brand PC (called a Systemax) starting from only £299 (exc VAT) with a 1.8 processor, 128MB RAM, 40GB hard disk and CD ROM, but without a monitor, which are available here for only £60 (exc VAT).

OUTER LONDON

Computer Warehouse (Macs only)
1 Amalgamated Drive, West Cross Centre,
Brentford, Middlesex, TW8
Tel: 020 8400 1234
Website: www.cwonline.co.uk
Tube: Boston Manor/Osterley Rail: Syon Lane
Open: Mon-Fri 9am-5.30pm, Sun 9am-5pm
This large warehouse specialises in Apple Macs and will attempt to match any quote. Brentford is quite a way to travel for most Londoners but ordering via their order line or the web is relatively painless and they provide an efficient delivery service. An easy and trusted outlet for all the latest Apple hardware and accessories.

COMPUTER FAIRS AND AUCTIONS

You can buy absolutely anything computer-related at computer fairs. They are great places to pick up bargain parts, accessories and software once you've got your PC or Mac, although it is not advisable to purchase your first actual computer at a fair, simply because after-sales, warranty and repairs are impractical to set up. For more information, including many one-off events, visit www.theshowguide.co.uk.

British Computer Fairs
UCL Windeyer Building, Cleveland Street, WC2
also at:
UCL Huntley Street, off Tottenham Court Road, WC2
Tel: 01943 817 300
E-mail: david@computerfairs.com
Website: www.britishcomputerfairs.com
Tube: Goodge Street or Warren Street
Bus: 10, 24, 29, 73, 134
Admission charge: £1.50 Adults, £1 Concessions
Open: Every Saturday 10am-5pm (Huntley Street till 4pm)
British Computer Fairs are a great opportunity to buy from a wide variety of computer traders selling both new and used equipment. All the traders have power supplies which allows you to see the equipment working before buying. There were also many traders dealing in accessories for computers with bargains such as 20 Verbatum CDs for only £8. BCF aim to provide the same consumer rights as you would find on the High Street. Visitors to the fair are given a free copy of the PCi guide listing products, prices and reviews. To find out about any of the fairs run by BCF, view their website which is regularly updated.

Schools Connect Auction

See full entry in the Auctions section (page 182)

Stratford Computer Fair

Carpenters & Dockland Centre, 98 Gibbins Road, Stratford, E15
Tel: 020 8552 1607
Tube: Stratford
Bus: 58, 69, 97, 158, 308
Open: Sat 10.30am-5.30pm, Sun 10.30am-4pm
Entry: £1.50 Adults, £1 Children (accompanied children free)

Fullact Computer Fair

TUC Building, Great Russell Street, WC1
Tel: 01747 854576
Bus: 10, 24, 29, 73, 134, 390
Open: Saturdays 10am-6pm
Entry: £2 Adults, Concessions £1

BUYING ON LINE

There are several UK based websites selling machines that have been refurbished and are re-sold at a significant discount with a full warranty.

Dell Outlet

Tel: 0870 905 0150
Website: www.euro.dell.com/countries/uk/enu/dfo

IBM

Tel: 0800 169 1485
Website: www.ibm.com/uk
Type in the key words "buy refurbished equipment" on the website's search engine, to get details of their refurbished sales scheme.

Lowcost Computers

Tel: 0845 108 0423
Website: www.lowcost-computers.co.uk
A useful independent website that also offers refurbished machines and is generally very good value.

INK CARTRIDGES AND REFILLS

The Ink Factory

Tel: 0870 7500 710
Website: www.theinkfactory.co.uk
This website has a good range of printer cartridges to fit most makes and models of printer. Check out their website for current offers.

HI-FI, VIDEO & TV

Richer Sounds
Branches at:

258 Fulham Road, SW10
Tel: 020 7352 8496

1A New Street, EC2
Tel: 020 7626 8006

29 Bloomsbury Way, WC1
Tel: 020 7831 2888

2 London Bridge Walk, SE1
Tel: 020 7403 1201

25 Northways Parade,
College Crescent, NW3
Tel: 020 7722 3359

48 East Street, BR1
Tel: 020 8466 6565

105 West Ealing Broadway, W13
Tel: 020 8566 4422

6 Farringdon Street, EC4M
Tel: 020 7329 7374

Mail order: 087001 12345

The clever way to acquire a good hi-fi is to construct a system from separates as this allows you to choose the best value parts and to upgrade your system easily later. The best place to buy new hi-fi separates is very likely to be Richer Sounds. It stocks recently discontinued lines at well below the original price, and buys new items direct from the factory. Richer Sounds guarantees to beat rivals' prices by at least £10. Most of their goods are in the middle ground (between £80-£200), but they also have a reasonable selection of the top-notch equipment to keep the hi-fi buffs happy. The recent development in home cinema systems is now reflected in Richer Sounds' copious stock of cinema sound systems.

NORTH

Audio T
190 West End Lane, NW6
Tel: 020 7794 7848
Website: www.audio-t.co.uk
Tube: West Hampstead
Bus: 139, 187, 268, 328, C11
Open: Tues-Sat 10am-6pm, Thurs till 9pm
A store that stocks amplifiers for over £3,000 may not seem a good place to find bargains, but they offer to match any price on the same item and they also have a selection of second-hand and ex-display items. The website is excellent and lists all the current offers.
Also at: 159a Chase Side, Enfield, Middlesex EN2, Tel: 020 8367 3132

Blue Audio Visual

61 Upper Street, N1
Tel: 020 7704 1124
Tube: Angel
Bus: 4, 19, 33, 43
Open: Mon-Sat 10am-7pm, Sun 12noon-6pm

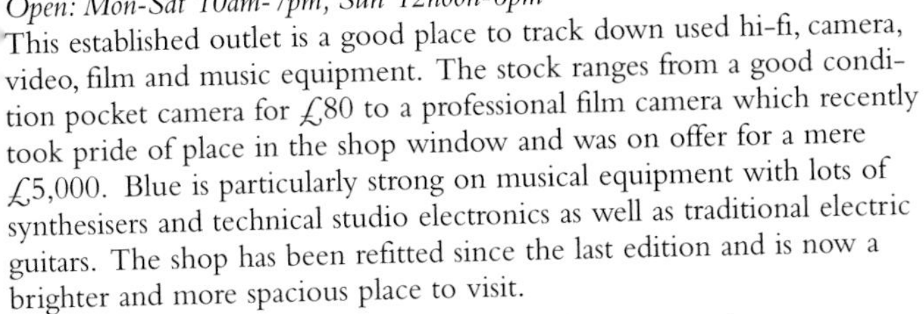

This established outlet is a good place to track down used hi-fi, camera, video, film and music equipment. The stock ranges from a good condition pocket camera for £80 to a professional film camera which recently took pride of place in the shop window and was on offer for a mere £5,000. Blue is particularly strong on musical equipment with lots of synthesisers and technical studio electronics as well as traditional electric guitars. The shop has been refitted since the last edition and is now a brighter and more spacious place to visit.

Church Street Electronics

44 Stoke Newington Church Street, N16
Tel: 020 7923 2522
Rail: Stoke Newington
Bus: 67, 73, 76, 149, 243
Open: Mon-Wed, Fri-Sat 9.30am-5pm, Thurs 9.30am-2pm

This long established shop has a good range of new and used televisions and videos. The service is friendly and helpful and second-hand goods come with a 3 month guarantee.

JBTV Services

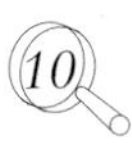

241 West End Lane, NW6
Tel: 020 7794 7887
Tube: West Hampstead
Bus: 139, 187, 268, 328, C11
Open: Mon-Sat 10am-6pm

This family-run West Hampstead shop offers worthwhile deals on all kinds of reconditioned electronic goods. As well as a popular repair service, they offer reconditioned TVs starting at £70, while videos start at around £75. All purchases come with a 6 month guarantee.

Satellite Electronics

104 Cricklewood Broadway, NW2
Tel: 020 8450 0272
Tube: Cricklewood
Bus: 16, 32, 245, 266, 316
Open: Mon-Sat 9.30am-7pm

A well-ordered shop offering reconditioned TVs and videos at very competitive prices. Any item under £100 gets a 6 month guarantee, anything over that price a full year.

Superfi London
2 Camden High Street, NW1
Tel: 020 7388 1300
Tube: Mornington Crescent
Bus: 168, 253
Open: Mon-Sat 10am-6pm
This shop is the only London branch of a chain of 19 stores, and offers a great selection of new quality hi-fi separates. There are always discounts available for special promotions and clearance stock. Among the bargains on a recent visit was a huge KEF KHT 2005 speaker system for £550 – reduced from £800.

TV4U
115 Cricklewood Broadway, NW2
Tel: 020 8450 9598
Tube: Cricklewood
Bus: 16, 32, 245, 266, 316
Open: Mon-Sat 9am-6.30pm
Reconditioned televisions, videos, DVDs and a selection of new hi-fi systems. A Sony Trinitron 21" colour TV was only £85, while other TVs were as little as £55. Guarantees depend on the item you're buying, and go up to a full year on some items.

WEST

Kays
280 King Street, W6
Tel: 020 8748 7238
Tube: Ravenscourt Park
Bus: 27, 190, 267, 391, H91
Open: Mon-Fri 10.30am-6pm (phone in advance)
This is a great shop selling used TVs, videos, hi-fi's , camcorders and cameras. The range and quality of electronic goods is impressive and all items come with a 3 month guarantee. They also offer a repair service. The strange and often irregular opening times make Kays a difficult shop to visit.

X Electrical
125 King Street, W6
Tel: 020 8563 7383
Tube: Hammersmith
Bus: 27, 190, 267, 391, H91
Open: Mon-Sat 10am-6pm

A second-hand music and home entertainment shop selling everything from guitars to digital recorders, laptops to digital cameras, SLRs to DVDs, PS2s to turntables. Among the bargains were a Technics SL1210 for £250, a Canon EOS 300 for £175 and a Compaq Ipaq for only £150.
Branches at:
4 Station Buildings, Fife Road, Kingston KT1, Tel: 020 8546 1233
43 Church Street, Croydon CR0, Tel: 020 8680 0007
Open: Mon-Sat 10am-6pm, Sun 11am-4pm

EAST

Hitachi Factory Shop

166 High Street North, E6
Tel: 020 8472 1373
Tube: East Ham
Bus: 101, 104, 147, 238, 300, 325, 372
Open: Mon-Sat 9am-6pm
This shop sells a wide range of Hitachi products from factory seconds to returned mail order deliveries. Reductions and levels of stock vary, but there are always bargains to be found here. It's a good idea to ring first to find out what they have in stock before making a special journey.

OUT OF TOWN

Centrax Direct Sales

Unit 17, 193 Garth Road
Morden, Surrey, SM4
Tel: 020 8330 7766
Tube: Morden
Bus: 54, 118, 154, 157, 163, 201, 293, 413, K5
Open: Mon-Sat 8.30am-5pm, Sun 10am-4pm
Centrax is an outlet for ex-showroom Phillips TVs, videos and hi-fi systems. It is quite a journey to either store and they have neither a website nor a catalogue, so it is a matter of ringing them to find out their latest stock and prices. All ex-showroom Phillips goods come with a 1 year shop warranty.
Also at: Unit E1-11, Tooting Broadway Market, SW17, Tel: 020 8672 444
Open: Mon-Sat 9am-5pm, Wed till 1pm

Other outkts for electronic goods:

The Catalogue Bargain Shop *on page 213.*

Pawnbrokers *on pages 256-57.*

MISCELLANEOUS

The shops reviewed here are difficult to classify, but very useful for those looking for blank audio and video tapes, batteries and CDs. All the stores featured also sell smaller electronic items, with Maplin offering a particularly wide range of goods. KVJ Fairdeal is the cheapest and the best of the lot although difficult to get to for some people as it is located in the East End.

KVJ Fairdeal

76 Whitechapel High Street, E1 (11)
Tel: 020 7247 6029
Website: www.kvjfairdeal.com
Tube: Aldgate East
Bus: 25, 67, 253
Open: Mon-Fri 9.30am-6pm, Sat 9.30am-1.30pm

KVJ is the best place in town to buy cheap video and audio tapes, CDs, batteries, camera film, ink cartridges, memory cards and even sticky tape. Although a small shop, it sells vast quantities via mail order and this allows it to keep its prices lower than anywhere in town. Among the bargains on a recent visit were 10 branded computer CDs for £3.99, and JVC 240 VHS videos for £1.25 each. They have now started stocking digital cameras including a Fujifilm A204 for only £180. The only disadvantage to shopping here is that they do not accept credit or debit cards and so you need to bring cash or a cheque book and card with you.

Maplin Electronics

186 Edgware Road, Marble Arch, W2 (3)
Tel: 0870 264 6000 (order line)
Website: www.maplin.co.uk
Tube: Marble Arch
Bus: 6, 7, 15, 16, 23, 36, 98
Open: Mon-Sat 9am-6pm, Sun 11am-5pm (times vary from store to store)

This chain of electronics stores sells all kinds of electronic goods, and always run promotions. Recent bargains included computer tool kits for £9.99 (half-price), printer cartridge refill kits for £14.99 (reduced by £8), and 50 Verbatum CDs for only £14.99 (half-price). They publish a regular sales catalogue that can be picked up from any store.

Branches at:
120-124 King Street, Hammersmith W6, 52-54 High Holborn WC1, 166-168 Queensway W2, 218-219 Tottenham Court Road W1
View website for other stores.

Stanley Productions
147 Wardour Street, W1
Tel: 020 7494 4545 / 7439 0311
Website: www.stanleyproductions.co.uk
Tube: Piccadilly Circus/Tottenham Court Road
Bus: 14, 19, 38
Open: Mon-Fri 9am-5.30pm
Catalogue available

This company is based in the heart of Soho and caters to the needs of the film and media industry whose offices are also located here. They offer lots of good deals on video and audio tapes, CDs and other forms of data storage. Among the bargains were Konica 180 VHS tapes for 89p each (exc VAT) and 10 TDK CDs for only £5 (exc VAT). They also sell a wide range of TVs, video recorders and video cameras as well as providing a data transfer service for those wanting to copy CDs or VHS tapes.

Tottenham Court Road

TOTTENHAM COURT ROAD

Tube: Tottenham Court Road & Goodge Street
Bus: 10, 24, 29, 73, 134
Open: Mon-Sat 9am-6pm, (some stores open Sunday)

This busy West End street has more electronics stores than anywhere else in London and it is therefore an excellent place to visit to find electronic bargains. Many of the shops house not one business but several trading under one roof from different counters, so you will find one company selling hi-fi equipment and another telephones and faxes. All this is not particularly relevant for the casual visitor to TCR, but it does explain the restless nature of the place with businesses frequently changing hands in a very competitive environment. The best way to find a good deal is by visiting each store in turn and bartering the price down, it usually takes about an hour of wandering from store to store before you get a price that makes retailers blanche and refuse to go any lower. In the course of your travels you will probably find a number of superceeded models which are on special offer and these are often a great deal.

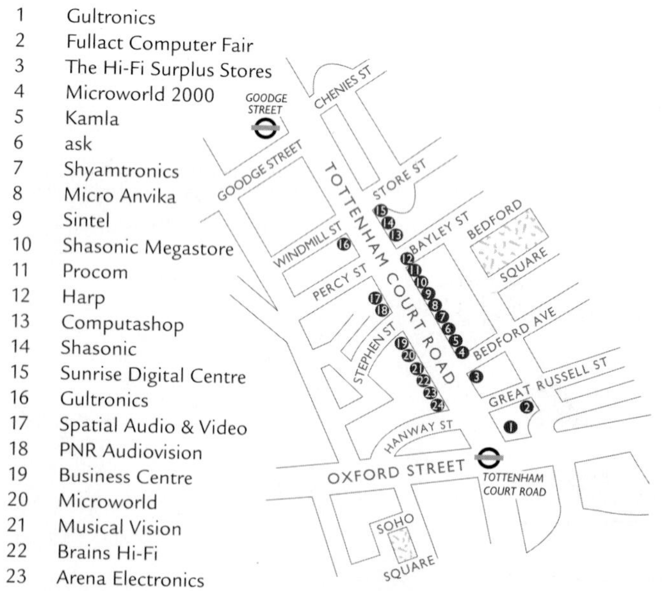

MAIN STORES ON TOTTENHAM COURT ROAD

Gultronics
264-267 Tottenham Court Road, W1
Tel: 020 7436 4120
Website: www.gultronics.co.uk
Branches at:
52 Tottenham Court Road, W1
45 New Oxford Street, WC1
42 Tottenham Court Road, WC1

Hi-Fi Surplus Store
260 Tottenham Court Road, W1
Tel: 020 7323 6712

Microworld 2000
256 Tottenham Court Road, W1
Tel: 020 7323 6712
Website: www.microworld2000.com
Branches at:
26 Tottenham Court Road, W1
27 Tottenham Court Road, W1

ask
248 Tottenham Court Road, W1
Tel: 020 7637 0353 / 020 7637 2690
Website: www.askdirect.co.uk

Kamla
251 Tottenham Court Road, W1
Tel: 020 7323 2747
Website: www.askdirect.co.uk

Brains Hi-Fi & Video
19 Tottenham Court Road, W1
Tel: 020 7631 1109

PNR Audiovision
28 Tottenham Court Road, W1
Tel: 020 7580 9098

Procom Electronics
239-40 Tottenham Court Road, W1
Tel: 020 7631 2020
Website: www.procomdirect.com

Shasonic Megastore
241-2 Tottenham Court Road, W1
Tel: 020 7323 0333
Branches at:
231 Tottenham Court Road, W1
42 Tottenham Court Road, W1

Procom Electronics
239 Tottenham Court Road, W1
Tel: 020 7631 2020
Website: www.procomdirect.com
Also at:
51 Tottenham Court Road, W1

Spatial Audio & Video
29 Tottenham Court Road, W1
Tel: 020 7637 8702

Sunrise Digital Centre
229 Tottenham Court Road, W1
Tel: 020 7637 3727
Website: www.sunrise-online.co.uk

Shyamtronics
246 Tottenham Court Road, W1
Tel: 020 7637 1961

Sintel
243 Tottenham Court Road, W1P

Musical Vision
20/21 Tottenham Court Road, W1
Tel: 020 7636 6025

Harp
237 Tottenham Court Road, W1
Tel: 020 7636 4611
Website: www.askdirect.co.uk

HEALTH & BEAUTY

CONTACT LENSES & GLASSES

CENTRAL

20/20 Optical Store

216-217 Tottenham Court Road, W1
Tel: 020 7596 2020
Website: www.20-20.co.uk
Tube: Goodge Street
Bus: 10, 24, 29, 73, 134
Open: Mon-Fri 9am-8pm, Sat 9am-7pm, Sun 11.30am-6pm

This modern and busy West End optician stocks a great range of frames and lenses. Besides offering interest-free credit, they also have great low prices on frames that are actually stylish. For contact lens wearers, they offer a free one-year aftercare service. Check out the annual summer sale with up to 70% off many products. They even have a café where clients can enjoy a nosh and a drink before or after shopping. Their one-hour service on grinding lenses and preparing contacts keeps busy people happy.

Specsavers Opticians

6-17 Tottenham Court Road, W1
Tel: 020 7580 5115
Website: www.specsavers.co.uk
Tube: Goodge Street
Bus: 10, 24, 29, 73, 134
Mon-Fri 10am-8pm, Sat 10am-7pm, Sun 10am-6pm

Plenty of attractive frames for £75 as well as Specsavers' cheapest range of £30 frames and some designer styles that go for about £175. They often offer deals like two pairs for the price of one so it's worth checking what's on offer. Check their website for the locations of the 23 other London branches. They allow drop-in appointments.

University Vision

University of London Union Building, Malet Street, WC1
Tel: 020 7636 8925
Tube: Euston Square
Bus: 10, 24, 29, 73, 134
Open: Mon-Fri 9am-5.30pm

The stock here runs the gamut from cheap and cheerful to expensive designer frames. They usually offer some sort of deal involving frames and lenses for less than £50. Two pairs of soft contact lenses with after care service can cost from £60. 10% discount for students and the promise to match prices elsewhere.

Vision Express
263-265 Oxford Street, W1
Tel: 020 7409 7880
Website: www.visionexpress.co.uk
Tube: Oxford Circus
Bus: 7, 8, 10, 25, 55, 73, 98, 176
Open: Mon-Sat 9.30am-8pm, Sun 12noon-6pm
Obviously, the emphasis here is on quick service. They stock a large variety of designer frames and often offer two for one specials. Prices for frames start at £39. If you want a reasonably priced frame with good lenses you'll pay about £189 for the package. They also do speciality eyewear like swimming goggles and ski masks with prescription lenses.
Also at:
Whiteley Centre, Queens Way, Bayswater W2, Tel: 020 7727 1888
Brent Cross Shopping Centre NW4, Tel: 020 8202 6715
Canada Square, Canary Wharf E14, Tel: 020 7513 2408
324 High Road, Chiswick W4, Tel: 020 8994 6534
82 The Broadway Centre, Ealing W5, Tel: 020 8840 1880
37-39 High Holborn WC1, Tel: 020 7831 2670
133A High Road, Woodgreen N22, Tel: 020 8889 8245

NORTH

Camden Contact Lens Centre (1)
32-36 Camden High Street, NW1
Tel: 020 7383 3838
Website: www.camdenopticians.co.uk
Tube: Camden Town
Bus: 24, 27, 29, 88, 134, 168, 214, 253
Open: Mon to Fri 9.30am-6.30pm, Sat 9am-5pm, Sun 11am-4pm
This shop offers great value contact lenses plus quick and efficient service. Good deals include 3 months' supply of Bausch & Lomb daily contact lenses for only £65. The shop also has a good range of prescription spectacles and sunglasses with offers like free lenses with every pair of designer frames and 25% off all designer sunglasses including top names such as Armani and Rayban.

Hackney Opticians
1 Northwold Road, N16
Tel: 020 7254 6978
Rail: Stoke Newington
Bus: 67, 73, 76, 149, 243
Open: Mon-Sat 9am-5.30pm
This unassuming and friendly opticians stocks excellent budget frames that start at £25. Contact lenses cost from £42 for a three month supply.

WEST

Optical World

3

166 Uxbridge Road, W12
Tel: 020 8740 7100
Tube: Shepherd's Bush
Bus: 49, 95, 207, 260, 272, 283, 607
Open: Mon-Fri 9am-5pm, Sat 9am-2pm

The most keenly priced plastic frames here sell for around £35-£40 and some frames are half-price. The contact lenses are also worth checking out, as there are bargains to be had. If you are in possession of a NHS voucher worth £29.30, expect to pay an additional £5 for the cheapest lenses and frames.

EAST

Bleetman Opticians

347 Bethnal Green Road, E2
Tel: 020 7739 2356
Tube: Bethnal Green
Bus: 8, D3
Open: Mon-Sat 9.15am-5.15pm

This friendly opticians stock the full spectrum from cheap frames to more expensive designer frames. Chunky plastic frames will set you back at least £15 while more delicate metal frames cost from £20. They offer a computer imaging system that allows customers to see their faces with a variety of different frame styles.

New Era Optical

114 High Street, E17
Tel: 020 8509 1935
Tube: Walthamstow Central
Bus: 123, 212, 275
Open: Thu-Sat 9.30am-5pm

54 Leather Lane, EC1
Tel: 020 7405 0618
Tube: Chancery Lane
Bus: 19, 38, 55, 243
Open: Mon-Fri 9.30am-5.30pm

Find a solid choice of economy and designer frames at these opticians. Plastic frames start at £29 and the cheapest metal frames are £39. Some of the better metal frames go for as little as £49-£59. The Leather Lane branch is much bigger and has better opening hours than the Walthamstow branch.

OUTER LONDON

Mr Scher's Spectacle Shop

278 High Road, Loughton, IG10
Tel: 020 8508 5852
Tube: Loughton
Bus: 20, 167, 397, 549

& 4 Jubilee Parade, Snakes Lane East, Woodford Green, IG8
Tel: 020 8504 9243
Tube: Woodford
Bus: 275, 549

Open Mon-Sat 9.30am-5pm, closed 1pm-2pm (both branches)
This friendly small family-run business supplies excellent frames at low prices. Plastic frames start at £10, fashion frames from £20, while lighter metal frames cost from £39 a pair. Daily wear contact lenses run from £70 for a 3 month supply. The opticians do both NHS and private care.

J.McAndrews Optician

HAIRCARE & COSMETICS

Remember to check out the High Street stores such as Superdrug and Boots for temporary seasonal knock-down prices and two-for-the-price-of-one offers. Body Shop's £1 sale in the new year is particularly good for bargain cosmetics. Don't forget to look at the markets for cheap cosmetics and hair products – Shepherd's Bush, North End Road and Whitechapel markets are particularly good for these types of bargains.

CENTRAL

Pure Beauty

19-20 Long Acre, WC2
Tel: 0845 129 6601
Website: www.purebeautystores.co.uk
Tube: Covent Garden
Bus: 1, 24, 29, 59, 68, 91, 168, 171, 176, 188
Open: Mon-Wed 10am-7pm, Thurs-Fri 10am-8pm, Sat 10am-7pm, Sun 12noon-6pm

Though selling top-name, high-priced cosmetic goodies, Pure Beauty (opened by Boots pharmacy) has taken a different road when it comes to selling. Luckily for bargain hunters, there is a policy of no hard-selling here and they don't even have counters. The biggest bargain is their series of "quick fixes," which are completely free. The five-minute aromatherapy head or hand massage is also free! Eyebrow reshaping is only a fiver. Makeovers without the pushy sales promotion afterwards costs £15 and last between 30 and 60 minutes. You should book ahead for the makeovers, but you can drop by for everything else.

Also at: 151 Oxford Street W1, Tel: 0845 129 6604

Sally Hair and Beauty Supplies

81 Shaftesbury Avenue, W1
Tel: 020 7434 0064
Website: www.sallybeauty.co.uk
Tube: Leicester Square
Bus: 14, 19, 38,
Open: Mon-Sat 8am-8pm, Sun 11am-5pm

More make-up, lotions, hairspray and other beauty accoutrements than one could ever need. Professionals and beauty mavens flock here to pick up everything from tooth whitening products to hair dye. Hairdressers are well catered for with an outstanding range of permanent hair colours, extensions and accessories. You can also stock up on essentials like shampoo, conditioner, hair gel or nail polish.

Also at:
18 Carlisle Road NW9, Tel: 020 8205 0111
44 Golders Green Road NW11, Tel: 020 8455 50 66
394 North End Road SW6, Tel: 020 7386 7863

9 7

NORTH

Salon Services
6 Penton Grove, off White Lion Street, N1
Tel: 020 7713 5000
Tube: Angel
Bus: 30, 73
Open: Mon-Wed, Fri 9am-5pm, Thurs 9am-8pm, Sun 10am-2pm
This small wholesale outlet serves the salon industry, but is open to the public for most purchases. A myriad of haircare products from shampoo (L'Oréal and generic brands) to rollers and brushes are for sale at a discount here. Revlon nail polish was a bargain at £3.79 and Mavala nail polish was just £1.79. A pack of bendy rollers goes for about £2.99.

Top Value Drug Store
see entry on page 217.

EAST

Beauty Collection
85 Whitechapel High Street, E1
Tel: 020 7375 2612
Tube: Aldgate East
Bus: 25, 67, 253
Open: Mon-Fri 10am-6.30pm, Sat-Sun 10am-4pm
This dinky little shop is quiet, but there are some bargains to be had, though it is mainly a wholesale outfit with some retail trade. Goodies like a Veet depilatory set is £3.99, a bottle of Vaseline lotion sells for £1.59 and Palmolive shower gel costs £1.99. Make-up is limited, but a Revlon pack of three nail polishes and two lipsticks goes for about £6 and brand-name perfumes from makes like Burberry and Polo sell for about half the department store price. Also does hair accessories and hair colouring kits.

East End Cosmetics
131 Middlesex Street, E1
Tel: 020 7626 4015
Tube: Liverpool Street
Bus: 67
Open: Mon-Fri 9.30am-5.30pm, Sun 9am-4pm
Bustling on Sundays when the market is open, East End Cosmetics draws the ladies in with booming speakers on the pavement advertising the amazing bargains inside and for the most part, there are indeed bargains to be found on the jam-packed shelves. Grab a basket and shop for every cosmetic under the sun. An excellent selection of hair accessories and belts lines one wall, and others are filled with brand name perfume at half-price, make-up displays and hair colouring kits. The staff will even assist you with choices. A tub of Olay double-action night cream costs £3.99, L'Oréal lipstick was marked down from £9.99 to £2.99 and four bottles of Revlon polish go for £3. This place has by far the biggest selection and best prices in the area.

South Molton Drug Store
53 Roman Road, E2
Tel: 020 8981 5040
Tube: Bethnal Green
Bus: 8, D6
Open: Tues, Thurs, Sat 9.30am-5.30pm, Mon, Wed, Fri 10am-5.30pm
Don't expect a load of help or young women attacking you with brushes and powder. Rather here at this unassuming shop, you will find deep discounts on end-of-lines from major cosmetic houses like Guérlain, Estée Lauder and Max Factor. They also sell cheap and cheerful Barry M cosmetics. No perfume, though.

Silverfields Chemist
141 Homerton High Street, E9
Tel: 020 8985 2030
Rail: Homerton
Bus: 236, S2, W15
Open: Mon-Wed, Fri 9am-7pm, Thurs & Sat 9am-6pm
This dispensing chemist is a great place to come for discounted brand name perfumes and aftershaves. Most perfumes are sold at a 50% discount. For men find a 30ml bottle of Calvin Klein's Contradiction eau de toilette at £14.99 and a 50ml bottle of Acqua di Gio eau de toilette for £24.99. Women are well catered for as well with bargains such as a 50ml bottle of Estée Lauder's Beautiful eau de toilette at £26.99 or Calvin Klein's Eternity for £26.99.

HAIRDRESSING

Opening hours listed are specifically for model/trainee haircuts only. Be aware that cuts or colouring can take up to three hours at the hairdressing schools since students tend be meticulous and careful.

CENTRAL

Nicky Clarke
130 Mount Street, W1
Tel: 020 7499 9023
Website: www.nickyclarke.com
Tube: Bond Street/Green Park
Bus: 3, 8, 25, 53, 55, 176
Open: Tues, Wed from 5.30pm for colour, from 6pm for cuts
Trainee hairdressers, supervised by a stylist (sometimes even Nicky Clarke himself) can cut and colour your hair during one of the training sessions at this sleek salon. Book your appointment at least a month in advance. Colour costs £20 and a cut is £10.

John Frieda
4 Aldford Street, W1
Tel: 020 7493 2693
Tube: Green Park
Bus: 8, 9, 14, 19, 22, 38

& 75 New Cavendish Street, W1
Tel: 020 7436 3979
Tube: Great Portland Street/Oxford Circus
Bus: 7, 8, 10, 25, 55, 73, 88, 98, 176, C2
Open: Wed & Thurs from 6pm
John Frieda is famous as a celebrity stylist and even worked on Halle Berry's Oscar night coiffure. To take advantage of the style expertise at this salon, you need to book in advance for their model evenings. Occasionally, it's possible to get same day service. A basic cut costs £5, colouring starts at £10.

Daniel Galvin
42-44 George Street, W1
Tel: 020 7486 9661
Website: www.danielgalvin.com
Tube: Baker Street/Bond Street
Bus: 2, 13, 30, 74, 82, 113, 139, 189, 274
Open: Tues, Wed 5pm-9pm by appointment

This salon is the place to get your hair coloured on the cheap during one of its model evenings. Daniel Galvin is renowned for his colouring techniques and his trainees (supervised by a teacher) can give a basic cut for £7, half a head of highlights for £25, a tint for £20 or vegetable colour for £20.

Andrew Jose and Jingles Academy
84 Lamb's Conduit Street, WC1
Tel: 020 7242 5057
Tube: Russell Square
Bus: 8, 25, 242, 501, 521
Open: Mon-Fri 9am-5.30pm
Clients are not restricted to odd hours at this very busy training academy, but you do need to ring a couple of days in advance to make an appointment. A haircut will set you back £7. Colouring, for £15-£30, is only done on Wednesday and Thursday afternoons.

Macmillan
33 Endell Street, WC2
Tel: 020 7240 4973
Website: www.macmillan-london.co.uk
Tube: Covent Garden
Bus: 14, 19, 24, 28, 29, 176
Open: Mon-Fri from 6pm
This trendy salon is home to Kene Franklin's 'invisible layers' technique that makes your hair look one length whilst adding volume and texture. Popular with celebrities for its full-price cuts, bargain hunters can book in for a trainee session for free at Factory, the academy here. More complicated cuts may require you to pay £10 and colouring by trainees can be done at cost for about £30. Book at least a week in advance.

Mr Toppers
148 Charing Cross Road, WC2
Tel: 020 7240 4744
Tube: Tottenham Court Road/Leicester Square
Bus: 14, 19, 24, 29, 38, 176
Open: Daily 10am-8.30pm
The flagship salon of this cut-rate hairdresser has the longest opening hours and the most chairs. Most of the stylists have trained at London's best salons and some have completed training academy courses elsewhere. £5 will get you a cut (no washing, no drying). On cold days, you are welcome to use a blow dryer before you leave. If you want your hair washed and then cut expect to pay £10. Prices are low because the turnover is high. No appointments necessary and don't expect a cutting-edge style.

Also at:
14 Moor Street, (off Cambridge Circus) WC2, Tel: 020 7434 4088
69 Berwick Street W1, Tel: 020 7287 5127
160 Tottenham Court Road W1, Tel: 020 7388 2601
13 Great Russell Street WC1, Tel: 020 7813 1856
80 Camden High Street NW1, Tel: 020 7813 4332
48 Goodge Street W1, Tel: 020 7436 1380

Toni & Guy
33 St Christopher's Place, W1
Tel: 020 7908 3825
Website: www.toniandguy.co.uk
Tube: Bond Street
Bus: 3, 8, 25, 53, 55, 176
Open: Appointments Mon-Fri 9.15am, 10.30am, 1.15pm or 3pm
This academy concentrates on basic techniques for beginner students. Cuts are just £5. A half-head of highlights goes for £20, tints for £15 and bleaches or colour corrections for £20. You can get a perm or hair relaxing for £15. Look out for vouchers to gain free admission in the publications Ms London or Girl About Town, both of which are handed out gratis at tube stations.

Toni & Guy Advanced Academy
75 New Oxford Street, WC1
Tel: 020 7836 0606
Tube: Tottenham Court Road
Bus: 1, 8, 14, 19, 24, 25, 29, 38, 55, 98, 176, 242
Open: Appointments Tues-Thurs 9.45am, 1.45pm or 2.45pm; Mon 1.45pm or 2.45pm, Fri 9.45am or 1.45pm
This is the advanced academy so the focus is on trend setting and innovation. Expect a complete change of style; the cost of a cut is £5. Colouring is £20, but occasionally can be free if the funky cut requires colour to emphasize it. Don't expect to have any input into your new style, but do expect something trendy, original and head turning.

Trevor Sorbie
27 Floral Street, WC2
Tel: 020 7395 2907
Tube: Covent Garden/Leicester Square
Bus: 24, 29, 176
Open: Mon-Tues 7-10pm (book 2 weeks in advance)
A practically unbeatable price, the colouring and cuts are free. Assistants supervised by teachers will style your hair for you, but the whole procedure costs an investment of time. Basically, you need to drop in for a

consultation and then an appointment for a cut or colour will be booked depending on when the student will be working and on what you need.

Vidal Sassoon Advanced Academy

20 Grosvenor Street, W1
Tel: 020 7491 0030
Website: www.vidalsasoon.co.uk
Tube: Bond Street
Bus: 3, 8, 25, 53, 55, 176
Open: Appointments Mon-Fri 9.30am or 1.30pm

This is most innovative of the salons and they look for models that are between 15-35 years old. Be prepared for a very high fashion, cutting-edge look. Cuts and colour are complimentary, but subject to availability and you must book in advance. Cutting is by fully trained staff as opposed to trainees.

Vidal Sassoon Creative School

17 Queen Street, W1
Tel: 020 7318 5205
Tube: Green Park
Bus: 8, 9, 14, 19, 22, 38
Open: Appointments Mon-Fri 9.30am or 1.30pm

This salon works on the same principle as the Advanced Academy meaning that you should be in the market for an avant-garde restyle. Cutting and colouring are complimentary and require an appointment in advance.

Vidal Sassoon School

56-58 Davies Mews, W1
Tel: 020 7318 5205
Tube: Bond Street
Bus: 3, 8, 25, 53, 55, 176
Open: Appointments Mon-Fri 9.30am or 1.30pm

Students from around the globe come here to learn the secrets of Vidal Sassoon. Occasionally, you can find a voucher in Metro or The Evening Standard. Otherwise, prices are as follows: £9.50 for a cut, students, OAPs and unemployed £6.50. Colouring costs £17.50 for basic colour; a half-head of highlights will set you back £32; and a perm is only £5.50. Unlike the other salons, you are welcome to have an input in your final style and bring along a photo of what you want.

NORTH

Cutting Bar

27b Islington High Street (on White Lion Street), N1
Tel: 020 7278 8720
Tube: Angel
Bus: 4, 19, 30, 38, 43, 56, 73, 341
Open: Mon-Sat 10am-7pm, Sun 11am-6pm

Drop in to this wee salon to get a quick cut for £5. If you want a shampoo or styling with a blow dry, the price skyrockets to £15 or £25 depending on hair length. In an innovative move, you provide the colouring product (you can have someone take you to nearby Boots or Superdrug to pick one out) and they do the colouring for £10. Highlights cost £20-£30 and they provide the chemicals. No appointment needed.

Also at:
23-25 Queensway W2, Tel: 020 7727 9594

Supreme Hair Design

10-12 West Green Road, N15
Tel: 020 8800 7459
Tube/Rail: Seven Sisters
Bus: 67, 41, 259, 279
Open: Mon-Thurs 9.30am-5.30pm, Fri 9.30am-7.30pm, Sat 8.30am-5.30pm

This salon specialises in Afro hair, but also works on European hair. Hair relaxing costs from £30. A trim is a paltry £5. Colouring a whole head or highlights is from £30 and tinting roots is £25. These bargain prices are for the salon and if you have more time and less money, prices are about 30% cheaper if you book in with one of the half a dozen students who train here.

WEST

L'Oréal Technical Centre

255 Hammersmith Road, W6
Tel: 020 8762 4292
Tube: Hammersmith
Bus: 9, 10, 27, 31, 295, 220, 391
Open: Mon-Fri 9.30am-1.45pm

The basic haircut is free, but if you want to colour your hair or get a perm then it's £13. You need to call in advance for an appointment and let them know what you want done. They will then book you into a class that is working on that type of style. You may have to wait a few weeks for your appointment.

Household Goods

BATHROOMS

NORTH

British Bathroom Centre
35-41 Market Place,
Hampstead Garden Suburbs, NW11
Tel: 020 8201 8811
Website: www.britishbathroomcentre.com
Tube: East Finchley
Bus: 102, 143, 234, H3
Open: Mon-Fri 9am-6pm, Sat 10am-4pm
This massive warehouse is an importer, supplier and retailer and promises to double the difference if you can find the same product cheaper elsewhere. The prices are very keen with a complete suite (plus taps) starting from £299 (inc VAT), and large steel baths (1.8m x 0.80m) for £161 (exc VAT). Although the prices are competitive you need to bear in mind that they charge between £15 and £30 for delivery.

Colourwash
165 Chamberlayne Road, NW10
Tel: 020 8459 8918
Website: www.colourwash.co.uk
Tube: Kensal Green
Rail: Kensal Rise
Bus: 6, 18, 23, 52, 187, 295, 302
Open: Mon-Fri 9am-5.30pm, Sat 10am-5pm
This is a well-known outlet for competitively priced designer bathroom suites and accessories. There are frequent special offers and a bathroom suite can start from as little as £450 (inc VAT), with a quality steel bath from only £160. They produce a regular brochure with details of all their core products and prices.
Also at:
Muswell Hill N10, Tel: 020 8365 3222
Fulham SW6, Tel: 020 7371 0911
Surringdale SL5, Tel: 01344 872 096
Wimbledon SW19, Tel: 020 8947 5578

7

WEST

Bathroom Discount Centre

297 Munster Road, Fulham, SW6
Tel: 020 7381 4222
Website: www.bathroomdiscount.co.uk
Tube: Parsons Green
Bus: 14, 74, 190, 220, 211, 295, 424
Open: Mon-Fri 8am-6pm, Sat-Sun 9am-5pm

This large and impressively stocked bathroom showroom has been providing great value and service since 1978. The staff here are very helpful, and they produce regular price lists and send out manufacturer's catalogues free of charge. They have loads of special offers including a complete whirlpool bath for £285 (exc VAT) and a complete bathroom suite for only £149 (exc VAT). All major brands are stocked and they guarantee to offer the lowest price on any item.

Bathstore.com

50 Sulivan Road, Fulham, SW6
Tel: 020 7736 1503
Brochure Line: 07000 228 478
Website: www.bathstore.com
Tube: Parson's Green
Bus: 11, 28, 295, 424
Open: Mon-Fri 9am-6pm, Sat 9am-5pm

This chain of bathroom outlets has a reasonable range of bathroom suites and fittings. The emphasis is on quality rather than the budget end of the market, but they are good value and guarantee to beat any written quote for the same item. They also have regular sales. Also at:
28 Rushgrove Avenue, The Hyde, Collindale NW9, Tel: 020 8200 0508
126-128 Uxbridge Road W13, Tel: 020 8567 7786
256 King Street, Hammersmith W6, Tel: 020 8748 6656

M & S Supplies Bathroom Centre
140 Horn Lane, Acton, W3
Tel: 020 8992 9653
Rail: Acton Central
Bus: 70, 95, 260, 266
Open: Mon-Fri 8am-5pm, Sat 9am-4pm

This is a very long established company, trading for over 50 years, but which moved to its present site in the last 8 years. They offer sound advice, excellent service and give the general public the same discounts as trade customers. They concentrate on recognised manufacturers, with suites starting from £350 (exc VAT).

Waterforce

103-7 Windmill Road, South Ealing, W5
Tel: 020 8568 7672
Rail: Brentford
Bus: E2, E8, H91
Open: Mon-Fri 8am-6pm, Sat 9am-5pm

This shop offers some cracking bathroom deals with suites including taps and fittings starting from £254 (exc VAT). They don't have a catalogue, but will try to match any price if you find the same product cheaper elsewhere.

SOUTH

Burge and Gunson

13-23 and 38 High Street, Colliers Wood, SW19
Tel: 020 8543 5166
Tube: Colliers Wood
Bus: 57, 152, 200, 219
Open: Mon-Fri 8am-5.30pm, Sat 8am-4pm

This large store offers a complete bathroom suite with a steel bath for £208 (inc VAT) and will match all quotes. The staff are generally helpful and on a recent price check this shop offered the lowest prices on a range of bathroom products. They produce a regular catalogue showing all their major lines and will offer free delivery in the London area for larger purchases.

Also at:

165 Garth Road, Morden, Surrey, SM4 4LH, Tel: 020 8330 0101

Diamond Plumbers Merchants

43-45 Acre Lane, SW2
Tel: 020 7274 6624/5
Tube/Rail: Brixton
Bus: 35, 37, P5
Open: Mon-Fri 8am-5.30pm, Sat 9am-5pm

This no-nonsense outlet offers good value with a standard sink and bath starting from £150 and steel baths from £66. They hold a small selection, but can order anything from their manufacturers' catalogues within two days. They also act as a plumbing suppliers with all the copper pipe, fittings and equipment you need to do the job yourself.

Plumbcraft Ltd
Unit 2, Ellerslie Square,
Lyham Road, SW2
Tel: 020 7274 0174
Website: www.plumbcraft.co.uk
Tube: Clapham North
Bus: 35, 37, 355, P5
Open: Mon-Fri 8am-5.30pm, Sat 8.30am-1pm
Plumbcraft is an established business offering helpful service, free delivery in the London area and some very good deals. A large steel bath (1.8m x 0.8m) was only £275 (inc VAT) and standard size baths start from only £75, while a budget white bathroom suite starts from £250. They have regular promotions on specific items and on a recent visit offered a bath shower mixer and mono basin mixer for £110 (reduced from £180). An excellent outlet for bathroom bargains.

EAST

A D Jones Ltd
857/861 Forest Road,
Walthamstow, E17
Tel: 020 8527 7189
Rail: Wood Street
Bus: 56, 123, 230, 275, 357
Open: Mon-Fri 9am-5.30pm, Thurs till 1pm, Sat 9am-5pm
This shop extends over three units on Forest Road and holds a reasonable range in stock as well as being able to source anything unusual. The shop offers advice and free delivery in the London area and complete bathroom suites start from a very reasonable £300 (inc VAT).

Mercury Discount
Plumbing and Heating Merchants Ltd
278 Cambridge Heath Road, E2
Tel: 020 8981 5445
Tube: Bethnal Green
Bus: 26, 48, 55, 106, 253, D6
Open: Mon-Fri 8am-5pm, Sat 9am-1pm
This trade counter offers everything the professional or DIY plumber needs from a simple washer to an entire bathroom suite. The novice plumber will be relieved to hear that staff are helpful and will usually take time to explain what it is you need for a job and dispense good advice. If things should go really wrong they always have details of skilled local plumbers to get you out of a fix.

OUTER LONDON

Discount Bathroom Warehouse

Unit 4 Brooklands Approach,
North Street, Romford, RM1
Tel: 01708 725 513
Website: www.discountbathroomcentre.co.uk
Rail: Romford
Bus: 86, 103, 128, 174, 193, 252, 499
Open: Mon-Sat 10am-5.30pm (closed Wed)

This large warehouse is a long journey for many Londoners, but worth the effort with a wide choice of bathroom fixtures and fittings all at competitive prices. Bargains included a steel bath for only £67, basins from only £30 and toilets for £100. As well as basic bathroom suites they also have more unusual items such as large steel baths (1.8m x 0.8m) for only £178 (exc VAT). They can send out catalogues on request and will attempt to match any price.

Other outlets for bathrooms:

See Builders' Merchants on pages 106-7, many of which sell good value bathroom suites and accessories.

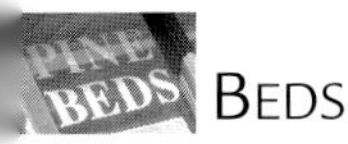

BEDS

If you are looking for a second-hand bed frame or headboard it might be worth trawling around a few junk shops (see pages 237-246) or visiting one of the many auctions reviewed later on in this book (see pages 181-187). Futon shops are also a good place to look for cheap places to sleep and we have reviewed Futon Company which is one of the best value outlets in the furniture section (see page 130 for further details).

SOUTH

Comfortably Off
70a Silverthorne Road, SW8
Tel: 020 7622 9393
Website: www.comfortablyoff.co.uk
Tube: Queenstown
Bus: 44, 137, 344
Open: Fri 12noon-6pm, Sat 10am-6pm, Sun 11am-4pm
These guys deal mostly with trade except at the weekend when they open to the public. The turnover is quick on the high quality sofas so arrive early. Prices are about £600 to £1200 for sofabeds and sofas. They carry mostly British maker Tetrad as well as a smattering of international furniture makers.

EAST

Citybeds Ltd
17-39 Gibbins Road, Stratford, E15
Tel: 020 8534 9000 or 0800 026 3414
Website: www.citybeds.co.uk
Tube/Rail: Stratford
Bus: 25, 52, 108, 276, D8
Open: Mon-Sat 8.30am-5pm
In business for more than two decades, this bed warehouse specialises in Duckers, Airsprung, Dico and Silentnight at discount prices. Find futon and sofa beds for £169, pine or metal beds for as low as £75, beds with storage for £99, sturdy bunk beds for £139 and mattresses for £38. Call their freephone for advice before trying to negotiate the warehouse on your own.
Also at:
20-22 Fowler Rd, Hainault Industrial Estate, Essex IG6, Tel: 020 8501 2426
Unit 2C, Claydons Lane, Rayleigh Weir, Essex SS6, Tel: 01268 772 422
Open: Mon-Sat 9am-5.30pm, Sun 11am-4pm

Litvinoff and Fawcett
281 Hackney Road, E2
Tel: 020 7739 3480
Website: www.litvinoffandfawcett.co.uk
Rail: Cambridge Heath
Bus: 26, 48, 55
Open: Mon-Sat 9am-6pm, Sun 10am-5pm
Litvinoff and Fawcett have been making beds since the 1970s and they put a lot of attention and care into their work. Solidly built and simply designed wooden frame beds with the option of a variety of headboards and under-bed storage are available. Considering the quality, the prices are very reasonable and the beds have a lifetime guarantee. A single, simple pine bed costs £90 or £115 with under-bed storage. Stacking beds go for £185 and bunk beds from £300. The staff are very helpful and well-informed.
Also at: 238 Grays Inn Road WC1, Tel: 020 7278 5391

Bargain beds can also be found at:
Big Table Furniture Co-Op Ltd (see page 224)
Moss Brothers Metal Design (see page 230)
Taurus Pine Beds and Mattresses (see page 226)
Big Bed & Pine Company (see page 129)

BEDDING

Below are some of the best outlets for quality bedding in London. If you are looking for top quality pre-war linen (which is beautifully made and much sought after) try The Portobello Cloth Shop (see page 103). If you don't mind the idea of buying hotel linen, there are several outlets on Sclater Street (part of Brick Lane Market) that sell these good condition 100% cotton sheets for just a few pounds.

NORTH

Bradleys Curtain and Linen Centre
184 Kentish Town Road, NW5
Tel: 020 7485 0029
Tube: Kentish Town Road
Bus: 46, 134, 214, C2
Open: Mon-Sat 9am-6pm
In business for over 30 years, Bradleys is a neighbourhood institution. The family-run shop is a good place to equip your bed with quality sheets at fair prices. They also stock every other household linen from towels to curtains. Find luxurious Egyptian cotton double sheets for £30.

WEST

Bedstock @ Puppy 4
26 Portobello Green Arcade
& 281 Portobello Road, W10
Tel/Fax: 020 8964 1547
Website: www.puppy-bedstock.co.uk
Tube: Ladbroke Grove
Bus: 7, 23, 52, 70
Open: Mon-Sat 10am-6pm
This quirky and eclectic shop stocks trendy and desirable linens and pillows for the home at reasonable prices. Their most popular sheets are 100% cotton with a white background printed with vibrant red roses. A graphic magenta and orange striped double bed set costs £48. The in-house plain-dye service means that you can order custom sheets. Slightly more expensive, but highly sought-after are the pillow cases with retro or photographic printed fabric. A 1950s cowboy pattern or a quirky sushi print on a pillow case costs £12.

Peacock Blue

7

201 New King's Road, SW6
Tel: 0870 333 1555
Website: www.peacockblue.co.uk
Tube: Parson's Green
Bus: 22, 39, 85, 93, 265, 270, 424
Open: Mon-Fri 10-6, Sat 10-5

Peacock Blue is excellent for budget shoppers willing to take a gamble and possibly pick up some first-rate sheets, duvet covers and pillowcases. Stocking high-end, internationally sourced bedding at full price, Peacock Blue usually has some discontinued lines on offer for less than half the original price. A fitted double sheet that was originally £22 was marked down to £6. Their website often offers a better selection of sale items than does the shop.

Shaukat Fabrics

168-172 Old Brompton Road, SW5
Tel: 020 7373 8956
Tube: Gloucester Road
Bus: 49, 70, 74, C1
Open: Mon-Sat 10am-6.30pm

As well as fabrics and bags, Shaukat also sell a great value selection of bedding from their basement. The good deals include a kingsize cotton sheet for £10.99, a 15 tog double duvet for £15.99 and a plain white cotton duvet cover for only £12.99. For more details about Shaukat's fabric and bags see pages 48 and 122.

EAST

Dreamland Linen

342 Bethnal Green Road, E2
Tel: 020 7739 0051
Tube: Bethnal Green
Bus: 8, 106, 253, D3, D6
Open: Mon-Sat 9am-6pm

Dreamland offer exceptional deals on bedding, including single 100% cotton sheets for £5.99 and double sheets for only £6.99. They also have great value duvet covers with a king size 100 % cotton duvet cover with 2 pillow cases for only £14.99. Quality pillows are only £4.99 each and cotton pillow covers are £2.99 a pair. The shop has both white linen and a range of colours, but avoids the excess of patterned bedding familiar to many discount bedding shops. Dreamland also offer a range of net curtains, heavy curtains and curtain track, pole and wire fittings at very competitive prices.

CARPETS, RUGS & TILES

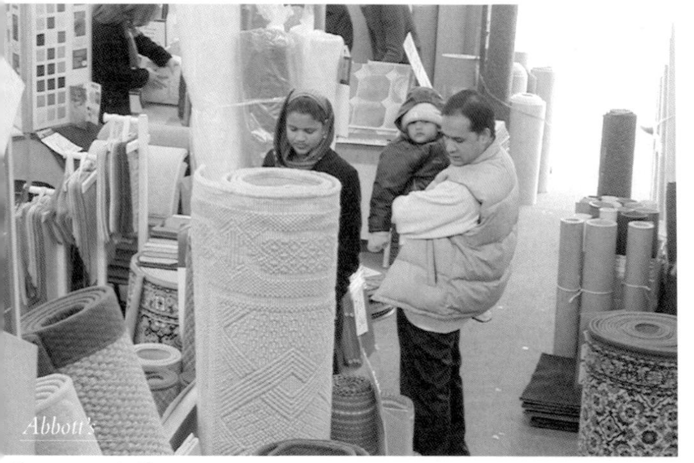

CARPETS & RUGS

CENTRAL

West End Carpets
1 Baker Street, W1
Tel: 020 7224 6635
Website: www.westendcarpets.co.uk
Sales Line: 0800 146 447
Tube: Baker Street
Bus: 2, 13, 30, 74, 82, 113, 139, 189, 274
Open: Mon-Fri 9am-5.30pm

& 928 High Road, North Finchley, N12
Tel: 020 8446 5331
Tube: Woodside Park
Bus: 125, 221, 263, 326, 383
Open: Mon-Fri 9am-5.30pm, Sun 10am-4pm
Dealing in high-quality carpets, West End carpets is one of the smarter carpet shops in the city. Bargains can be found in their stock of room-size remnants and choice mixed fibre carpeting starts at £10 per square metre. In general, prices here are good considering the excellent carpets on offer.

NORTH

Battens Carpets & Wood Floors
413 Holloway Road, N7
Tel: 020 7609 4268
Tube: Holloway Road
Bus: 43, 153, 271
Open: Mon-Sat 9am-5.30pm, Sun 10.30am-4.30pm
Alongside a regular priced selection of wood flooring, Battens sells carpet remnants at a 50% discount with prices running from £4.99 to £7.99 a square metre. Heavy-duty domestic carpet both plain and patterned starts at £3.99 a square metre. In general, mostly plain carpet rolls available.

Carpet Tile Centre 8
227 Woodhouse Road, N12
Tel: 020 8361 1261
Tube: Arnos Grove
Bus: 34, 184, 232, 251, 298
Open: Mon-Sat 9am-5pm, Sat 9am-1pm
A wide range of perfect tiles at reasonable prices can be had here, but the real bargains are the seconds. You can pick up a discounted Huega tile from £1.95 each and that's about half the original price.

Leebanks Carpet Centre
71-75 Essex Road, N1
Tel: 020 7359 6482
Tube: Angel
Bus: 38, 56, 73, 341
Open: Mon-Fri 9am-5pm, Sat 9am-4.30pm
Mostly selling high-end carpets, they do have a limited stock of cord carpet rolls from £1.99 per square metre.

S & M Myers
100-106 Mackenzie Road, N7
Tel: 020 7609 0091
Website: www.myerscarpets.co.uk
Tube: Caledonian Road
Bus: 17, 91, 259, 274
Open: Mon, Wed, Fri 10-5.30pm, Tues & Thurs 10am-5pm, Sat 9.30am-2pm
This family business started in 1819 and still offers good quality new carpets and a wide range of remnants at very keen prices. Among the bargains an 80% wool mix carpet was only £13.50 a square metre and seagrass started for as little as £8.99 a square metre. The remnants are

displayed on a board and labelled with the dimensions and price, making it easy to choose what you want. A 2.9m x 4m 80% wool remnant was found here for only £128. The East End Road branch has a wider range of rugs, but all remnants can be cut and the edges sewn at very little cost to make a bespoke rug. Probably the best budget carpet outlet in the capital.

Also at:
81-85 East End Road N2, Tel: 020 8444 3457
Open: Mon-Fri 8am-5.30pm, Sat 9.30am-5pm

Palace Floorings UK Ltd
20 Palace Gates Road, N22
Tel: 020 8881 2538
Rail: Alexandra Palace
Bus: 184, W3
Open: Mon-Sat 9.15am-5.30pm
This small shop has been trading for over 20 years and offers a good range of carpets and vinyls as well as an expert fitting service. Hardworking, synthetic carpets cost as little as £3.99 per square metre, but natural fibre carpets are less of a good deal at £45 per square metre.

Soviet Carpet and Art Galleries
303-305 Cricklewood Broadway, NW2
Tel: 020 8452 2445
Website: www.russian-art.co.uk
Tube: Cricklewood Broadway
Bus: 16, 32, 245, 266, 316
Open: Sun 10.30am-5.30pm (other times by appointment)
This former trade warehouse has been opening its doors to the public since 1992, offering large discounts on paintings from the former Soviet Union and rugs from Eastern Europe as well as Afghanistan, Iran, China and Turkey. There are thousands of hand-made rugs to choose from and all are sold at roughly half the usual retail price. The quality is so high on their items that many are auctioned at Sotheby's.

West End Carpets
922-928 High Road, North Finchley, N12
See main entry in Central page 91

David J. Wilkins
27 Princess Road, Regent's Park, NW1
Tel: 020 7722 7608
Website: www.orientalrugexperts.com
Tube: Camden Town
Bus: 27, 31, 274, C2
Open: Mon-Fri 9am-5pm (by appointment only)
Not your everyday retailer, this family-run business sources their stock from wholesale warehouses and passes on the savings to customers. The choice is immense compared to High Street retailers and prices are at least 25% less. Iranian and Afghan carpets are well represented and sell for as little as £100. The personal service and expert advice come as a bonus.

WEST

The Carpetstore
167 King Street, W6
Tel: 020 8563 2221
Tube: Hammersmith
Bus: 27, 190, 267, 391, H91

& 156 Goldhawk Road, W12
Tel: 020 8749 9340
Tube: Goldhawk Road
Bus: 94, 237
Open: Mon-Sat 9am-5pm

Visit the Goldhawk Road branch for a wide range of remnants. The rest of their carpets and linos represent a good selection of flooring options. Call to check what special offers are on as they don't normally discount regular stock. However, one established good value buy is the Sultan Berber carpet for £10.75 per square metre plus a free fitting service.

Gray and Lowe
91 Uxbridge Road, W12
Tel: 020 8743 5854
Tube: Shepherd's Bush
Bus: 49, 95, 207, 237, 260, 272, 607
Open: Mon-Wed, Fri 7am-5.30pm, Sat 8am-5.30pm
Bargain hunters should start with a search through the room-size remnants before moving on to the decently priced natural and synthetic carpets that go as low as £2.40 per square metre. Top quality wool carpet weighs in at a hefty £65 per square metre.

Hani Wells Carpets
452 Edgware Road, W2
Tel: 020 7723 5522
Website: www.haniwells.com
Tube: Edgware Road
Bus: 6, 16, 98
Open: Daily 9am-6pm
Serious bargains await you at this retailer offering carpets, vinyls, laminates and wood flooring at a minimum 30% discount. Carpet prices start at the unbelievably low price of 89p per square metre. Extra-wide carpet rolls are also on offer. Dedicated bargain hunters might like to take advantage of their price-matching guarantee.

SOUTH

Carpetman
7A Putney Bridge Road, SW18
Tel: 020 8875 0232
Website: www.carpetman.co.uk
Rail: Wandsworth Town
Bus: 220, 270, 77A
Open: Mon-Sat 8am-6pm
Carpets in plenty of styles and colours sell for as little as £3.99 per square metre at this warehouse-style shop that is one of the best outlets in London. Remnants represent a good bargain at a 50% discount from the original price and there is usually a fair selection. Seagrass, jute and sisal flooring comprises the bulk of the stock and start at around £10.75 per square metre.

L.W. Carpet Warehouse
239-241 Balham High Road, SW17
Tel: 020 8672 1902
Tube: Tooting Bec
Bus: 155, 249, 355
Open: Mon-Sat 9am-5.30pm
In business for more than three decades, this Balham shop offers good value flooring and beds and the helpful staff provide a fitting service and express delivery within the city. Find carpets, vinyls and wood laminates at a discount.

Discount Carpets
382 Streatham High Road, SW16
Tel: 020 8677 7010
Rail: Streatham
Bus: 57, 109, 118, 133, 159, 201, 250, 255, 315, 319, P13
Open: Mon-Fri 9am-6pm, Sat 9am-5pm
This south London shop stocks over 100 room-size remnants to choose from as well as about forty end-of-line carpet rolls with varying colours and designs. Prices drop as low as £2.80 a square metre.

H Dourof & Sons Ltd
70-72 Rushey Green, Catford, SE6
Tel: 020 8690 3938
Rail: Catford/Catford Bridge
Bus: 75, 124, 138, 171, 181, 185, 202
Open: Mon-Wed, Fri-Sat 9am-5pm, Thurs 9am-1pm
A favoured local shop, this family-run business has been trading for over 45 years. Prices for carpet start at a reasonable £2.99 per square metre and there is plenty of choice. The best value is represented in the discounted end of rolls.

EAST

Abbott's
470-480 Roman Road, E3
Tel: 0800 716 783
Website: www.abbottscarpets.co.uk
Tube: Mile End/Bethnal Green
Bus: 8, 277, 339, D6
Open: Mon-Fri 8.30am-5.30pm, Sat 8.30am-5pm
Cheap rugs (for as little as £14), trendy Dalsouple rubber flooring for £39 a square metre and heavily discounted room-size remnants keep customers happy at this shop that has been trading for over a century. The selection of carpets, lino and laminate all comes at competitive prices and is worth looking at for top-value flooring solutions.

Marcon & Co
14 Leytonstone Road, E15
Tel: 020 8503 1115
Tube/Rail: Stratford
Bus: 69, 257, 308
Open: Mon-Sat 8.30am-5.30pm
This very busy shop sells carpets and vinyl flooring. The best deals are on the room-size remnants. They also offer a fitting and delivery service.

TILES

NORTH

The Reject Tile Shop

2A England's Lane, NW3
See main entry in West London page 98 for further details.

Topps Tiles

Unit 2, 92-94 Stamford Hill, N16
Tel: 020 8806 4688
Website: www.toppstiles.co.uk
Rail: Stoke Newington
Bus: 149, 243, 67, 76, 73
Open: Mon & Fri 8am-8pm, Tues-Thurs 8am-6pm,
Sat 9am-5.30pm, Sun 11am-5pm

Covering over 7,500 square feet, this warehouse tile outlet will beat any price by 5%. If you're not into price-matching schemes, you can still come away with a bargain such as simple white tiles for £4.40 per square metre. Better quality, coloured tiles are about double that price at £10.89 per square metre. Call in advance to check special promotions that lower prices by 30%.

Also at:
Rookery Way, The Hyde, Collindale NW9, Tel: 020 8200 8100
78-79 Goding Street, Vauxhall SE11, Tel: 020 7820 8882
Station Road, New Southgate N11, Tel: 020 8368 2400
596-598 Old Kent Road SE15, Tel: 020 7732 7272
Unit 1 Meridian Trade Estate Lombard Wall, Charlton SE7, Tel: 020 82931233
2-6 Rushey Green, Catford SE6, Tel: 020 8690 2917
124 Oakfield Road, Penge SE20, Tel: 020 8778 6447
Unit 25, Carnwath Industrial Estate, Carnwath Rd SW6, Tel: 020 7384 1300
Unit 3 Becton Retail Park (off Alpine Way), Beckton E6, Tel: 020 7511 2663

TWS Ceramics Ltd

270 Kentish Town Road, NW5
Tel: 020 7485 9455/7605
Tube: Kentish Town
Bus: 134, 214, C2
Open: Mon-Fri 9.30am-5.30pm, Sat 9.30am-5pm

Basic white tiles cost £10 per square metre, but with that price you'll get friendly, informed advice from the staff at this shop, which has been trading for 20 years. In general, the floor and wall tiles are priced competitively and they offer cool rubber and glass tiles.

WEST

The Reject Tile Shop
178 Wandsworth Bridge Road, SW6
Tel: 020 7731 6098
Website: www.criterion-tiles.co.uk
Tube: Parson's Green
Bus: 28, 295
Open: Mon-Fri 9.30am-5.30pm, Sat 10am-5pm

& 2A England's Lane, NW3
Tel: 020 7483 2608
Tube: Belsize Park
Bus: 46, 168, 268, C11
Open: Mon-Fri 10am-6pm, Sat 10am-5pm
This is the best place to buy discount tiles in London. Most High Street tile shops sell on their very slight seconds to the Reject Tile Shop so you'll encounter many elegant, fashionable and interesting tiles at low prices. Among the bargains here, find hand-made tiles that usually retail for £100 per square metre at about £50 per square metre. Look out for their regular clearance sales that dramatically reduce the already low prices. The Reject Tile Shop is part of the full-price Criterion Tiles company.

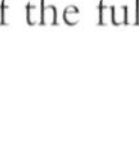

Tile Superstore
157-159 Goldhawk Road, W12
Tel: 020 8749 1115
Tube: Goldhawk Road
Bus: 94, 237

& Unit 6
Sergeants Industrial Estate
102 Garratt Lane, SW18
Tel: 020 8877 3919
Tube: Wandsworth Town
Bus: 44, 270
Open: Mon-Fri 8am-5pm, Sat 9am-4pm

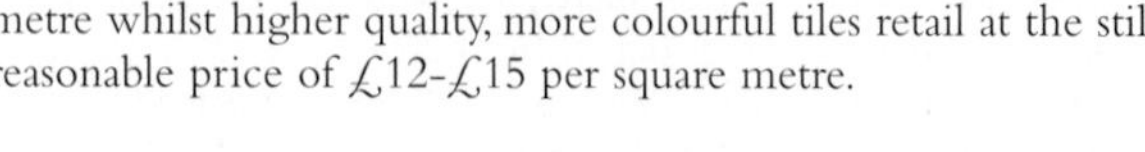

Imported, continental tiles at a 20% discount are for sale at this superstore. Basic white bathroom tiles go for as little as £5.99 per square metre whilst higher quality, more colourful tiles retail at the still very reasonable price of £12-£15 per square metre.

SOUTH

Tile Superstore

102 Garratt Lane, SW18
See main entry in West London (page 98) for full details.

Topps Tiles

78-79 Goding Street, Vauxhall, SE11
See main entry in North London (page 97) for full details.

EAST

Bargain Tile Centre

150 Plashet Road, E13
Tel: 020 8472 5780
E-mail: bargaintiles@hotmail.com
Tube: Upton Park
Bus: 104, 238
Open: Mon-Sat 9am-6pm

Luckily, this East End shop offers a free delivery service within London. Prices are so low that you may end up with more than you can carry home. Ceramic tiles of varying quality are all discounted with basic white tiles going for £2 per square metre. Designer tile prices rise to about £40 per square metre.

N & C Tile Style

3-10 Shoreditch High Street, E1
Tel: 020 7247 5432
Website: www.nichollsandclarke.com
Tube/Rail: Liverpool Street
Bus: 35, 47, 78
Open: Mon-Fri 7.30am-5pm, Sat 8.30am-12.30pm

Part of a huge building materials distribution company, this massive shop stocks a dizzying range of wall and floor tiles. While prices are competitive, the real bargains are the special offers on the end of ranges.

Topps Tiles

See main entry in North London (page 97) for full details.

Ward & Stevens Tiles & Decorating Supplies

248 High Street North, E12
Tel: 020 8472 4067
E-mail: info@wardandstevens.co.uk
Website: www.wardandstevens.co.uk
Tube: East Ham
Bus: 101, 104, 147, 238, 300, 325, 376
Open: Mon-Sat 9am-5.30pm

Ward & Stevens is a definite must for those decorating a bathroom or kitchen on a budget. By purchasing in bulk directly from manufacturers, they are able to sell seconds (from brand names like Pilkington and H R Johnson) and perfect tiles to the public at really low prices. Seconds are discounted by 75%. Simple white wall tiles go for £1.98 per square metre; floor tiles are a bargain at £3.99 per square metre. Border tiles are only 30p each. Laminate flooring and mosaic tiles are also priced competitively.

OUTER LONDON

Just Tiles

142 Kenton Road, HA3
Tel: 020 8907 3020
Website: www.just-tiles.co.uk
Tube: Harrow on the Hill, Northwick Park
Bus: 140, 182, 186, 223, H10, H11, H14, H18
Open: Mon, Tues, Thu-Sat 9am-5.30pm, Sun 10am-4pm

The real bargains to be had here are the end of line promotions. They don't sell seconds, but since they import directly prices are competitive. Choose from a selection of quality bathroom, kitchen and floor tiles in all sizes. They also offer a kiln service where you can get custom-made tiles.

CURTAINS

Curtains can cost a small fortune if you don't know where to shop. London offers dozens of outlets for cut-price fabrics both from UK designers and imported from India and the Far East. You could also explore the shops that sell second-hand curtains, usually supplied by local people moving home or rejected from big hotels. In addition to the outlets listed below some of the most reasonably priced curtain materials and ready-made curtains can be found at John Lewis branches, Ikea, Habitat, M&S, British Home Stores, Homebase or Laura Ashley. Otherwise sale time at department stores like Harrods and Selfridges can produce bargains.

CENTRAL

Alexander Furnishings

51-61 Wigmore Street, W1
Tel: 020 7935 2624
Tube: Bond Street
Bus: 7, 8, 10, 25, 55, 73, 98, 176, 2, 13, 30, 74, 82, 113, 139, 189, 274
Open: Mon-Sat 9am-6pm, Thurs 9am-7pm

The largest independent curtain retailer in London, established fifty years ago, offering an assortment of soft furnishings, upholstery, wallpaper and blinds and curtain fabrics at prices discounted by up to 60%. Housed in a warren of six connecting shops just behind Oxford Street, discontinued fabrics and clearance lines are bought here direct from factories in Italy, India and Belgium. Fabrics that were originally sold at up to £18 a metre are on offer at £4.95 to £5.95. Up-to-date branded stock with discounts on quantities of over 40 to 50 metres. They also offer a making-up service.

NORTH

Changing Curtains

186 Archway Road, Highgate, N6
Tel: 020 8340 9801
Tube: Highgate
Bus: 43, 134, 263
Open: Tues-Sat 10am-4pm, Thurs 10am-8pm

Quality second-hand curtain agency supplied by local people moving home and the odd hotel with constantly changing stock and a made to measure new curtains and blinds service. Some designer fabrics. Second-hand curtains from £60 up to £1,500.

The Curtain Factory Outlet (8)
269 Ballards Lane, North Finchley, N12
Tel: 020 8492 0093
Tube: West Finchley
Bus: 82, 125, 260
Open: Mon-Sat 9am-6pm, Sun 10am-4pm

A curtain wholesalers and exporters with over half a million metres of top designer names on offer in a warren of rooms in a converted house (next to Waitrose). They stock upholstery fabrics as well as curtain material, calico and vibrant coloured voiles. At the back is a trade warehouse which the public are allowed into when business is quiet. The most you will pay is £6.99 per metre (plus VAT) for top names, regardless of the retail price, which could be £50 a metre upwards. They also sell ready-made curtains, have a made to measure service for both curtains and blinds on the premises and new rolls arrive daily. The staff are attentive and very helpful.

The Cloth Shop

Curtain Mill Ltd
15-17 Colindale Avenue, NW9
Tel: 020 8205 2220
Tube: Colindale
Bus: 32, 142, 204, 303
Open: Mon-Sat 9am-5.30pm, Sun 10am-4pm
Factory outlet off the Edgware Road with 1000s of metres of fabrics in rolls from £2 to £30 a metre. They also stock ready-made curtains and offer a wide range of materials including weaves, prints and velvets, linings plus all the trimmings, poles and tie-backs. Making-up service available.

WEST

The Cloth Shop

290 Portobello Road, W10
Tel: 020 8968 6001
Tube: Ladbroke Grove
Bus: 7, 23, 28, 31, 52, 70, 295, 328
Open: Mon-Sat 10am-6pm
Set among the market stalls of Portobello, this small shop is crammed full of amazing, mostly plain, fabrics with nothing over £14 a metre. Lots of linens, muslins, calicoes, and Indian cottons ideal for making up into stylish curtains. Also antique French linen sheets and Welsh wool blankets; furnishing and clothing fabrics, vintage and new.

The Curtain Exchange
129-131 Stephendale Road, SW6
Tel: 020 7731 8316
Website: www.thecurtainexchange.co.uk
Tube: Fulham Broadway/Parson's Green
Bus: 11, 28, 295, 391, 424
Open: Mon-Sat 10am-5pm
There are relatively few outlets for second-hand curtains in London. The Curtain Exchange will only take high quality fabrics (usually inter-lined) in tiptop condition and offer them for about a third of their original price. A warren of eight rooms is lined floor to ceiling with rich velvets, patterned textiles and other sumptuous fabrics. Prices start at around £80 a pair to over £1,000 and provided you leave a cheque for the full amount you can take your chosen curtains home on approval for 24 hours to see how they look. Take detailed measurements of your rail rather than the window, plus the drop, before you visit. Lots of swags, cushions, tie-backs and other accessories. Helpful staff will give advice. Sellers get 60% of sale price for curtains priced at over £200 a pair, 50% for those less than £200. There is a made to measure service (available in any fabric), home fitting service and easy parking within reach.
Also at: *80 Park Hall Road, Dulwich SE21, Tel: 020 8670 5570*

The Curtain Fabric Factory
236a North End Road, W14
Tel: 020 7381 1777
Tube: West Kensington
Bus: 28, 391
Open: Mon-Sat 9.30am-5.30pm
This busy shop near the market has a huge warehouse behind it full of fabrics supplied direct from manufacturers. Some seconds and samples. From £2.99 to £20 a metre. If what you want is not in stock they will order it in. Made to measure service for curtains and blinds, plus tracks and fitting. Also see entry in Discount Outlets on page 217.

SOUTH

Wall to Wall
549 Battersea Park Road, SW11
Tel: 020 7585 3335
Rail: Clapham Junction
Bus: 44, 49, 319, 344, 345
Open: Mon-Sat 10am-4pm
Full-price fabrics and a selection of designer clearance ranges from stock from £9.95 to £15.95 per metre. They also offer a full curtain making and fitting service.

EAST

Fancy Curtains
65 Queens Market, E13
Tel: 020 8470 1331
Tube: Upton Park
Bus: 58, 330, 104, 376
Open: Tues-Fri 10am-5.30pm, Sat 9.30am-6pm
Over 700 fabrics and swatches of all descriptions crammed into a little shop opposite West Ham football ground. Everything you could possible need from nets and trimmings to made to measure blinds with fabrics from 50p to £95 a metre. They specialise in metal tracks for bay windows. Happy hunting!

OUTER LONDON

Corcoran & May
31-35 Blagdon Road, New Malden, Surrey, KT3
Tel: 020 8949 0234
Rail: New Malden

Bus: 131, 152, 213, 726, K1, K9, K10
Open: Mon-Sat 9.30am-5.30pm, Sun and Bank Holidays 11am-5pm
A vast store filled with overstocks from well-known curtain fabric designers (Osborne & Little, Crowson, G.P. & J. Baker, Monkwell, Malabar Cotton Company) from £1.99 to £19.99 per metre. They also have fabric from some of the brightest newcomers. A reputable make-up service is available.

Fabric World
287-289 High Street, Sutton, Surrey, SM1
Tel: 020 8643 5127
Tube: Morden Rail: Sutton
Bus: 151, 213, 408, 413, 726
Open: Mon-Sat 9am-5.30pm
Over 3,000 rolls of cut-price designer fabrics in stock, both from the UK and imported from all over the world. Retail prices discounted by 75%. Making-up workroom and an interior design service.
Also at:
6-10 Brighton Road, South Croydon, Tel: 020 8688 6282

London Curtain Agency
298 Sandycombe Road, Kew, Surrey, SM6
Tel: 020 8940 5959
Tube: Kew Gardens
Bus: 65, 190, 391, 419
Open: Tues-Fri 10am-4pm, Sat 10am-5pm
Well-established agency that specialises in curtains from refurbished hotels as well as donations from local homes and show houses. Curtains from £30 a pair. £800 will buy a sumptuous pair of interlined curtains for a large bay window including a pelmet. They also sell wrought iron poles, blinds, bed covers and cushions and offer a made to measure service.

South London Fabric Warehouse
Unit F2 Felnex Trading Estate
Hackbridge Road, Hackbridge, Wallington, Surrey, SM6
Tel: 020 8647 3313
Rail: Hackbridge
Bus: 151, 127
Open: Mon-Sat 9am-5pm, Sun 10am-4pm
Large warehouse on two floors (18,000 square feet) between Croydon and Sutton. Stocks of competitively priced named brands from the UK and abroad by the roll. From £2.99 to £30 a metre. Made to measure service and ready-made curtains. Plus blinds, poles and all the trimmings, bed linen, towels and cushions.

DIY & EQUIPMENT

BUILDERS MERCHANTS & GENERAL DIY SUPPLIERS

NORTH

Mr C. Demetriou DIY
132 Balls Pond Road, N1
Tel: 020 7354 8210
Tube: Highbury & Islington
Bus: 30, 38, 56, 277
Open: Mon-Fri 9am-5pm, Sat 9am-4pm, Sun 10am-3pm
This shop is an unusual mix of old and new DIY equipment and materials. The stock comes from all kinds of sources including auctions and markets and there is also part-exchange on power tools. The shop seems small from the outside, but extends back a long way. Mr Demetriou lives for his shop and even shows up for a few hours on Christmas Day to sell batteries to the kids in the neighbourhood for their new toys.

E.D. Elson Ltd
304 Essex Road, N1
Tel: 020 7226 6422
Tube: Angel or Highbury & Islington
Bus: 38, 56, 73, 341
Open: Mon-Fri 8am-5pm, Sat 9am-5pm
This shop offers a good value mix of decorating and building materials, tools and also features a well stocked timber yard.

M.P. Moran & Sons Ltd (10)
293/301 Kilburn High Road, NW6
Tel: 020 7328 5566
Website: www.mpmoran.co.uk
Tube: Kilburn
Bus: 16, 32, 189, 316
Open: Mon-Fri 7am-5.30pm, Sat 7am-4pm
Moran's is a huge independent building suppliers offering plumbing and electrical equipment, painting and decorating materials, power and hand tools, all kinds of glass cut to size and a large timber yard which is situated just around the corner. All materials are competitively priced with regular promotions. *Also at:*
Rear of 5-23 Iverson Road NW6 (Timber Yard), Tel: 020 7328 5566
449-451 High Road, Willesden NW10, Tel: 020 8459 9000
198-200 Kennington Park Road SE11, Tel: 020 7735 9291

Chris Stephens Ltd
545-561 Holloway Road N19
Tel: 020 7272 1228
Tube: Holloway
Bus: 17, 271, 43
Open: Mon-Fri 7am-6pm, Sat 8am-6pm
This huge shop has four departments specialising in bathrooms, tiles, plumbing, paint and wallpaper. They provide excellent value across the board with bathroom suites starting from only £142 (inc VAT) and white tiles for as little as £2.99 per square metre. They also offer further discounts when you spend £50 or more.

West

Nu-Line Builders Merchants
315 Westbourne Park Road, W11
Tel: 020 727 7748
Tube: Ladbroke Grove
Bus: 7, 23, 28, 31, 52, 70, 295, 328
Open: Mon-Fri 7am-5.30pm, Sat 8am-1pm
This massive shop covers all aspects of buiding and decorating including paints, electrics, powertools, ironmongery and plumbing. It also has a large timber yard. The prices are competitive and they produce a colour catalogue of all their products.

East

N & C Building Materials
3-10 Shoreditch High Street, E1
Tel: 020 7247 5432
Website: www.nichollsandclarke.com
Tube: Liverpool Street
Bus: 8, 26, 35, 43, 47, 48, 78, 149, 242
Open: Mon-Fri 7.30am-5pm, Sat 8.30am-12.30pm
This shop offers general building materials, power tools, locks and a great selection of bathroom fixtures and fittings. Bargains include a large belfast sink for only £60 and an economy bathroom suite for only £169.92. A section of the store is dedicated to tiles with lots of special offers. The shop is difficult to get to by car, but worth the effort as it one of the best value outfits in town.
Also at:
Unit 1a-b Alexander Place, Lower Park Road N11, Tel: 020 8361 6050
Unit 14 Meridian Trading Estate, Bugsby Way, Charlton SE7, Tel: 020 8269 5960

Paint & Wallpaper

Central

Foxell & James
57 Farringdon Road, EC1
Tel: 020 7405 0152
Tube: Farringdon
Bus: 17, 45, 46, 63
Open: Mon-Fri 7am-5pm, Sat 7am-12.30pm
This is just about the best paint, varnish and woodstain outlet in the capital and offers all the products and advice the novice DIY person requires. For example they sell the hard resin varnishes you need to seal a wood floor and cannot get in the usual DIY outlets. The place is always busy and yet the staff are unfailingly helpful and if for some reason they do not have what you need they will recommend other shops where you might get it. Although not specifically a bargain outlet, the quality of their service and goods make Foxell & James worthy of a mention in this book.

Leyland Paint

371-373 Edgware Road, W2
Tel: 020 7723 8048

6-8 Warwick Way, SW1
Tel: 020 7828 8695

683-685 Finchley Road, NW2
Tel: 020 7794 5927

89-90 Farringdon Road, EC1
Tel: 020 7278 8933

335-337 King's Road, SW3
Tel: 020 7795 0054

7-15 Camden Road, NW1
Tel: 020 7284 4366

1

365 Kensington High Street, W14
Tel: 020 7602 9099

167-169 Shaftesbury Avenue, WC2
Tel: 020 7836 7337

Ealing Broadway, 9 The Mall, W5
Tel: 020 8566 0481

SDM Interiors, 424 Edgware Rd, W2
Tel: 020 7706 1099

25 Goodge Street, W1
Tel: 020 7636 2995

314-316 Old Brompton Road, SW5
Tel: 020 7370 6600

Open: All branches Mon-Fri 7am-6pm, Sat 7.30am-5.30pm
Leyland are a specialist paint outlet selling their own brand of paint at competitive prices. Good deals include 5 litres of white emulsion for

£12.75 (inc VAT), 5 litres of masonry paint for £15.80 (inc VAT), and 5 litres of eggshell wood paint for £19.45 (inc VAT). They also have a paint mixing service if you are after a particular colour.

G. Thornfield
321 Gray's Inn Road, WC1
Tel: 020 7837 2996
Tube/Rail: King's Cross
Bus: 17, 45, 46
Open: Mon-Fri 8am-6pm, Sat 9am-2pm
This shop has been trading for nearly 50 years and has a reputation for excellent value wallpapers, paints and fabrics as well as in-store picture framing. The discounts on wallpapers and fabrics range from between 10%-30%.

NORTH

Colour Centre
29a Offord Road, N1
Tel: 020 7609 1164
Website: www.colourcentre.com
Rail: Caladonian Road & Barnsbury
Bus: 17, 91, 259, 274
Open: Mon-Fri 8am-5pm, Sat 9am-1pm
This large warehouse sells a huge range of paints and decorating materials and offers trade prices to all its customers. It is a particularly good place to try for unusual things like anti-graffiti paint, cellulose car paint and specialist hard-wearing industrial floor coverings. For those with less exacting requirements, they also stock standard emulsions and wood paints. One of the best paint outlets in town.

Dave's DIY
296-8 Firs Lane, N13
Tel: 020 8807 3539
Rail: Palmers Green
Bus: 121, 329, W6
Open: Mon-Wed & Fri 7.30am-5pm, Thurs 7.30am-1pm
This company sells paints and wallpapers to the trade but also offers the same discounts to the public. There are many brand name wallpapers, and considerable savings to be found on most items. Both branches have a wide range of paints and offer 3 mixing systems.
Also at:
4 Enfield Road, Enfield, Tel: 020 8363 1680
Open: Mon-Tues, Thurs-Fri 8am-5pm, Wed 8am-1pm

WEST

Askew Paint Centre

99-103 Askew Road, W12
Tel: 020 8743 6612
Tube: Stamford Brook
Bus: 207, 266, 272, 607
Open: Mon-Fri 7am-5pm, Sat 8am-1pm

3

This shop offers great value paints with Dulux, Leyland, Sanderson and William Morris all kept in stock. They also provide a mixing service. It might be a long way to go just for paint, but could be worth the journey as there are a number of DIY shops on nearby Uxbridge Road.

SOUTH

Discount Decorating

157-159 Rye Lane, SE15
Tel: 020 7732 3986
Rail: Peckham Rye
Bus: 12, 37, 63, 78, 312, P12, 343
Open: Mon-Fri 8am-5.30pm, Sat 9am-5.30pm

This shop has a good selection of quality wallpapers and paints at competitive prices. The stock caters for all pockets, but even the brand names like Dulux paints and Sanderson's wallpapers are discounted. They also have a paint mixing service.

EAST

Bargain Wallpapers

203 Plashet Road, E13
Tel: 020 8470 7261
Tube: Upton Park
Bus: 104, 238, 376
Open: Mon-Sat 10am-7pm, Sun 10am-4pm

This no-nonsense shop offers great value for wallpapers with prices starting from only £1 per roll, and they also sell brand name paints for below the usual price. Among the good deals are 2.5 litre tins of Dulux gloss for£10 and a 10 litre tin of Johnstones silk emulsion for the same price. A terrific place to come for decorating bargains.

Discount Decor
159 High Street, Walthamstow, E17
Tel: 020 8521 1999
Tube/Rail: Walthamstow Central
Bus: 123, 212, 275, W12
Open: Mon-Sat 9.30am-6pm, Sun 10.30am-3pm
This shop has deals on brand name paints and wallpapers and can mix colours from the Dulux and Berger paint ranges. The shop also offer good deals on small power tools.

POWER TOOLS

EAST

Toucan Tools Co.
373-375 Church Road, Leyton, E10
Tel: 020 8539 4163
E-mail: toucan@mcmail.com
Tube: Leyton
Bus: 58, 158
Open: Mon-Fri 8am-5pm, Sat 9am-3pm
This large tool suppliers stocks all the major brand names at competitive prices and usually has a few special offers. Recently they had a promotion on a Makita circular saw and hammerdrill which were being sold for £85 each (exc.VAT), which is nearly half the usual price. The company will deliver free in the London area, have a large ironmongery and lock department and will also repair tools.

C W Tyzack
79/81 Kingsland Road, E2
Tel: 020 7739 7126
Tube: Old Street
Bus: 67, 149, 242, 243
Open: Mon-Fri 8am-5.30pm, Sat 8am-1pm
C W Tyzack is a very well-stocked DIY store with a particularly wide selection of powertools. The prices are competitive and they have regular promotional discounts as well as a catalogue. The shop is usually busy and the staff do not have the time to discuss things in detail, so it's a good idea to know what you're looking for before visiting.

SOUTH

A. Gatto & Son

206-12 Garratt Lane, SW18
Tel: 020 8874 2671
Rail: Earlsfield
Bus: 44, 270
Open: Mon-Fri 9am-4.45pm, Sat 9am-11.30am

6

This tool distributor has been in business since 1933, and is happy to deal with the public. The savings are massive, and the range of tools bewildering to those uninitiated in the art of shelf erection. Among the bargains was a Black and Decker Workmate 825 for £59.95 and an 18V Bosch drill for £99.95, both of which are about half the usual retail price. A great value power tool outlet.

S.J. Carter Electrical Tools Ltd

Gloucester House, 10 Camberwell New Road, SE5
Tel: 020 7587 1222
E-mail: info@sjcarter.co.uk
Website: www.sjcarter.co.uk
Tube: Oval
Bus: 36, 155, 185
Open: Mon-Fri 8am-5pm, Sat 8am-12.30pm

S.J. Carter are a large, well-stocked and very competitively priced tool shop. They sell both hand and power tools, have a mail order service, hire tools and will also deliver in the London area. Just about the most central major tool supplier in London and one of the best.

London Power Tools and Fixings

190 Lower Road, Rotherhithe SE16
Tel: 020 7237 9884
Website: www.londonpower.co.uk
Tube: Canada Water/Surrey Quays
Bus: 1, 199, 395, P13
Open: Mon-Fri 8.15am-5pm, Sat 8.30am-12.30pm

This shop stocks lots of different brands, but is one of the largest Bosch power tool retailers in the country and has the entire range in stock, all sold at significant discounts. On a recent visit a 12v Bosch drill was only £39.99 (exc VAT) the normal price being around £70. The company offers free delivery in the London area.

OUTSIDE LONDON

Croydon Powertool Centre

Units 9 & 10 Roman Industrial Estate,
Tait Road, Croydon, CR0
Tel: 020 8683 0550
E-mail: sales@croydonpowertools.co.uk
Open: Mon-Fri 8am-5pm, Sat 9am-1pm

This large shop buys tools in bulk and sells to the trade and public at large discounts. They were recently selling a Makita circular saw for only £89.99 (inc VAT), which is a huge saving on the usual retail price of £143. They offer free delivery in the London area regardless of the amount spent, so give them a call for their best price.
They also have a sister company:
Lakedale Power Tools, 217-223 Plumstead High St SE18, Tel: 020 8854 9894

Gill & Hoxby

131-137 St Mark's Road
Enfield, Middlesex, EN1
Tel: 020 8363 2935
Open: Mon-Fri 8am-5.30pm, Sat 8.30am-2pm

This shop boasts the largest display of power tools in the country and stocks every major and minor name, from professional equipment by Makita and DeWalt to tools made for domestic use by the likes of Black & Decker and Bosch. The company buys in bulk and sells at considerable discounts to the public. The savings you make on larger items may make the trip to Enfield worthwhile.

Impact Power Tools Ltd

Unit 10, Trowers Way
Holmthorpe Industrial Estate, Redhill, Surrey, RH1
Tel: 01737 772 436 / Fax: 01737 765 944
E-mail: sales@impactpt.co.uk
Website: www.impactpt.co.uk
Open: Mon-Fri 8.30am-5.30pm, Sat 8.30am-12.30pm

DIY bores will gag at the bargains available at this large power tool warehouse. It has a comprehensive price list, and offers free delivery for orders over £100. A recent bargain was the De Walt 12V cordless drill for only £79 (exc.VAT) – the list price being around £120. For more details phone for a specific price or ask them to send you a price list.

DOMESTIC APPLIANCES

Kettles, toasters, microwaves, fridge freezers and washing machines can vary in price from store to store. Comparing like with like is often difficult with subtle changes introduced with each new model number. If you're not too fussy about the latest model and can do without some of the extra special features you can get a bargain. For a large choice start by looking in big outlets like John Lewis, Argos, B&Q, Dixons, Homebase, Currys, Comet or Powerhouse to work out what you want and then compare prices in any of the shops below before you make your decision. If you're prepared to go for a machine that is 'graded', i.e. scratched or dented or an ex-showroom model, there are good savings to be made. Check out delivery charges, guarantees and whether installation and removal of your old machine is included.

NORTH

Capital Appliances Ltd

10

198 West End Lane, NW6
Tel: 020 7793 5359
Tube: West Hampstead
Bus: 139, 328, C11
Open: Mon-Sat 9am-7pm

Small well-established shop that supplies local estate agents, landlords and developers with re-conditioned, ex-display and graded household appliances at very reasonable prices. Washing machines from £250, fridge freezers from £140, dishwashers and cookers from £200. They also offer a repair service.

CES

936-938 High Road, N12
Tel: 020 8343 8288
Tube: Woodside Park
Bus: 125, 263, 383
Open: Mon-Fri 9am-6pm, Sat 9.30am-5.30pm

Busy outlet (established over 20 years) for new and reconditioned fridges, washing machines and cookers, all at great prices. Fridges from £69, fridge freezers from £89. Guaranteed for six months for parts and labour. They have a large showroom with new furniture including beds from £59. CES will also deliver free in the London area.

Domestic Gas Appliances

110-112 Hoxton Street, N1
Tel: 020 7708 4347
Website: www.domesticgasappliancesn1.co.uk
Tube: Old Street
Bus: 43, 55, 243
Open: Mon-Fri 7am-5pm, Sat 9am-4pm

This is a smart showroom, offering good value new gas cookers and boilers. On a recent visit they had a Cannon Oakley, two-oven gas cooker for £340 and a stylish stainless steel White-Westinghouse range cooker for only £900. The company also offers the full range of gas and plumbing services and is Corgi registered.

Finchley VAC Centre

660 & 646-648 High Road, N12
Tel: 020 8492 7500
Tube: East Finchley/Woodside Park
Bus: 125, 263, 383
Open: Mon-Sat 8.30am-6pm, Sun 10am-4pm

One outlet, two shops. No. 660 deals in slightly damaged or scratched new appliances, mostly Indesit and Ariston. While Finchley VAC Supercentre, five doors down at 646-648 High Road deals in new machines straight from the manufacturers at prices you'll find hard to beat. All sorts of white goods: American fridges, old fashioned ranges, washing machines, dishwashers and some fancy styles and colours. Ask about special offers. Choose the make and model you want from your nearest dealer and then give Finchley VAC Centre a call. They will deliver and fit.

London Domestic Appliances

4 Mordaunt Road, NW10
Tel: 020 8961 5695
Tube: Harlesden
Bus: 187, 206, 224, 226, 260, 487, PR1
Open: Mon-Sat 9am-6pm (closed Fri 12-3pm)

Long-established shop offering new, graded and reconditioned white goods. Washing machines from £100-£175, graded from £200-£350. Reconditioned fridges from £60-£75 with 6 months guarantee, graded from £110-£165. Corgi registered for gas appliances.

Magnet Discount Warehouses Ltd
79 Fore Street N18
Tel: 020 8807 9211
Tube: Seven Sisters
Bus: 149, 259, 279
Open: Mon-Sat 9am-6pm
Large stores selling new appliances at reasonable, but not necessarily the cheapest prices.
Also at: 17 Lymington Avenue N22, Tel: 020 8889 3600

WEST

Buyers & Sellers

120-122 Ladbroke Grove, W10
Tel: 020 7243 5400
Tube: Ladbroke Grove
Bus: 7, 23, 52, 70
Open: Mon-Fri 9am-5.30pm (Thurs 9am-6.30pm), Sat 9am-4.30pm
Buyers and Sellers adopt a travel agency approach to selling household appliances with a busy office/showroom, hundreds of brochures, helpful staff and a determination to offer the lowest possible price. Established over thirty years ago they can supply anything from the cheapest to the most sophisticated machines, integrated or free standing. Everything is fully guaranteed and delivery is fast. Worth calling in or phoning with the model number of the machine you fancy to get a comparative quote. Special offers on the shop floor.

Cooker Centre Ltd
420 Edgware Road, W2
Tel: 020 7723 6444
Tube: Edgware Road
Bus: 6, 16, 98
Open: Mon-Sat 8.30am-5.30pm
Friendly family run business offering 'massive' discounts and immediate delivery on new kitchen appliances. Located at the Maida Vale end of the Edgware Road near to Church Street market, the firm has a fast turnaround of discounted goods, many going to local builders and rental agencies. All fully guaranteed. Not averse to haggling!
Also at: 69 Cricklewood Broadway NW2, Tel: 020 8452 8709

Hot & Cold Inc

13-15 Golborne Road, W10
Tel: 020 8960 1200/1300
Tube: Westbourne Park
Bus: 23, 28, 31, 328
Open: Mon-Fri 10am-6pm, Sat 10am-4.30pm

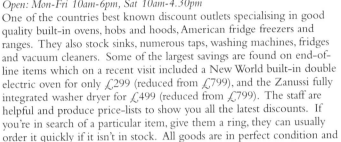

One of the countries best known discount outlets specialising in good quality built-in ovens, hobs and hoods, American fridge freezers and ranges. They also stock sinks, numerous taps, washing machines, fridges and vacuum cleaners. Some of the largest savings are found on end-of-line items which on a recent visit included a New World built-in double electric oven for only £299 (reduced from £799), and the Zanussi fully integrated washer dryer for £499 (reduced from £799). The staff are helpful and produce price-lists to show you all the latest discounts. If you're in search of a particular item, give them a ring, they can usually order it quickly if it isn't in stock. All goods are in perfect condition and are fully guaranteed.

Icetech Appliance Ltd

1-3 Barons Court Road, W14
Tel: 020 7381 2303/3119
Tube: West Kensington
Bus: 28, 74, 391, 190
Open: Mon-Fri 9.30am-6pm, Sat 9am-5pm

Large choice of electrical appliances of all makes including ranges and American fridges. New machines at heavily discounted prices and 'graded' machines (with the odd dent or scratch) greatly reduced. Full manufacturers' guarantees. If they haven't got what you want they'll send you to their warehouse in Filmer Road, SW6.

Sun Hill Electric

117 Fulham Palace Road, W6
Tel: 020 8748 1861
Tube: Barons Court/Hammersmith
Bus: 190, 211, 220, 295
Open: Mon-Sat 9am-6pm

All makes of fully reconditioned appliances (cooker, fridge/freezers, washing machines) guaranteed for 3 months or, for an extra £20, a year. Around 500 machines usually in stock (there's a garage full at the back). Bosch, Neff, AEG, Hotpoint. Expect to pay about £100 for a 2 year old Bosch washing machine (£380 new) or £120 for a four year old Zanussi fridge/freezer (£300 new). Repairs and free delivery.

South

Cookerama
137 Lewisham Way, SE14
Tel: 020 8692 6668
Tube: New Cross
Bus: 21, 36, 136, 321
Open: Mon-Sat 9am-5pm
Fully reconditioned second-hand cookers, fridges and other white goods with 6 month guarantees, free delivery and fitting. Also a selection of vintage and retro appliances.

Discount Cookers
97 Rushey Green, SE6
Tel: 020 8461 5273
Tube: New Cross   Rail: Catford
Bus: 47, 54, 75, 136, 185, 199, 208
Open: Mon-Sat 9am-6pm
Twenty year old family business (family members run Cookerama in New Cross, see above) selling mostly new but also some 'graded' cookers and white goods at a 10-30% discount. A large shop with a lot in stock including range cookers and American fridge/freezers. If they haven't got what you want they will order it for you, as well as delivering and fitting your new appliance.

Iceland Clearance Centre
120-132 Camberwell Road, SE5
Tel: 020 7708 4347
Tube: Elephant & Castle
Bus: 12, 35, 40, 42, 45, 68, 171, 176, 468
Open: Mon-Sat 9am-5.30pm, Sun 10am-4pm
Clearance centre for shop-soiled, slightly damaged or discontinued fridges, fridge freezers, microwaves, cookers, TVs and other appliances from Iceland showrooms countrywide. Several hundred appliances in stock including Bosch, Hot Point, Whirlpool and their own brand Kyoto. Also some second-hand goods.

EAST

Eastern Domestic Appliance
271 Bethnal Green Road, E2
Tel: 020 7613 4575
Tube: Bethnal Green
Bus: 8, D3
Open: Mon-Sat 10am-6pm
Large shop selling graded kitchen appliances. Most brands in stock but will order in if necessary. Special deals when we visited included Servis fridge freezers from £180 and cookers from £160.
Also at: 572 Green Street E13, Tel: 020 8552 0056

Power Giant
353 Hoe Street, E17
Tel: 020 8520 2300
Tube: Walthamstow
Bus: 20, 48, 69, 97, 230, 257, 357
Open: Mon-Sat 10am-7pm
Graded washing machines and fridge freezers at a 'good, fair price'. They specialise in Bosch and Siemens as well as other brands.
Also at: Barking Road E13, Tel: 020 8470 4488

New & Second Hand Furniture
24/26 Amhurst Road, E8
See main entry in Junk Shop section on page 247.

FABRICS & HABERDASHERY

Below are reviewed many of the most interesting and good value fabric and haberdashery shops in the capital. Several of the shops offer both furnishing and dress fabric, but we have also included more specialist outlets dealing only in household fabrics. Although not classified by neighbourhood it is worth noting that Brixton and Green Street have several fabric retailers and are therefore worth a special trip if you want a bit more choice. Brick Lane and Petticoat Market are also a good source for African and Indian fabrics. Any High Street retailer is worth checking out for remnants if you only need small pieces.

CENTRAL

Alexander Furnishings

51-61 Wigmore Street, W1
See review in Curtains section on page 101

Barber Green

Room 17, 33-35 St John's Square, EC1
Tel: 020 7608 0362
Tube/Rail: Farringdon
Bus: 55, 153, 243
Open: By appointment

Bargain hunters should call these tailors in advance of a visit to arrange to check out the remnants and end-of-line fabrics such as lace, velvet, woollens and trimmings that they sell to the public at a hefty discount. If you slip out of bargain shopping mode, keep in mind that the tailors at this busy workshop also make wonderful, tempting, high-quality bespoke clothing.

Russell & Chapple

68 Drury Lane, WC2
Tel: 020 7836 7521
Website: www.russellandchapple.co.uk
Tube: Covent Garden
Bus: 1, 59, 68, 91, 168, 172, 188
Open: Mon-Fri 9am-5.30pm

Suppliers to the surrounding theatres, Russell and Chapple have an excellent selection of hard-to-find fabrics at extremely competitive prices. While domestic seamstresses may find little need for the flame retardant fabrics, there are several that are very practical. Cotton duck suitable for upholstery costs £3.66 per metre and muslin costs just £1.30 per metre.

NORTH

Bargain Centre

93 Upper Street, N1
Tel: 020 7226 1741
Tube: Angel
Bus: 4, 19, 30, 43
Open: Mon-Sat 10am-5.30pm, Sun 10am-1pm

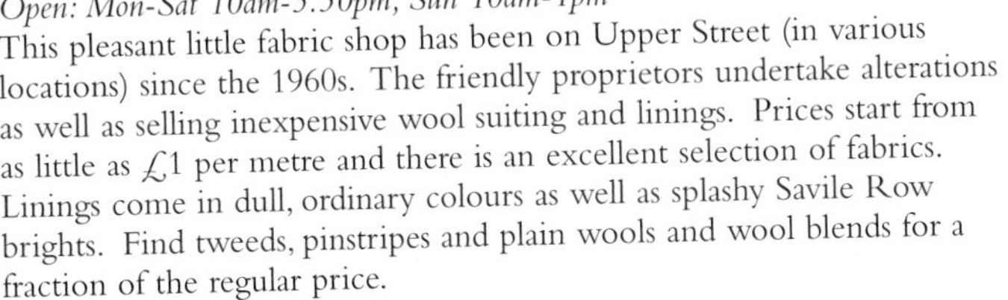

This pleasant little fabric shop has been on Upper Street (in various locations) since the 1960s. The friendly proprietors undertake alterations as well as selling inexpensive wool suiting and linings. Prices start from as little as £1 per metre and there is an excellent selection of fabrics. Linings come in dull, ordinary colours as well as splashy Savile Row brights. Find tweeds, pinstripes and plain wools and wool blends for a fraction of the regular price.

Martin's Fabric
24-26 South Mall, Edmonton Green Shopping Centre, N9
Tel: 020 8807 4222
Rail: Edmonton Green
Bus: 102, 144, 191, 259, W6
Open: Mon-Wed, Fri-Sat 9am-5.30pm

Sheeting, upholstery and curtain fabrics are the forte here where fabrics are piled high and sell for as little as £1 a metre. A great place for budget-conscious DIY enthusiasts who want to re-do a room quickly with some new curtains or upholstery.

Sew Fantastic!

2

107 Essex Road, N1
Tel: 020 7226 2725
Tube: Angel
Bus: 38, 56, 73, 341
Open: Mon-Wed, Fri-Sat 10am-5.30pm

A great little local fabric shop selling everything you might need. The owner is helpful and informative. Bargain hunters should check out the remnants at just £1 a piece. Otherwise, there are plenty of fabrics of all kinds for reasonable prices. The selection of fleeces is rather good. As well as fabrics, they also sell buttons, ribbons, patterns and other sewing essentials.

Rolls & Rems

12 The Concourse,
Edmonton Green, N9
Tel: 020 8803 6532
Rail: Edmonton Green
Bus: 102, 144, 191, 259, W6
Open: Mon-Sat 9am-5.30pm

As the name suggests, this small chain of fabric shops sells rolls of fabrics as well as a good selection of remnants. The choice is top-notch with plenty of printed and plain natural fabrics from £3.50 per metre as well as synthetics like fake fur at £4 per metre and bridal fabrics. They also sell all the stitching accoutrements from patterns to zippers.

Also at:
21 Seven Sisters Road, Holloway N7, Tel: 020 7263 3272
111 High Street, Lewisham SE13, Tel: 020 8852 8686

WEST

The Cloth Shop

290 Portobello Road, W10
Tel: 020 8968 6001
Tube: Ladbroke Grove
Bus: 7, 23, 52, 70
Open: Mon-Thurs 10.30am-6pm, Fri and Sat 10am-6pm
See review in Curtains and Fabrics section on page 103

Shaukat Fabrics

168-172 Old Brompton Road, SW5
Tel: 020 7373 8956
Tube: Gloucester Road
Bus: 49, C1
Open: Mon-Sat 10am-6.30pm

This large shop has a cosy atmosphere which is largely provided by the reams of fabric that are piled high and sold at a very reasonable price. There is every conceivable type of fabric here with corduroy for £5 per metre, cotton drill for £5.99 per metre and bright coloured poly-cotton fabric for £3.50 per metre. They are also the only London outlet for Liberty remnants with 90cm wide reams for £6.99 per metre – a huge saving on the original price. As well as fabrics, Shaukat also sell great quality bags and bedding (see pages 48 and 90 for further details).

South

Atlantic Silk Fabric

28 Electric Avenue, SW9
Tel: 020 7274 6040
Tube/Rail: Brixton
Bus: 35, 37, 109, 118, 196, 250, 355, P4, P5
Open: Mon, Tues, Thurs-Sat 9am-5.45pm, Wed 9am-5pm

This shop sells silks as well as every other fabric you might want, from African prints to plain cotton shirting sourced from around the globe. They've got a small selection of remnants as well as fabrics as cheap as £1 per metre. As expected, they also sell trimmings, buttons, and patterns as well as handing out free advice.

Bits of Cloth

22 Electric Avenue, SW9
Tel: 020 7274 0224
Tube/Rail: Brixton
Bus: 35, 37, 109, 118, 196, 250, 355, P4, P5
Open: Mon-Sat 9.30am-5.30pm

If you've got £1 to spend, you will be spoilt for choice at this shop selling a wide range of European fabrics. Lycras, jerseys and suiting start at £1 per metre and there are even some super cheap fabrics for the paltry sum of 50p per metre. Prices are consistently low and the choice is decent, which makes this a great place for bargain hunters.

Field Fabrics

17 Atlantic Road, SW9
Tel: 020 7738 3333
Tube/Rail: Brixton
Bus: 35, 37, 109, 118, 196, 250, 355, P4, P5
Open: Mon-Tues, Thurs-Sat 9am-5.30pm, Wed 9am-4pm

From curtaining to shirting, this shop has it covered. While many of its competitors stock more exotic fabrics, this shop sticks with a wide range of fabrics from all over Europe and the world. Lining fabric goes for as little as 99p per metre while something more ornate like embroidered lace costs from £15 per metre. Serious bargain hunters should go straight for the end-of-line fabrics that are sold at a hefty discount.

Also at:
56 High Street, Weldstone, Harrow, Middlesex HA3, Tel: 020 8427 4488

Nasseri Fabrics
38 Atlantic Road, SW19
Tel: 020 7274 5627
Tube/Rail: Brixton
Bus: 35, 37, 109, 118, 196, 250, 355, P4, P5
Open: Mon-Sat 9.30am-5pm
Something of a Brixton institution, the long-established Nasseri Fabrics is a great place to come for African fabrics. Purchases require a six-yard minimum, but the prices are low with a bright, colourful cotton print going for £5 per yard.

Rolls & Rems
111 High Street, Lewisham, SE13
Tel: 020 8852 8686
See entry in North London (page 122) for full details.

Yemmy Textiles
73 Granville Arcade,
Coldharbour Lane, SW19
Tel: 020 7738 3552
Tube/Rail: Brixton
Bus: 35, 37, 109, 118, 196, 250, 355, P4, P5
Open: Mon-Sat 9.30am-6pm
Shoppers can stock up on multi-coloured, brightly hued African fabrics at this shop in one of the arcades at Brixton Market. In general, prices are competitive, but there are especially good bargains to be had in the discontinued lines.

EAST

Bhopal Fabrics

98 Brick Lane, E1
Tel: 020 7377 1886
Tube: Aldgate
Bus: 8, 25, 67, 253
Open: Mon-Fri 9am-6pm, Sat 10am-4pm, Sun 9am-4pm
Like many Brick Lane area fabric shops, customers are required to buy at least five metres of fabric here. Elegant, vibrant silks start at just £5 per metre. The stock is varied and there is a particularly good selection of Indian fabrics in plain, bright colours or with pretty embroidery. A great place to find some ethnic chic.

Empee Silk Fabrics Ltd

Z. Butt Textiles 2001

24 Brick Lane, E1
Tel: 020 7247 7776
Tube: Aldgate East/Shoreditch
Bus: 8, 25, 67, 253
Open: Mon-Fri 9am-6pm, Sun 9.30am-2.30pm

This is an established fabric outlet on Brick Lane offering great value fabrics and a lot of choice. Among the bargains on offer are blue Cotton Drill for £2.95 per metre, 65" width Calico for 95p per metre and quality Velvet for £4.95 per metre. The shop has a good reputation and is popular with designers who emerge laden with reams of fabric. Well worth visiting, particularly with the closure of R.Halstuk just a few doors down.

Empee Silk Fabrics Ltd

42-44 Brick Lane, E1
46-48 Fashion Street, E1
Tel: 020 7247 1094
E-mail: empeesilks@bsnet.co.uk
Tube: Aldgate East/Shoreditch
Bus: 8, 25, 67, 253
Open: Mon-Fri 9am-5.30pm, Sun 8am-2pm

This well-stocked group of shops are excellent for all kinds of material from plain cotton fabric for £1 per metre to fine silks from £5.25 per metre. The staff are very friendly and helpful and always prepared to do a deal. The store is largely wholesale, but they welcome individual customers with a minimum purchase of 10 metres per fabric.

Also at:
Somersby Textiles, 55 Fashion Street E1, Tel: 020 7247 8008

Epra Fabrics

52/56 Brick Lane, E1
Tel: 020 7247 1248
Tube: Aldgate East/Shoreditch
Bus: 8, 25, 67, 253
Open: Mon-Fri 9am-5.30pm, Sun 8am-2pm

Epra is a large fabric store with a wide selection of very cheap fabrics. Prices start at 75p per metre for simple calico and go up to a very modest £3.25 per metre for a kitsch synthetic fur fabric. They have a selection of curtain fabrics which are kept in a separate room and lots of colourful fabrics for children's' clothes and furnishing. The shop does a good deal of wholesale business and has a minimum order of 10 metres per fabric, so its' a good place to visit for curtaining and other big projects.

Hardwick Textiles

369 Green Street, E13
Tel: 020 8472 1284
Tube: Upton Park
Bus: 58, 104, 330, 376
Open: Mon-Tues, Thurs-Sat 11am-6pm

On Green Street since before the First World War, this is a local institution. For fine fabrics take the journey to Upton Park to find this classic material shop just opposite the tube station. Selling suiting, special occasion fabrics and linen, this shop has a great selection of timeless fabrics at good, old-fashioned prices. The proprietor aims to sell his goods at half the price of High Street retailers. Irish linen costs from £6 per yard and wool suiting goes for around £10 per yard.

Hussain Fabrics

123 Green Street, E7
Tel: 020 8548 4601
Tube: Upton Park
Bus: 58, 104, 330, 376
Open: Daily 10am-8pm

Plenty of fabrics from curtaining to dress are available at this modest shop. Linens start at £2 per yard and there is a big selection of fabrics for just £1 a yard. Occasionally, there is a small array of reasonably good fabric for the bargain price of 50p per yard. This is a great place for the novice or serious bargain hunter as you can pick-up a lot of fabric at ridiculously low prices.

Mermaid Fabrics

364 Mare Street, E8
Tel: 020 8985 3694
Rail: Hackney Central
Bus: 30, 276, 236, W15
Open: Mon-Sat 9.30am-5.30pm

This is a large fabric outlet with an established reputation and loyal customer base. There are many hundreds of reams to choose from and on fine days reduced items are placed on the pavement to attract trade. Among the stock felts, cords and velvets were all £3.95 per metre and there were lots of remnant reams for just £1. The shop is even bigger than it looks from the pavement with two large rooms at the back for furnishing and curtain material. Mermaid also offer a curtain making service.

Textiles Le Prestige
41 Wentworth Street, E1
Tel: 020 7375 2706
Tube: Aldgate/Aldgate East
Bus: 25, 67, 253
Open: Mon-Fri 9.30am-5.30pm, Sun 9am-3pm
One of a bevy of shops along Wentworth Street and in the area that specialises in West African fabrics, the goods here vary from the vibrant to the gaudy. Luckily for bargain hunters, prices are low. However, like its neighbours, the minimum order here is six yards. Prices start from £10 for six yards.

OUTER LONDON

Corcoran & May
31-35 Blagdon Road,
New Malden, Surrey, KT3
See main entry in Curtains section on page 104.

Field Fabrics
56 High Street, Weldstone, Harrow, Middlesex, HA3
Tel: 020 8427 4488
Open: Mon-Sat 9am-6pm
See main entry in South London (page 123) for full details.

Jersey Vogue
14 Station Road, Edgware, Middlesex, HA8
Tel: 020 8952 7751
Tube: Edgware
Bus: 32, 142, 204, 251, 288, 292, 303, 614
Open: Mon-Fri 9am-5.30pm, Sun 9.30am-1pm
Take advantage of trends and changing tastes at Jersey Vogue where the public can get end-of-season fabrics from major manufacturers at a cut-rate price. Cheap fabrics cost as little as £1 per metre while better stuff goes for just £5 per metre. Two warehouses mean that there is always plenty of choice.

FURNITURE

NORTH

Big Bed & Pine Co
125 Essex Road, N1
Tel: 020 7359 9614
Tube: Angel or Highbury & Islington
Bus: 38, 56, 73, 341
Open: Mon-Sat 9am-5pm
This shop sells beds and quality pine furniture. A kingsize pine bed frame is only £170 with a good mattress an additional £115, while a single pine frame is £89 with a mattress for £49. All the chests have solid wood backs and drawers. A medium chest of drawers was £199 and a large one £229. As well as having very good prices the shop will also stain the furniture to your liking, deliver in the London area, and when necessary assemble the furniture – all without charge. A great value shop.

EAST

Bohemia
Gate 1 Old Spitalfields Market, E1
Tel: 020 8875 1228
E-mail: pzeph@aol.com
Tube: Liverpool Street
Bus: 8, 26, 35, 43, 47, 48, 67, 78, 149, 242
Open: Sun 10.30am-6pm
This little shop in the heart of Spitalfields Market has a great selection of retro furniture and houseware at prices considerably less than you would pay at some similar outlets in the fashionable East End. On a recent visit a large 70s leather sofa was a great buy at £450. There is a quick turnover of stock so it's always worth a visit to see what they have available.

Little Book of Furniture Ltd
11 Lamb Street, Old Spitalfields Market, E1
Tel: 020 7247 4445 / 020 7247 4448
E-mail: ibofurniture@aol.com
Website: www.littlebookoffurniture.com
Tube: Liverpool Street
Bus: 8, 26, 35, 43, 47, 48, 67, 78, 149, 242
Open: Tues-Thurs 9.30am-5.30pm, Fri 9.30am-5pm, Sun 10am-5.30pm
This business imports quality leather (and some fabric) sofas, chairs, footstools and bean bags and sells to the public at very competitive

prices. The sofas are great looking and a leather 3-seater starts from £695, with armchairs in leather for £475. To get an idea of the quality and designs available phone for one of their colourful catalogues, view their website or better still visit the showroom in Spitalfields Market.

WEST

Futon Company

138 Notting Hill Gate, W11
Tel: 020 7727 9252
Website: www.futoncompany.co.uk
Tube: Notting Hill Gate
Bus: 12, 31, 94
Open: Mon-Sat 10am-6pm, Thurs till 7pm, Sun 11am-5pm

5

The Futon Company is a rather smart chain of stores that offers well-made and surprisingly good value futons. A large 3 seater futon can be found here for only £399 which is a considerable saving when compared with rival futon companies. As well as being generally very good value, Futon Company also have regular sales usually in the spring and winter when futons are reduced by a further £50. They also offer a reasonably priced range of accessories and small items of furniture.
Branches at:
102 Chiswick High Road W4, Tel: 020 8995 2271
59 Muswell Hill Broadway N10, Tel: 020 8883 5657
169 Tottenham Court Road W1T, Tel: 020 7636 9984
60-62 London Road KT2, Tel: 020 8546 4868

The Galleries

157 Tower Bridge Road, SE1
Tel: 020 7407 5371
Website: www.antiques-uk.co.uk
Tube: London Bridge
Bus: 21, 35, 40, 133, 343
Open: Mon-Fri 9am-5pm, Sat-Sun 12noon-6pm

This huge warehouse has all kinds of furniture from fine antiques to modern furniture. Among the four to five thousand pieces of furniture there are enough bargains to make this place worth a visit. It is also located very close to Bermondsey Market (see page 248 for details).

Maison du Monde
22-24 Ariel Way, Shepherd's Bush, W12
Tel: 020 8740 1314
Website: www.maisondumonde.com
Tube: Shepherd's Bush, White City
Bus: 72, 95, 220, 272
Open: Mon-Sat 10am-6pm, Sun 10am-5pm
This large warehouse outlet, tucked away in an industrial estate in Shepherd's Bush, imports furniture from India, Indonesia and Morocco and sells direct to the public at considerable discounts. They have a variety of styles from a traditional hardwood cupboard and chest for only £295 to a contemporary solid teak chest of drawers for £125 (reduced from £295). They also stock wrought iron furniture. The store's website is a useful resource and offers the opportunity to buy on line.

Other outlets for furniture:

Bucks Warehouse
125 Evelyn Street, SE8
See full entry in the Discount Outlet section (page 215)
Poetstyle Ltd
Unit 1 Bayford Street Industrial Units, E8
See full entry in the Factory Shops section (page 225)

KITCHENWARE & CUTLERY

CENTRAL

Denny's
55a Dean Street, W1
Tel: 020 7494 2745
Tube: Piccadilly Circus
Bus: 14, 19, 38
Open: Mon-Fri 9.30am-6pm, Sat 10am-4pm
Denny's sells mostly chefs' and waiters' clothes at cheap prices. A pair of chequered chef's trousers cost just £10. There are a few items that can be used in a domestic kitchen such as a white bib apron for £3.40 and white cotton damask napkins £1.65 each. To encourage the budding chef, pick up a child's chef hat for £5.50. High quality knives from Henckels,Victorinox and others go for about 15% off the normal price, but you should still expect to shell out for these top of the range blades.

Leon Jaeggi & Sons
77 Shaftesbury Avenue, W1
Tel: 020 7580 1974
Tube: Leicester Square/Piccadilly Circus
Bus:14, 19, 38
Open: Mon-Sat 9am-5.30pm
Most amateur, domestic chefs will never need any of the heavy-duty, professional equipment sold here. However, the shop's excellent range of smaller items are tops. A dozen simple wine glasses cost £7.50 and plain white china plates go for as little as £1.85 each and bowls for £2.50 each. Plate clips for holding a wine glass on a plate at a cocktail party cost 36p each and sponges are just 90p. To host a really professional dinner party, pick up the table crumb sweeper for £12: The enthusiastic amateur chef will certainly find dozens of inexpensive items to buy for their next culinary adventure. Prices are quoted without VAT.

Pages
121 Shaftesbury Avenue, W1
Tel: 020 7379 6334
Tube: Leicester Square/Piccadilly Circus
Bus: 14, 19, 38
Open: Mon-Fri 9am-6pm, Sat 9.30am-5pm
Bigger than nearby Leon Jaeggi & Sons, Pages stocks the same types of things, but has a bigger selection. From prepping to cleaning up, the shop is full of gadgets and major appliances to make the job easier. Discount cookbooks from celebrity chefs are on offer. If you fancy

white porcelain dishes, they carry a large and diverse stock of tableware from makers like Apilco. A giant iron frying pan costs just £16. Keen home bartenders might find the wine racks, cocktail shakers and ice crushers tempting. Expect to pay at least 25% less than High Street prices.

David Richards and Sons

10 New Cavendish Street, W1
Tel: 020 7935 3206
Tube: Baker Street/Bond Street
Bus: 88, C2
Open: Mon-Fri 9.30am-5.30pm

All things silver are sold at this wholesale shop. The stock consists of tableware like cutlery and candlesticks as well as gift items like christening mementos and jewellery. All items are either silver or silver plate and they stock both antique and new objects. They also offer a wedding list service and a restoration and repairs service.

NORTH

A & K Warehouse Ltd

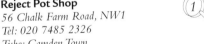

152 Camden High Street, NW3
Tel: 020 7267 3805
Tube: Camden Town
Bus: 24, 27, 29, 88, 134, 168, 214, 253
Open: Mon-Sat 9am-6pm, Sun 11am-5pm

Kit out your kitchen with basic, good value items. There is a wide selection of excellent gadgets, pots and pans, and utensils at this bright, spacious shop. From pizza pans to ice crushers, the friendly staff will help you find what you need.

Reject Pot Shop

56 Chalk Farm Road, NW1
Tel: 020 7485 2326
Tube: Camden Town
Bus: 24, 27, 31, 168
Open: Tues-Sun 11am-5.30pm

A shop that offers a great selection of simple white crockery with slight and often difficult to spot defects. The crockery is made with the intention of decorating it with patterns and any slight blemish in the glaze will show up when decorated, so must be rejected. Many people find the plain white look attractive and with large plates for only £1.50, half pint mugs for only 60p and 10" pasta serving bowls for £3.50, it is possible to get good quality kitchenware at a budget price. If you're setting up home they sell a 12 piece table set for only £15. Cheap blinds and reasonably priced kitchen utensils are at the back of the store.

WEST

Hansens

306 Fulham Road, SW10
Tel: 020 7351 6933
Website: www.hansens.co.uk
Tube: Fulham Broadway
Bus: 14, 211
Open: Mon-Fri 9.00am-5.30pm

This huge shop is dedicated to professional cooking, but anyone can take advantage of the reasonable prices and wonderful selection of goods. Every little gadget, dish and appliance a chef might ever need is here from cheap plasticware to expensive, heavy-duty appliances. This is a good West London alternative to the central Pages and Leon Jaeggi & Sons catering shops.

SOUTH

Chomette

See main entry in the Factory Shops section on page 224.

Dentons Catering Equipment

2 Clapham High Street, SW4
Tel: 020 7622 7157
Tube: Clapham North
Bus: 88, 345, 355, P5
Open: Mon-Fri 8.30am-5.30pm, Sat 8.30am-1pm

In business for 65 years, this shop is family run and stocks more than the amateur chef will ever need. They cater to the restaurant and professional catering trade, but also offer good deals to ordinary punters. Among the interesting gadgets were professional cake dividers for £5.99 and cake decorating kits for £6.99. They have a great selection of white tableware, small appliances, gadgets, utensils and even chef's clothing.

EAST

Kitchen Warehouse

12 Bacon Street, E1
Tube: Shoreditch
Bus: 67
Open: Daily 9am-5pm

This large warehouse is crammed with used professional kitchenware and kitchen furniture. Among the bargains on a recent visit were 4-way electric extension leads for £4 each, a huge stainless steel shelving unit for £170 and massive industrial cookers and mixers for a fraction of the original price. The best deal was good quality used bar and bracket shelving, with 7ft bars for £5 and bracket fittings for £1, which is about 25% of the usual price. Just about the best place in London to get cheap kitchen equipment and next door is a very good junk shop (see review on page 246 for further details).

Pot Luck

Pot Luck
84 Columbia Road, Shoreditch, E2
Tel: 020 7722 6892
Tube: Shoreditch, Old Street
Bus: 26, 48, 55
Open: Fri 10am-3pm, Sun 8am-12.30pm
There's no such thing as perfect china and this shop, opened by Linda Solomon 25 years ago, sells what are called 'blanks' in the trade, though you'd never guess there was anything wrong with them. All the china, bone and porcelain on sale is white. A $10^{1}/_{2}$ inch plate costs £4.50 (£12.50 in shops) or you can buy 8 for £32. The shop also sells Italian oven to table ware at about a quarter of store prices and plain white 'flokati' wool rugs from £15. Open to the public on Fridays and Sundays (combine it with a visit to the Columbia Road flower and plant market on Sunday mornings), the rest of the time Linda sells direct to hotels and restaurants.

KIDS' TOYS, CLOTHES & EQUIPMENT

Buying second-hand can sometimes prove a false economy, but in the case of children's clothing and equipment it makes very good sense because the little darlings outgrow things so quickly. Below are reviewed the best shops specialising in such second-hand items in the London area; many are also useful places for selling your children's things when finished with. Markets and car boot sales (see pages 248 and 253) and charity shops (see page 190) are also rewarding hunting grounds for children's things. Other useful shops are listed with page references at the end of this section.

CENTRAL

Little Badger
Unit 206 Oxo Tower Wharf, Barge House Street, SE1
Tel: 020 7620 2422
Website: www.littlebadger.com
Tube: Waterloo or Southwark
Bus: 4, 26, 45, 63, 100, 243, 501, 521
Open: Mon-Fri 9.30am-5.30pm (mail order)
Sales: End of January and July
This mail order company specialises in stylish knitwear and logo T-shirts for children. Their studio sample sales take place twice a year and offer up to 50% off the usual catalogue price. Phone to put your name on their mailing list.

NORTH

Jo Jo Maman Bébé

3 Ashbourne Parade,
1259 Finchley Rd, NW11
Tel: 020 8731 8961
Website: www.JoJoMamanBebe.co.uk
Tube: Golders Green
Bus: 82, 102, 260
Sales: January, April and July each year

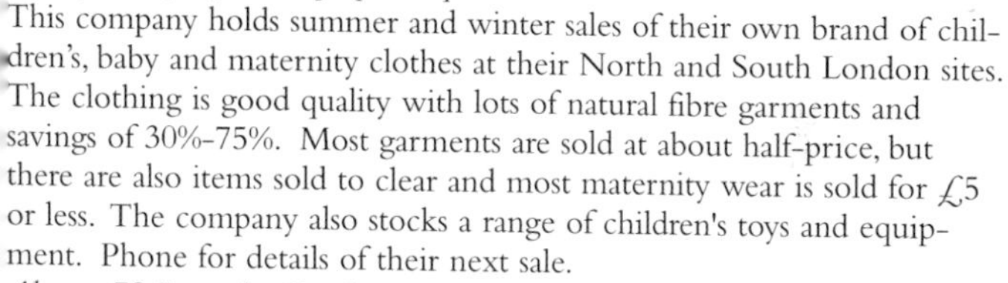

This company holds summer and winter sales of their own brand of children's, baby and maternity clothes at their North and South London sites. The clothing is good quality with lots of natural fibre garments and savings of 30%-75%. Most garments are sold at about half-price, but there are also items sold to clear and most maternity wear is sold for £5 or less. The company also stocks a range of children's toys and equipment. Phone for details of their next sale.

Also at: 72 Bennerley Road SW11, Tel: 020 7924 3144

Rainbow

249 & 253 Archway Road, N6
Tel: 020 8340 8003
Tube: Highgate
Bus: 43, 134, 263
Open: Mon-Sat 10.30am-5.30pm

At no. 253 you'll find traditional and unusual new toys at reasonable prices, while the used clothes and toys are at no. 249. It's at the latter that the real bargains can be found with good quality kids' clothes and toys (such as Duplo and Brio) at a fraction of their original cost. There is a loading bay right outside the shop and free parking in the side streets.

Rub-a-Dub-Dub

198 Stroud Green Road, N4
Tel: 020 7263 5577
Tube/Rail: Finsbury Park
Bus: 210, W3, W7
Open: Mon-Sat 10am-5pm

This small shop is surprisingly well stocked with new and used kids' clothing and equipment. On a recent visit they had a used trip-trap chair for only £50 and new trikes for £85. There is also a good selection of used kids' clothes with used designer labels for no more than a third of the original price. All the used goods have been checked and come with a guarantee. Check out their new store which only sells new goods (review on the following page).

Rub-a-Dub-Dub
15 Park Road, N8
Tel: 020 8342 9898
Rail: Hornsey
Bus: 91, W5, W7
Open: Mon-Sat 10am-5pm
This is a new shop which sells only new kids' clothing and equipment. Although you will not get the kind of bargains you can find buying second-hand, the stock is very competitively priced. Among the good deals are Baby Bjorn Slings for £45 (usual price £50) and Maxi Cosi Car Seats for £61.99 (usual price £65). A great place to stock-up on clothing and equipment for your little sprog/s.

Simply Outgrown Nursery Equipment & Toys
360 Lordship Lane, N17 (opposite Lordship Recreation Ground)
Tel: 020 8801 0568
Tube: Wood Green
Bus: 144, W3
Open: Mon-Fri 10.30am-5pm, Sat 10.30am-4pm
This shop buys and sells nearly new baby equipment and toys. All goods are clean, checked for safety and under 2 years old. Specialising in toys and equipment and being pretty fussy about the goods they buy, this is one of the best places in London to kit out a nursery on a budget.

WEST

Boomerang (3)
69 Blythe Road, W14
Tel: 020 7610 5232
Tube: Hammersmith, Kensington (Olympia)
Bus: 9, 10, 27, 391
Open: Mon-Sat 9.30am-6pm
This established shop is tucked away from the bustle of Shepherd's Bush Road, but is well worth a visit if you're on the hunt for good quality second-hand kids' clothing, toys and equipment. The goods are thoroughly checked and reasonably priced with car seats starting from £20 and prams from only £25.

The Little Trading Company
7 Bedford Corner, The Avenue, Chiswick, W4
Tel: 020 8742 3152
Tube: Turnham Green
Bus: 237, 267, 391, 440, H91, E3
Open: Mon-Fri 9am-5pm, Sat 9am-4.30pm

Located in the back streets of Chiswick, this wonderful children's dress agency is easily missed. It's worth taking the trouble to visit because it's the main repository for high quality used clothes, toys, shoes and equipment from the surrounding leafy avenues. The shop also offers children's haircuts by appointment from £8.50.

Pixies
14 Fauconberg Road, W4
Tel: 020 8995 1568
Tube: Chiswick Park
Bus: 94, 237, 267, 391, 440
Open: Tues-Fri 10am-4.30pm, Sat 10am-3pm
This shop is crammed to the gunnels with good quality new and used kids' clothes and equipment, but nevertheless manages to appear tidy and well-ordered. Situated in a rather upmarket part of West London the shop gets more than its fair share of designer labels, but they are all affordably priced and there are always cheaper garments to suit those on a tight budget. Bargains found on a recent visit included a Britax car seat for £27.50 (about £60 new) and a Little Tikes Activity Easel for £15 (£30 new). The place is also very child friendly.

SOUTH

The Anerley Frock Exchange
122 Anerley Road, SE20
Tel: 020 8778 2030
See main entry in Dress Agencies section on page 41.

Jo Jo Maman Bébé
72 Bennerley Road, SW11
Tel: 020 7924 3144
See entry in West London (page 137) for full details.

Swallows & Amazons
91 Nightingale Lane, SW12
Tel: 020 8673 0275
Tube: Clapham South
Bus: 155, 255, 355, G1
Open: Mon-Sat 10am-5.15pm
This large and well-stocked shop offers a fantastic range of used kids' clothes, toys and equipment. A lot of garments are good as new and the quality of clothes is high with plenty of High Street and designer labels. The prices are at least half the new price and the stock caters for new borns to 12 year olds. They also offer haircuts by appointment for around £7-£8.

EAST

Chocolate Crocodile
39 Morpeth Road, E9
Tel: 020 8985 3330
Tube: Bethnal Green
Bus: 26, 277
Open: Mon-Sat 11am-5pm
This small shop manages to cram a vast quantity of kids' clothing, toys and equipment into a limited space. The clothing ranges from cheap basic items for a few pounds to designer labels such as Oilily, Paul Smith and Moschino for between half and one-third the original price. There is also a mix of new and used equipment with bargains like a second-hand Britax car seat for £30 (new price £109), and new buggies starting from £16. Crocodile also sells a large number of good condition shoes, with sandals for £2.99 and smart leather boots for £6.99. The shop has also recently started selling new books and wooden toys, both at competitive prices. An excellent children's dress agency and just around the corner from Victoria Park.

Chocolate Crocodile

Merry-Go-Round
12 Clarence Road, E5
Tel: 020 8985 6308
Rail: Hackney Central
Bus: 56, D6, W15
Open: Mon-Sat 10am-5.30pm
This children's clothing and equipment agency is located in a rough area, but inside the shop it is reassuringly clean and well organised. The stock includes a great selection of clothes, toys, books and equipment, extending over two floors. Among the bargains on a recent visit were a large cot for £45, denim jackets for only £4, a wide choice of wellington boots for £2.50-£3 and cotton baby-grows for £2.50. If your children are over 3 years old, the basement caters for you with a similar mix of clothing, books and equipment. One of the best value children's shops in town.

Other outlets for kids' things:

Benny Dee (City) Ltd
74-80 Middlesex Street, Liverpool Street, E1
Tel: 020 7377 9067
See main entry in the Basic Clothing section on page 11.

The Catalogue Bargain Shop
252 Green Lane, N15
Tel: 020 8886 9532
See main entry in the Discount Outlets section on page 213.

David Charles
2-4 Thanes Works,
Thane Villas, N7
Tel: 020 7609 4797
See main entry in the Designer Sale section on page 25.

Choice
Unit 11, Arcadia Centre, Ealing Broadway, W5
Tel: 020 8567 2747
See main entry in the Basic Clothing section on page 10.

La Scala
39 Elystan Street, SW3
Tel: 020 7589 2784
See main entry in the Dress Agencies section (lots of clothing for children up to 6 years old) on page 39.

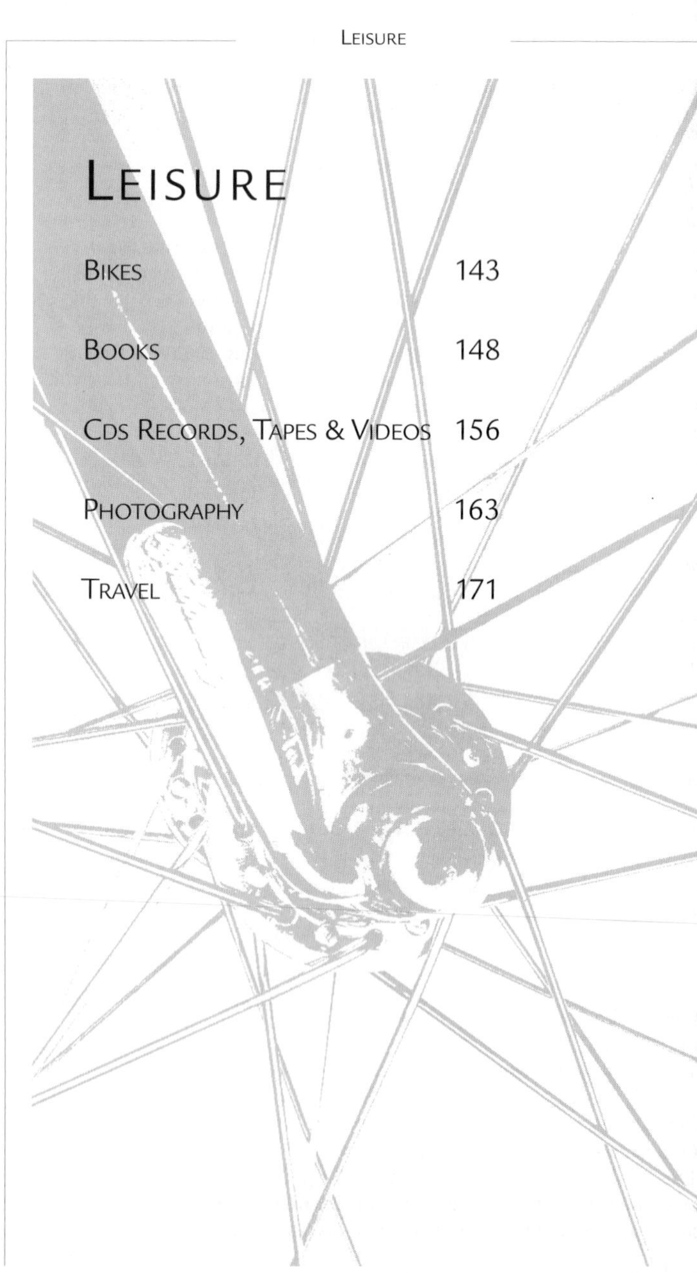

LEISURE

BIKES

It's difficult to find new bikes at a discount – bicycle manufacturers attempt to control the retail price charged by outlets selling their bikes. One way to get a bargain is to buy your bike in the autumn when new models are introduced and the superseded ones are cleared at considerable discounts. Below are featured many bike shops that say they will better the price offered by other outlets and it is a good idea to use this promise to beat the price down even lower. You can also try some of the websites listed below which market themselves as very price competitive. A good tip when buying a new bike is to get the bike with all the specifications you want. The bike shop wants your business and will usually be willing to change the saddle, tyres and other peripherals at no extra cost. Another good tip is to avoid very cheap new bikes with unrecognisable brand names. These bikes look OK to the novice cyclist, but are badly made South East Asian copies and are not worth buying. If you don't know a good bike from a bad one it's a good idea to bring a bikie friend with you to give advice.

If you want a real bargain then it's best to buy second-hand and there are lots of places to look. There are quite a few specialist second-hand bike outlets in London which are reviewed below, but they are not the cheapest places in town. I found that some of the best deals were to be found at new bike shops that sell part-exchange bikes. These bikes are sold to clear and the retailer is not trying to make a profit from them so they are often great value. If you fancy being a bit more adventurous you could try Lloyds International Auction which sells bikes on behalf of the Metropolitan Police (see their entry on page 185). There are also cycle jumbles which are mysterious events where second-hand bikes and parts are sold to more serious cycle enthusiasts. To find out more about cycle jumbles check the classified pages of Cycling Weekly where they are intermittently advertised.

WEST

Mend-a-Bike (7)
Effie Road, SW6
Tel: 020 7371 5867
Tube: Fulham Broadway
Bus: 11, 14, 28, 211, 295, 391, 424
Open: Mon-Fri 9am-7pm, Sat 9am-6pm
This large bike workshop has been selling good quality new and used bikes on this site for 14 years. It is a particularly good place to find ex-showroom bikes and slight seconds for less than half the new price.

Recent bargains included a brand new Gary Fisher mountain bike that had been returned because it had the wrong coloured spokes, the new price was £1,400 and it was on offer for £900. Those with more modest biking ambitions could find a used Ridgeback mountain bike (over £300 new) for £130. All bikes come with a 3 month guarantee and used bikes are fully serviced. The shop also offers an excellent repairs service which is usually next day, depending on how busy they are.

SOUTH

Compton Cycles

23-25 Catford Hill, Catford, SE6
Tel: 020 8690 0141
Website: www.comptoncycles.co.uk
Rail: Catford, Catford Bridge
Bus: 75, 124, 181, 202
Open: Mon-Fri 9am-6pm, Sat 9am-5pm

Compton Cycles are an established shop who sell a wide range of new and used bikes. They usually have about 20 second-hand bikes in stock with prices starting at around £80 for a well used Marin mountain bike and going up to £300 for a good condition Cannondale. The new bikes are good value with regular promotions such as the Raleigh Spirit recently on offer for £200 (£100 off the usual price).

Der Ver Cycles

630-634 Streatham High Road, Norbury, SW16
Tel: 020 8679 6197
Website: www.devercycles.co.uk
Rail: Streatham Hill
Bus: 50, 109, 255, G1
Open: Mon-Sat 10am-6.30pm (closed Wed and Sun)

Der Ver Cycles is a great bikeshop run by former British cycling champion Maurice Burton featuring a range of bikes from standard town bikes to £3,000 racing machines. Bargain hunters' should have a look at the 20 or so part-exchange, second-hand bikes that the shop stocks which cost anything from £30 to £200. If you are after a shiny new bike at a discount you should wait for their October sale which offers substantial discounts on superseded models. Der Ver Cycles sometimes offer special deals through the e-Bay web auction site, to find out more view their website which has a link to e-Bay.

Edwardes
221/225 Camberwell Road, SE5
Tel: 020 7703 5720 / 020 7703 3676
Tube: Kennington
Bus: 12, 35, 40, 42, 45, 68, 171, 176, 468, X68
Open: Mon-Sat 8.30am-6pm
This family business has been trading since 1908 and now occupies four shop fronts on Camberwell Road stocking many reputable makes like Scott and Ridgeback as well as serious racing bikes from names like Pinello and Principia. They have regular sales and always have bikes on promotion, such as the good quality Dawes road bike reduced from £200 to only £139. They also accept part-exchange bikes which means that they always have about thirty second-hand cycles for those on a budget. On a recent visit a good condition used Marin hybrid was only £79.

Global Esprit
525 Garratt Lane, Earlsfield, SW18
Tel: 020 8946 2352
Rail: Earlsfield
Bus: 44, 77, 270
Open: Mon Sat 9am-6pm, Sun 11am-4pm
This shop offers a solid range of bikes with established names like Giant, Trek and Ridgeback among their stock. Although they don't sell second-hand bikes, they will beat any written quote for new bikes. Their January sales knock as much as 30% off the list price.

Recycling
110 Elephant Road, SE17
Tel: 020 7703 7001
Tube: Elephant and Castle
Bus: 1, 53, 63, 172, 188
Open: Mon-Fri 9am-6.30pm, Sat 9am-6pm, Sun 11am-4pm
This large showroom has a grunge atmosphere with thumping bass music and the scent of tobacco smoke and bike oil in the air. This is the kind of shop where you would expect to get a bargain, but it actually appears a little expensive with old upright bikes for no less than £70 and second-hand kids' bikes for around £25. Likewise, the mountain bikes seemed a bit pricey with a well-used Gary Fisher bike for £250. Worth a visit perhaps, but not the first port of call for the bargain hunter.

South London Cycle Surgery
Arch 840 Consort Road, Peckham, SE15
Tel: 020 7639 9515
Rail: Peckham Rye
Bus: 12, 37, 63, 78, 312, 343, P12
Open: Mon-Sat 10am-6pm, Sun 11am-4pm
This shop is situated under the railway arches behind Peckham Rye bus station and holds about 150 used bikes. The stock ranges from scrappy old uprights for around £70 to serious off-road bikes like the Muddy Fox for £299. As the name suggests, this is a good place to get your two-wheeled friend serviced.

EAST

The Bike Station
1 Upper Walthamstow Road, E17
Tel: 020 8520 6988
Rail: Wood Street Walthamstow
Bus: 56, 230, 357
Open: Mon-Sat 9am-6pm
This friendly local bike shop offers new bikes at reasonable prices, but also has a selection of top quality second-hand cycles. Recent bargains included a dual suspension Cannondale mountain bike for £500 (half the new price) and a very good condition Klein mountain bike which was £790 new, for only £300. There is usually a better choice of second-hand bike in the summer when they are displayed on the street. They also offer a good value repairs service.

OUTER LONDON

Ciclos Uno
37 New North Road,
Hainault, Ilford, Essex, IG6
Tel: 020 8500 1792
Website: www.ciclosuno.com
Open: Mon-Sat 9am-4.30pm (closed Wed)
This shop is not for the everyday cyclist as it specialises in top quality racing bikes but if you are looking for a serious racing machine on a budget this is definitely a good place to visit. They always have a selection of used racing bikes to choose from and can offer great deals on bike parts as well as detailed advice about anything to do with serious cycling.

SOUTH
LONDON
SURGERY
NEW AND SECOND-HAND
CYCLE SALES
SERVICING+REPAIRS

BOOKS

There are lots of places in London to find cheap second-hand books and below are reviewed some of London's best second-hand bookshops as well as Soho Books which sells cheap remaindered books. For those in search of real bargains it's always best to pay attention to the tables outside most bookshops. It is from such tables that booksellers' clear surplus stock at a discount and hope to attract passing custom. Other places to seek out cheap reading matter include London's street markets, the best being Camden Passage (on Thursdays) and Riverside Walk (on the Southbank), as well as the larger markets like Spitalfields, Merton Abbey Mills and Portobello (see markets section on pages 248-252). Charity shops (pages 190-210) are another source of low cost, interesting books, with the Oxfam Books and Music on Marylebone High Street (page 192), Oxfam Books (page 206) and Bookshops for Amnesty (pages 198 and 204) being the best in the capital. Bloomsbury Book Auctions (page 188) is a good place to look for rare and collectable books.

CENTRAL

Any Amount of Books
56 Charing Cross Road, WC2
Tel: 020 7836 3697
E-mail: anyamountofbooks@aol.com
Website: www.anyamountofbooks.com
Tube: Leicester Square
Bus: 24, 29, 176
Open: Mon-Sat 10.30am-9.30pm, Sun 11.30am-8.30pm
A small general bookshop with enough quality paperbacks and clearance stock to catch the bargain hunter's eye. The £1 trays on the pavement are always worth a browse.

Judd Two
82 Marchmont Street, WC1
Tel: 020 7387 5333
Tube: Russell Square
Bus: 59, 68, 91, 168
Open: Mon-Sat 11am-7pm, Sun 11am-6pm
This is a fantastic bookshop ranging over two floors with an emphasis on the humanities, but also featuring lots of quality fiction. Remaindered books are discounted for 20-50% and even greater discounts are to be found from tables on the pavement. The shop also offers a 10% discount for students.

Quinto
48a Charing Cross Road, WC2
Tel: 020 7379 7669
E-mail: sales@haycinemabookshop.co.uk
Tube: Leicester Square
Bus: 24, 29, 176
Open: Mon-Sat 9am-9pm, Sun12am-8pm
An established feature of the West End book scene, covering most subjects and a good range of fiction. Although it makes no claim to be a bargain outlet, Quinto offers enough choice to reward the eager bargain hunter.

Quinto of Great Russell Street
63 Great Russell Street, WC1
Tel: 020 7430 2535
E-mail: sales@quintogrs.co.uk
Tube: Tottenham Court Road
Bus: 1, 8, 19, 25, 38, 55, 98, 242
Open: Daily 9.30am-6.30pm
Over 50,000 second-hand academic and remaindered books in all subjects. There's a selection of 50p bargain books outside.

Rees and O'Neill
27 Cecil Court, WC2
Tel: 020 7836 3336
Website: www.rees-oneill.com
Tube: Leicester Square
Bus: 24, 29, 176
Open: Mon-Fri 10am-6pm, Sat 10am-5pm
This shop has a very modern interior and specialises in fine books. The main stock is a treat for bibliophiles, but not for bargain hunters. Those looking for bargains should take a look at the tables outside where good quality books are sold for as little as £1. Nigel Williams is next door and has a similar discount policy.

Skoob Russell Square
10 Brunswick Centre, WC1
Tel: 020 7278 8760
Website: www.skoob.com
Tube: Russell Square
Bus: 59, 68, 91, 168, 188, X68
Open: Mon-Sat 11am-7pm, Sun 12am-5pm
Not the cheapest bookshop in London, but rated by many as the best. It has a wide range of books with a particular emphasis on academic subjects and an unrivalled stock of second-hand arthouse and World Cinema videos.

Soho Original Bookshop

11-12 Brewer Street, W1
Tel: 020 7494 1615
Tube: Piccadilly Circus
Bus: 3, 6, 12, 13, 15, 23, 53, 88, 94, 139, 159
Open: Mon-Sat 10am-1am, Sun 11am-11pm

This chain of bookshops sell new books at about 10% discount or in many cases £1 off the published price, as well as quality remaindered books at much greater discounts. The Brewer Street store is more art orientated, with city branches having a more general stock. Those of a prudish disposition should avoid the basement which is stocked with top quality porn.

Branches at:
23/25 Leather Lane EC1, Tel: 020 7404 3594
124 Middlesex Street E1, Tel: 020 7377 5309
63 Cowcross Street EC1, Tel: 020 7251 8020

Unsworths Booksellers

12 Bloomsbury Street, WC1
Tel: 020 7436 9836
E-mail: books@unsworths.com
Website: www.unsworths.com
Tube: Tottenham Court Road
Bus: 10, 24, 29, 73, 134
Open: Mon-Sat 10am-8pm, Sun 11am-7pm

This well-laidout shop carries a large stock of literary and academic titles with an emphasis on the humanities, with classics and history being especially well represented. The prices are low, usually at 50-90% off the published price and clearly marked. There is also a rare and antiquarian department in the basement.

NORTH

Archive Second-hand Books and Music

83 Bell Street, NW1
Tel: 020 7402 8212
Tube: Marble Arch
Bus: 6, 7, 15, 16, 23, 36, 98
Open: Mon-Sat 10.30am-6pm

If you like bookshops to be musty establishments piled to the ceiling with books, this shop will not disappoint. The varied stock fills two floors and the cheaper stuff can be found on the pavement outside for as little as 10p. The music referred to in the shop's name is not records but a basement full of printed music and related books.

Church Street Bookshop

142 Stoke Newington Church Street, N16
Tel: 020 7241 5411
Rail: Stoke Newington
Bus: 67, 73, 76, 149, 243
Open: Daily 11.30am-6pm

A second-hand bookshop with a fine stock of well-priced books, and a particularly impressive choice of paperback fiction. They usually have several boxes of books for £1 each or 3 books for £2.

Hoxton Books Depository

97 Hoxton Street, N1
Tel: 020 7613 4841
Tube/Rail: Old Street
Bus: 43, 55, 67, 149, 242, 243
Open: Mon-Sat 12noon-7pm

This shop is stuffed full of discounted new and remainder books, second-hand books, vintage magazines, comics, videos and old vinyl, with an emphasis on popular culture.

Keith Fawkes

1-3 Flask Walk, NW3
Tel: 020 7435 0614
Tube: Hampstead
Bus: 46, 268
Open: Mon-Sat 10am-5.30pm, Sun 1pm-6pm

The books in this shop are reasonably priced, but the conversation, advice and bookish atmosphere are priceless and free. A blissful refuge from the hustle and bustle of Hampstead High Street.

Ocean Books

127 Stoke Newington Church Street, N16
Tel: 020 7502 6319
E-mail: oceanbooksn16@yahoo.co.uk
Rail: Stoke Newington
Bus: 67, 73, 76, 149, 243
Open: Mon-Sat 11.30am-6pm, Sun 12noon-6pm

This establishment may look small from the street but behind the main shop there is a well-stocked back room with discounted books on most subjects, making it an enjoyable place for the serious bargain hunter to rummage.

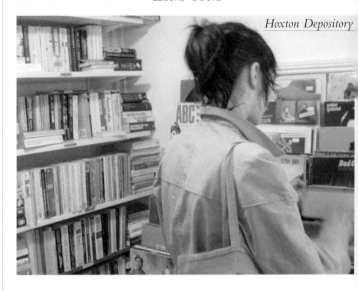

Hoxton Depository

Walden Books

38 Harmood Street, Camden, NW1
Tel: 020 7267 8146
E-mail: waldenbooks@lineone.net
Website: www.ukbookworld
Tube: Camden Town/Chalk Farm
Bus: 24, 46, 168, C11
Open: Thurs-Sun 10.30am-6.30pm
Situated just off busy Chalk Farm Road, this is a great place to escape the Camden crowds and browse for second-hand books at reasonable prices.

WEST

Book & Comic Exchange

(5)

14 Pembridge Road, W11
Tel: 020 7229 8420
Tube: Notting Hill Gate
Bus: 12, 27, 28, 31, 52, 94, 328
Open: Daily 10am-8pm
Part of the Music and Video Exchange group, selling an interesting mix of fiction and non-fiction.

Gloucester Road Bookshop
123 Gloucester Road, SW7
Tel: 020 7370 3503
E-mail: manager@gloucesterbooks.co.uk
Tube: Gloucester Road
Bus:49, 74
Open: Mon-Fri 9.30am-10.30pm, Sat-Sun 10.30am-6.30pm
This is a friendly second-hand bookshop offering lots of book bargains. The shop has a good reputation for art, history and literature, but if you're after cheap paperback fiction look at the stands outside, where prices start from only 20p. They publish a regular catalogue.

Notting Hill Books
132 Palace Gardens Terrace, W8
Tel: 020 7727 5988
Tube: Notting Hill Gate
Bus: 12, 27, 28, 52, 70, 94, 328
Open: Mon-Wed, Fri and Sat 10.30am-6pm, Thurs 10.30am-1pm
A small shop, but packed full of discounted and second-hand books on a variety of serious subjects, with excellent coverage of art, literary criticism, architecture, design, history and travel. The small selection of quality fiction is offered at half the publisher's price and there are trays of bargain books outside.

Portobello Bookshop

328 Portobello Road, W10
020 8964 3166
Tube: Ladbroke Grove
Bus: 7, 23, 52, 70
Open: Mon-Fri 12noon-5pm, Sat 9am-5pm
This is one of the best second-hand bookshops in London. There are books on every possible subject and the stock is well displayed and competitively priced. A gem of a shop.

World's End Bookshop
7
357 King's Road, SW3
Tel: 020 7352 9376
Tube: Fulham Broadway/South Kensington
Bus: 11, 19, 22, 49, 211, 319
Open: Daily 10am-6.30pm
This is a fine little bookshop with a broad general stock. There are lots of discounted titles sold from tables outside with prices starting from 50p. Between Saturday and Monday there's a further 20% off all titles. If you're in the area don't forget the two charity shops on the same corner.

SOUTH

Book Mongers
439 Coldharbour Lane, SW9
Tel: 020 7738 4225
Tube/Rail: Brixton
Bus: 35, 45, 109, 118, 196, 250, 345, 355, P4, P5
Open: Mon-Sat 10.30am-6.30pm
This bookshop in the heart of Brixton has an impressive range of titles on most academic and general subjects as well as plenty of good value fiction.

Enigma Books
16 Church Road, SE19
Tel: 020 8771 9572
Rail: Crystal Palace
Bus: 157, 249, 358, 410, 417
Open: Wed-Sat 11am-6pm, Sun 11am-5pm
Excellent second-hand bookshop with a wide range of paperback fiction from classics through to popular genres and literary stuff. Prices are fair and there are plenty of titles in the £2-£3 range. The more academic philosophy and collectable stock is now in their new sister shop called Renaissance Books just a few doors down.

Marcet Books
4A Nelson Road, Greenwich, SE10
Tel: 020 8853 5408
Website: www.marcetbooks.co.uk
E-mail: info@marcetbooks.co.uk
Rail/DLR: Greenwich
Bus: 177, 180, 188, 199, 286
Open: Daily 10am-5.30pm
In one of the alleyways leading off Greenwich Craft Market, this is a small shop packed with a good choice of mostly second-hand but some discounted new books in a broad range of subjects. It is particularly strong on maritime books, fiction, history, art and also stocks literary magazines.

My Back Pages
8-10 Balham Station Road, SW12
Tel: 020 8675 9346
Tube/Rail: Balham
Bus: 155, 219, 249, 319, 355
Open: Mon-Fri 10am-8pm, Sat 10am-7pm, Sun 11am-6pm

This shop offers used books, review copies and some discounted new books. Just about every subject is covered and prices start from 50p for a tatty but still readable paperback. They also have a range of new books at reduced prices prices.

The Spread Eagle Bookshop
8 Nevada Street, SE10
Tel: 020 8305 1666 ext.23
Website: www.spreadeagle.org
Rail/DLR: Greenwich
Bus: 177, 180, 188, 286
Open: Daily 10.30am-5.30pm
This large bookshop sells ephemera, collectables and books over three floors of an 18th century coaching inn. The stock covers every conceivable subject with a particular emphasis on travel, topography and the arts. There are always cheap books being sold to clear.

Tlon Books
Elephant & Castle Shopping Centre, SE1
Tel: 020 7701 0360
Tube: Elephant & Castle
Bus: 1, 53, 63, 133, 155, 172, 188
Open: Mon-Sat 9am-7pm, Sun 11am-6pm
A gem of a second-hand bookshop set in the unpromising surroundings of this pink monstrosity of a shopping centre. The shop is well laid out and has a decent general and academic stock. The selection of paperback fiction of all kinds is impressive and prices are competitive. Subject catalogues are issued regularly.

EAST

Beedell Coram Antiques
7 Lamb Street, Spitalfields, E1
Tel: 020 7377 1195
Tube: Liverpool Street
Bus: 67
Open: Wed-Fri 12noon-4.30pm, Sun 9am-5.30pm
This antiques shop is situated in Spitalfields Market and has a few tables displaying books outside as well as a whole basement dedicated to second-hand books. Among the crammed shelves there is a good selection of paperback and hardback fiction, reference and art books, as well as a limited collection of old magazines. The prices are reasonable and there are always a few bargains to be found.

CDS RECORDS, TAPES & VIDEO

CENTRAL

Cheapo Cheapo Records Ltd

53 Rupert Street, W1
Tel: 020 7437 8272
Tube: Piccadilly Circus
Bus: 14, 19, 38
Open: Mon-Sat 11am-10pm

A cavernous second-hand music shop selling a variety of CDs for cheap, cheap prices. Expect to pay as little as £3 for a CD, £2 for a record and £5 for videos. Be prepared to hunt as the selection is enormous and not very well presented. Patience and time will be repaid by great savings on your entertainment needs.

Harold Moores Records and Video

2 Great Marlborough Street, W1F
Tel: 020 7437 1576
Website: www.hmrecords.co.uk
Tube: Oxford Circus
Bus: 7, 8, 10, 25, 55, 73, 98, 176
Open: Mon-Sat 10am-6.30pm, Sun 12noon-6.30pm

This established classical record shop is renowned for its basement of over 60,000 well catalogued and priced, used and collectable CDs and LPs. They are particularly good for Jazz, Film Sound Tracks, Show and 'Personality' LPs. The discount boxes are always kept well filled and there's even more clearance stock on the pavement outside. LPs start from as little as 50p and go up to over £50 for a rarity. Mail order service available from their website.

Music & Video Exchange

95 Berwick Street, W1
Tel: 020 7434 2939
Tube: Leicester Square
Bus: 14, 19, 38
Open: Daily 10am-8pm

A branch of the exchange specialising in Soul and Dance music.

Reckless Records

2

30 Berwick Street, W1
Tel: 020 7437 4271
Website: www.reckless.co.uk

Tube: Leicester Square
Bus: 14, 19, 38
Open: 7 days a week 10am-7pm, records cannot be sold to the shop after 6pm
Reckless Records sells second-hand CDs and vinyl as well as videos and DVDs. They buy or exchange used records and CDs too. Dance is particularly well catered for, but they've got loads of mainstream music. Everything is well presented and in good condition.

Steve's Sounds
20-20a Newport Court, WC2
Tel: 020 7437 4638
Tube: Leicester Square
Bus: 24, 29, 176, 14, 19, 38
Open: Mon-Sat 10.30am-7.30pm, Sun 12noon-7pm
Centrally located, Steve's Sounds specialises in bargain CDs with all stock for less than £10 a piece. If you are looking for real bargains, check out their £1 CDs. They have a small selection of vinyl as well. The stock is mostly mainstream music.

NORTH

Flashback

50 Essex Road, N1
Tel: 020 7354 9356
Website: www.flashback.co.uk
Tube: Angel
Bus: 38, 56, 73, 341
Open: Mon-Sat 10am-7pm Sun 12noon-6pm

This shop has an excellent collection of second-hand music, video, DVDs and video games. The basement is devoted to vinyl, where anything from Krautrock to Hip Hop can be found, with a special accent on rare and collectable items. Prices for vinyl range from £1 upwards. Upstairs is where the CDs are kept, with an equally impressive range. Recent releases can be bought for around £8. There's also an impressive selection of videos, averaging at around £4 as well as DVDs and video games. They give a fairly good deal if you want to trade in your old records and CDs, but can be quite picky as to what they buy – ultimately a good thing for the overall quality of the stock.

Haggle Vinyl

114-116 Essex Road, N1
Tel: 020 7704 3101
Website: www.hagglevinyl.com
Tube: Angel
Bus: 38, 56, 73, 341
Open: Mon-Sat 9am-7pm, Sun 9am-4pm

If you are one of those that still treasure your vinyl collection and keep your turntable dust-free and in working order, then this shop will prove a useful place to add to your collection. They claim to have over 21,000 albums and taking a look at the packed display units and large piles of records on the floor it is easy to believe. Among the stock is every type of music, but with a slant toward soul, reggae and jazz. The records on the floor are usually £2, while those in the units can range from £5 to £20 for a signed collectable. Haggle often has boxes outside with records reduced to clear.

Music & Video Exchange

208 Camden High Street, NW1
Tel: 020 7267 1898
Tube: Camden Town
Bus: 24, 27, 29, 88, 134, 168, 214, 253
Open: Daily 10am-8pm

This is one of the largest and best stocked record shops in town with two floors offering CDs, vinyl, DVDs and videos. They claim to have an emphasis on contemporary music, but in reality every kind of music is represented here and the less favoured styles, like classical and folk, are often sold at greater discounts. All stock is competitively priced and they keep a corner of the ground floor and the entire basement for bargain items. In the bargain areas all LPs are less than £5, with many for as little £1, there are piles of CDs for 50p each and the novel idea of 10 singles for £1 (the packs of 10 are wrapped so you can't see what you get). Even in the main areas there are numerous records that have been reduced in price to below £5. They also have a large stock of videos for £3-£4.

Out on the Floor

10 Inverness Street, NW1
Tel: 020 7267 5989
Tube: Camden Town
Bus: 24, 27, 31, 88, 168, 274, C2
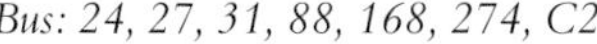
Open: Daily 10am-6.30pm

Two floors of collectable and second-hand vinyl, with an emphasis on soul, funk, reggae, indie, rock and pop. The stock is very well organised with most CDs and LPs for around £7. They buy good condition stuff and also offer part-exchange.

Music & Video Exchange Camden

Reckless Records
79 Upper Street, N1
Tel: 020 7359 7105
Tube: Angel
Bus: 4, 19, 30, 43
Open: Daily 10am-7pm, records cannot be sold to the shop after 6pm
See entry in Central London (page 157) for full details.

Totem
168 Stoke Newington Church Street, N16
Tel: 020 7275 0234
Website: www.totemrecords.com
Rail: Stoke Newington
Bus: 67, 73, 76, 149, 243
Open: Mon-Sat 10:30am-6.30pm, Sun 12noon-5.30pm
Their strength lies in their great stock of second-hand vinyl, but Totem also excels with their mail order service available through their website. With every genre covered, you are sure to find some CDs or records here. They also buy records with 40% of an item's saleable value in cash or 33% in exchange.

WEST LONDON

KCD (3)
142 Uxbridge Road, W12
Tel: 020 8740 7500
Tube: Shepherd's Bush
Bus: 207, 260, 283, 607
Open: Mon-Sat 11am-7pm
A no-nonsense outlet selling a reasonable range of CDs for discount prices. Most CDs sell for £10-£12. Worth a visit if you're passing.

CD Warehouse
51 New Broadway, Ealing, W5
Tel: 020 8567 2122
Tube: Ealing Broadway
Bus: 83, 112, 207, 607, E11
Open: Daily 10am-7pm (both branches)
Sell your old CDs here for up to £4 cash per item or £1 in trade at the shop. The CD Warehouse stocks both new and second-hand CDs and prices are exceptionally reasonable with CDs selling for between £3.99 and £14.99.
Also at:
46 The Broadway, Wimbledon SW19, Tel: 020 8543 2355

Honest Jon's Records

276-278 Portobello Road, W10
Tel: 020 8969 9822
Tube: Ladbroke Grove
Bus: 7, 23, 52, 70
Open: Mon-Sat 10am-6pm, Sun 11am-5pm

Specialising in world music and dance, bargain hunters can find a plethora of good quality tunes here. The stock comprises new and some second-hand records and CDs. Not everything is dirt cheap since some of their stock is highly prized.

Music & Video Exchange

Tube: Notting Hill Gate
Bus: 12, 27, 28, 31, 70, 94, 328

General:
38 Notting Hill Gate, W11
(Bargain Basement)
Tel: 020 7243 8573

28 Pembridge Road, W11
Tel: 020 7221 1444

Classical:
36 Notting Hill Gate
Tel: 020 7229 3219

Singles & Memorabilia:
40 Notting Hill Gate
Tel: 020 7792 9393

Soul & Dance:
42 Notting Hill Gate
Tel: 020 7221 2793

Videos:
Stage & Screen
34 Notting Hill Gate
Tel: 020 7221 3646

Computer Games:
56 Notting Hill Gate
Tel: 020 7229 4805

Open: Daily 10am-8pm

This chain of shops has colonized a sizeable chunk of Notting Hill Gate with a variety of music, video and computer game outlets. The shops are plain, the staff a little surly, but the selection of vinyl and CDs is enormous. The general store at 38 Notting Hill Gate also has videos and a bargain basement with discounted CDs and vinyl. For even more discounts don't forget the store at no.56 which sells discounted video games, but also thousands of clearance LPs for 50p. Although many of the albums are worthless dross, there are enough little gems to make the search worth while. If you like classical music, the Classical Music Exchange at 36 is a good place to look for bargains with many quality LPs, CDs and tapes gradually reduced in price until they sell. Stage & Screen at 34 specialises in second-hand videos, with films for between £1 and £14. There is also a small general music outlet on Pembridge Road. Bring ID if you want to trade your old records or CDs in.

SOUTH LONDON

Beanos

7 Middle Street
Croydon, Surrey
Tel: 020 8680 1202
Website: www.beanos.co.uk
Rail: East Croydon
Bus: 197, 312, 726, 410
Open: Mon-Fri 10am-6pm, Sat 9am-6pm

Beanos is the largest second-hand record shop in Europe, and therefore worth trekking out to Croydon to visit. The shop has a vast selection of vinyl, CDs and videos (which are housed in a separate store next door to the main branch). Prices start from as little as £2 for a record, while current release CDs can be had for only £9.

Music & Video Exchange

Dance/General
23 Greenwich Church Street, SE10
Tel: 020 8858 8898
Rail/DLR: Greenwich
Bus: 177, 180, 188, 199, 286, 386
Open: Daily 10am-8pm

A South London branch of this chain (see entry in West London section), with a great value bargain basement.

Rat Records

348 Camberwell New Road, SE5
Tel: 020 7274 3222
Tube: Oval
Bus: 36, 185, 484
Open: Mon-Fri 11am-6pm, Sat 10am-6pm

This is one of South London's best kept secrets with second-hand vinyl and CDs, piled high and sold cheap. There are at least 500 fresh records arriving every Saturday including Soul, Reggae, Hip-Hop, R&B, Jazz, Rock, Indie, Folk, Blues and much more. Most CDs are sold for £5-£8, but many are reduced to clear for £3 or less. Well worth going out of your way to visit.

PHOTOGRAPHY

CAMERA EQUIPMENT

CENTRAL

Camera World
14 Wells Street, W1
Tel: 020 7636 5005
Website: www.cameraworld.co.uk
Tube: Oxford Circus/Tottenham Court Road
Bus: 7, 8, 10, 25, 55, 73, 98, 176
Open: Mon-Fri 9am-6pm, Sat 10am-5pm
This shop offers a large selection of SLR cameras and lenses, digital cameras, used equipment, camerabags and accessories at very competitive prices. They give a personal service with independent advice and run an excellent digital and 35mm printing service.

Jessops
63-69 New Oxford Street, WC1
Tel: 020 7240 6077
Website: www.www.jessops.com
Tube: Tottenham Court Road
Bus: 1, 8, 19, 25, 38, 55, 98, 242
Open: Mon-Sat 9am-6pm, Thurs till 8pm
Jessops is the largest camera chain in the UK and has a good reputation. They sell every type of camera plus all the accessories and offer to match any local price. Many of the branches stock second-hand equipment and both buy or part-exchange quality used camera equipment. All used goods are sold with a 30 day no quibble exchange policy.
Branches at:
89 King Street W6, Tel: 020 8741 2670 (3)
42 Upper Street N1, Tel: 020 7354 4144
Jessops Classic, 67 Great Russell Street WC1, Tel: 020 7831 3640
281 Regent Street W1, Tel: 020 7491 1055
43 Strutton Ground, Victoria SW1, Tel: 020 7222 0521
124 High Holborn, WC1, Tel: 020 7405 3364
360 Kensington High Street W14, Tel: 020 7602 5311
443 The Strand WC2, Tel: 020 7379 6522
154 Tottenham Court Road W1, Tel: 020 7387 7001
Unit 28, Whiteleys Ctr, 133-165 Queensway W2, Tel: 020 7221 1784
Opening times vary, call branch for details. For other branches view their website.

Leeds Camera Centre
24-26 Brunswick Centre, WC1
Tel: 020 7833 1661
Tube: Russell Square
Bus: 59, 68, 91, 168
Open: Mon-Fri 8am-6pm
This shop caters for the professional and serious photographer with a wide range of new and second-hand camera equipment including mid and top-end digital cameras. The used equipment is very largely professional medium-format stuff and is not aimed at the casual snapper. Leeds holds a huge stock of film and always has film reduced to clear.

R G Lewis Ltd
9 Southampton Row, WC1
Tel: 020 7242 2916
Fax: 020 7831 4062
Tube: Holborn
Bus: 1, 59, 68, 91, 168, 188
Open: Mon-Fri 8.15am-6pm, Sat 9.30am-4pm
This company has been trading since before the war, and although they have moved to this site in recent years, the premises still have a traditional feel with lots of wood and glass display units. The shop specialises in Leica cameras but also has a range of second-hand cameras at very competitive prices. Among the bargains found here on a recent visit was a Leica III with lens for only £269. They also sell an extensive range of vintage cameras as well as digital cameras from £50 to £800. All the used goods come with a 6 month warranty and they offer a mail order service.

Vic Oddens (Photographic) Ltd
4 & 5 London Bridge Walk, SE1
Tel: 020 7407 6833 (no.5)
Tel: 020 7378 6149 (no.4)
E-mail: sales@vicoddens.co.uk
Tube/Rail: London Bridge
Bus: 17, 21, 43, 48, 133, 149, 343, 501, 521
Both branches open Mon-Fri 8.30am-6pm
Number 5 caters for amateurs, while number 4 deals mainly in professional equipment. Both branches have an excellent range of digital cameras and scanners, SLR, medium format and compact cameras as well as telescopes, binoculars and accessories. There are lots of sales and special offers, and there is a ratio of about 80% new to 20% second-hand equipment. Odden's is a particularly good place to find deals on camera film.

Sonic Foto Centre Ltd
256 Tottenham Court Road, W1
Tel: 020 7580 5826
Tube: Tottenham Court Road
Bus: 10, 24, 29, 73, 134
Open: Mon-Sat 9.30am-6.30pm
This established camera shop is located at the back of a large computer retailers on Tottenham Court Road. Sonic only consists of a counter and display cabinets but it does stock a good range of new cameras at competitive cameras, as well as a few second-hand items. On a recent visit they had a good condition Nikon EM body for only £80.

NORTH

Camden Camera Centre

28 Parkway, NW1
Tel: 020 7485 7247
Tube: Camden Town
Bus: 24, 27, 31, 168, 274, C2
Open: Mon-Sat 9am-6pm
An excellent camera shop offering quality camera equipment at good prices. All second-hand items come with a 6 month guarantee, and a repair service is available.

Nicholas Camera Company
15 Camden High Street, NW1
Tel: 020 7916 7251
Tube: Mornington Crescent
Bus: 24, 27, 29, 88, 134, 168, 214, 253
Open: Mon-Sat 10am-6pm
A good little camera shop with lots of used SLR cameras at reasonable prices and a more limited range of darkroom equipment.

Photocraft
4 Heath Street, NW3
Tel: 020 7435 9932
Tube: Hampstead
Bus: 46, 268
Open: Mon-Sat 9am-5.30pm
A general photographic store, which has a large range of second-hand cameras sold on commission, rather than bought in and then sold with a mark-up. This makes the possibility of finding a quality bargain very likely. Although no guarantees are available on used gear, refunds or repairs can be offered if purchases are brought back within two weeks.

WEST

Film Plus

216 Kensington Park Road, W11
Tel: 020 7727 1111
Tube: Ladbroke Grove/Notting Hill Gate
Bus: 23, 52, 70, 295
Open: Mon-Fri 9am-6pm, Sat 10am-12.30pm

A shop for the professional photographer, specialising in equipment rental. They have a small selection of second-hand cameras, and while happy snappers probably won't find anything to fit the bill here, budding David Baileys will.

Mac's Cameras

262 King Street, W6
Tel: 020 8846 9853
Tube: Ravencourt Park
Bus: 27, 190, 266, 267, 391, H91
Open: Mon-Sat 8.45am-5.45pm

A large camera shop with a reasonable selection of used cameras. On a recent visit a Canon 500N with 50mm lens was only £220. A good place to look for camera bargains, and only a few doors down from Kays which also sells second-hand cameras and electronics (see page 62).

Nes Cameras

16 Beadon Road, W6
Tel: 020 8741 5359
Tube: Hammersmith
Bus: 9, 10, 27, 33, 209, 211, 391, 419
Open: Mon-Fri 8am-6.30pm, Sat 8am-6pm

The affable Mr Samoon has a wide selection of second-hand cameras in this well-run little shop. Among the bargains on a recent visit was a Pentax P30n body for a mere £69. Well worth a visit for those seeking camera bargains.

EAST

College Cameras

623 Forest Road, E17
Tel: 020 8527 4633
Website: www.collegecameras.co.uk
Tube: Walthamstow Central
Bus: 123, 275
Open: Mon-Sat 9am-5.30pm

This large, well-stocked shop covers every aspect of the photographer's art. From sturdy SLRs to discreet digital cameras, along with all the hardware, chemicals and papers for the darkroom, this is a convenient and good value place to stock up. They also offer on site film processing and digital printing.

OUTER LONDON

Mr Cad

68 Windmill Road, Croydon
Surrey, CR0 2XP
Tel: 020 8684 8282
E-mail: sales@mrcad.co.uk
Website: www.mrcad.co.uk
Rail: East Croyden, West Croyden
Bus: 130, 154, 166, 194, 367, 403, 405, 412, 450, 494
Open: Mon-Sat 9am-5.30pm

This huge warehouse is way out in the London suburbs but has hundreds of new and used cameras and lenses as well as darkroom and studio equipment. There are lots of bargains on offer and a very efficient mail order service.

Photomarket

397B High Street, Wembley
Middlesex, HA9
Tel: 020 8903 0587
E-mail: sales@photomarket.co.uk
Website: www.photomarket.co.uk
Tube: Wembley Central
Bus: 79, 204, 223, 297
Open: Mon-Sat 9am-5.30pm

This large photographic retailer has a fine stock of second-hand cameras and accessories, details of which can be found on their easy to use website. Recent used bargains found on the website included a Nikon F601 body, with a 35-80mm Nikon lens for only £199, and an Olympus OM101 with 50mm lens for £89. New cameras and equipment – including a good range of digital cameras – are sold at very competitive prices, with special offers on certain items. Photomarket welcomes part-exchange.

WEBSITE/MAIL ORDER

Lee's Cameras
PO Box 35519, London, NW4 1YF
Tel: 020 8202 9918
E-mail: sales@leescameras.demon.co.uk
Website: www.leescameras.demon.co.uk
Open: Mon-Fri 10am-5pm
Lee's Cameras is now run as a mail order business. The mail order service still offers great advice and very good value with a large stock of cine cameras and accessories as well as a fine selection of conventional SLR cameras and lenses. They also offer a hire and repair service and are willing to part-exchange. View their website or give them a call.

www.internetcamerasdirect.co.uk
Unit 14 New Mill, Brougham Road,
Marsden, Huddersfield, HD7 6BJ
Tel: 0870 745 1036 / 0870 752 2566
This internet site offers a wide selection of digital cameras with lots of independent reviews to help you make your choice. Among the deals recently on offer was a Konica KD500Z for £448 (£50 cheaper than on the High Street). Another good feature of the site is the link with the online auction QXL with lots of used and discounted camera available.

CAMERA REPAIR

Camera Care
20 Hanway Street, W1
Tel: 020 7436 8655
Tube: Tottenham Court Road
Bus: 7, 8, 10, 25, 55, 73, 98, 176
Open: Mon-Fri 9.30am-6pm, Sat 10am-3pm
Repairs are done on site to cameras, digital video cameras and computer equipment. Specialists in notebook repairs. All repairs are guaranteed.

Sendean Camera Repair
9-12 St Anne's Court, W1
Tel: 020 7734 0895/020 7437 8746
Tube: Tottenham Court Road
Bus: 7, 8, 10, 25, 55, 73, 98, 176
Open: Mon-Thurs 9.30am-5.30pm, Fri 9.30am-6pm
Good quality camera repairs at reasonable prices, with a selection of second-hand equipment as well. Same-day estimates can be given on most repairs.

London Camera Repair Centre
72 Golbourne Road, W10
Tel: 020 8968 5554
Tube: Westbourne Park
Bus: 28, 31, 328
Open: Mon-Fri 11am-7pm
An established camera repair shop which offers a 6-month guarantee on all work and also sells a limited stock of second-hand cameras.

DARKROOM SUPPLIES

Process Supplies
13-25 Mount Pleasant, WC1
Tel: 020 7837 2179
Tube: Farringdon
Bus: 19, 38, 63, 341
Open: Mon-Fri 9am-5.30pm
Substantial reductions on film, paper, chemicals and processing accessories, most of which is sold at or below trade prices. B&W paper comes with a 10% reduction on manufacturer's prices, and some out-of-date film is on sale with a large discount. They also now sell papers and inks for digital reproduction – all at substantial discounts.

RK Photographic
161 Ballards Lane, N3
Tel: 020 8349 4568
Tube: Finchley Central
Bus: 82, 125, 143, 260, 326
Open: Mon-Sat 9am-5.30pm
RK sells all the main makes of enlargers, plus all the darkroom accessories, with a large range of papers, including the budget brand Barclays. Some second-hand cameras are also on offer.

DARKROOM HIRE

The Camera Club
16 Bowden Street, SE11
Tel: 020 7587 1809
Website: www.thecameraclub.co.uk
Tube: Kennington
Bus: 133, 155
Open: Mon-Fri 11am-10pm, Sat & Sun 11am-6pm
Once you have paid the annual membership fee of £75, plus a £20 joining fee, you can make use of this club's extensive services. Facilities include a B&W darkroom at £3 per hour, and a studio for £10 per hour. The club now has a Digital Suite for £6 per hour and runs courses all year round.

Drill Hall Arts Centre
16 Chenies Street, WC1
Tel: 020 7307 5061
Website: www.drillhall.co.uk
Tube: Goodge Street
Bus: 10, 24, 29, 73, 134
Open: Daily 10am-10pm
Since the last edition the Drill Hall has undergone a major re-development of its darkroom facilities and now has a photography studio. Annual darkroom membership is still only £65 (£55 concessions) with use of the darkroom for £3 per hour and hire of the photography studio (including equipment) from £7 per hour. There is a compulsory induction course. Ring or refer to the website for future dates.

TRAVEL

BUDGET AIRLINES (from London)

The key to getting the great prices from any airline (including the low-cost, no-frills airlines) is to book as early as possible for the best choice of fares, book online as most airlines give a slight discount for doing so and sign up for their newsletters to get information about sales and specials. Always check that all taxes and charges are included before comparing prices. Remember that most of their telephone reservation numbers are toll calls. It's always worth checking British Airways' sales as their discounted flights often beat the low-cost airlines' fares.

Air Berlin
Tel: 0870 738 88 80
Website: www.airberlin.com
From London Stansted, Air Berlin flies to every conceivable city in Germany as well as Vienna for as little as £20 one-way. Aimed at business travellers, they do fly to some touristy destinations such as the Canary Islands.

Air Europa
Website: www.air-europa.co.uk
Tel: 0870 240 1501
This is Spain's largest private airline and they fly from London Gatwick to destinations in Spain and as far as the Americas. If the Balearic islands are your destination, try Air Europa's direct flight to Palma de Mallorca that cost as little as £32 roundtrip if booked in advance. They also fly directly from London Gatwick to Madrid. From both cities, you can then transfer onto a multitude of destinations.

Easyjet
Tel: 0870 600 00 00
Website: www.easyjet.com
Distinguished by their bright orange logo, Easyjet is one of the biggest no-frills airlines flying from Britain. They fly to over 100 cities in the UK, France, Spain, Switzerland, the Netherlands, Denmark, Italy, the Czech Republic, Greece, Germany, and Portugal. They also operate a ski holiday travel booking service through their website or on Tel: 0845 070 0203. There is no office in London, so booking is best done by phone or on the website (you get a small discount for booking on-line). Join their mailing list to receive up-to-date route information. London Luton is their hub, but they also fly from Gatwick and Stansted.

Flybe
Tel: 08705 676 676
Website: www.flybe.com
Once called British European, Flybe has a large network of flights between destinations in the UK, Ireland, France, Spain, Switzerland, Belgium and Italy all sold at competitive prices.

Hapag-Lloyd Express
Tel: 0870 606 0519
Website: www.hlx.com
This small airline bills its airfares as cheaper than a taxi ride and offers direct flights from London Luton to Cologne/Bonn airport. From there, they offer connections to a few other cities in Germany, Italy, Spain and France.

Meridiana
Tel: 020 7839 2222
Website: www.meridiana.it
This low-fare Italian airline runs flights from London Gatwick to Florence and Olbia in Sardinia. Within Italy, their flights link all major cities and they also fly to Paris, Barcelona and Amsterdam.

Now
Tel: 0845 4589737
Website: www.now-airlines.com
This brand-new airline flies from London Luton. Flights are charged according to how far you travel so flights within their "Zone A" such as Manchester cost £35 and flights in "Zone F" such as Tenerife cost £75. They fly to the UK, Italy, Germany and Spain, but will add more destinations. They promise to fly into well-known airports and have back-up planes to keep schedules running smoothly.

Ryanair
Tel: 0871 246 0000
Website: www.ryanair.com
Ryanair nearly always have some special fare offer whether it be £1 seats within the UK or £10 roundtrips to destinations to Europe. Remember that these fares do not include airport taxes, which can significantly raise the fare. Keep abreast of sales by registering with them on their website. London Stansted is their hub, but they also fly from Gatwick and Luton.

Volare Airlines
Tel: 0800 032 0992
Website: www.volareweb.com
Volare, Italy's low-cost airlines fly from London Gatwick to Venice and Rimini and then you can catch connections all over Italy as well as to Belgium, the Czech Republic, Germany, France and Spain. Prices cost as little as £15 one-way from Gatwick to Venice.

TRAVEL AGENTS

Cheap flights are always available and finding them is often a matter of scanning publications such as Time Out and The Evening Standard and phoning around to get the best quote. You could also take a look at the travel pages on Teletext which offer lots of up-to-date flight bargains or check out their website: www.teletextholidays.co.uk
Below you'll find reviews of many of the established discount travel agents to help you in your search. If you're under the age of 26, always ask about youth fares. Often they are up to 50% less than a full-priced economy fare.

Egyland Travel
167 Stoke Newington High Street, N16
Tel: 020 7254 4994/7241 3955
Rail: Stoke Newington
Bus: 67, 73, 76, 149, 243
Open: Mon-Sat 9.30am-6pm
This neighbourhood travel agency is helpful and friendly. They advertise the latest deals in their shop window, but if you want an even better deal, visit them a few days before you want to travel to get rock-bottom prices.

Flight Centre
5 Regent Street, SW1
Tel: 020 7925 1114
Website: www.flightcentre.co.uk
Tube: Piccadilly Circus
Bus: 3, 6, 12, 13, 15, 23, 53, 88, 94, 139, 159
Open: Mon-Fri 9.30am-6pm, Sat 10am-4pm
This international chain of travel agents sells discount flights to destinations all over the globe. They also promise to beat any lower fare that you find either at another agent or online. Besides flights, the company can also arrange lodging and transportation at your destination.
For other branches throughout London Tel: 0870 8908 099

Student Travel Centre
24 Rupert Street, W1
Tel: 020 7434 1306
Website: www.student-travel-centre.com
Tube: Piccadilly
Bus: 14, 19, 38
Open: Mon-Fri 9am-6pm, Sat 10am-2pm
This company was recommended by a friend as a great value travel agents for students and those under 26. They offer flights throughout Europe and world-wide, tickets for Eurostar as well as accommodation and tours. Other services include travel insurance and car hire. A great value independent travel agents.

Travelwise
51 Fortis Green Road, N10
Tel: 020 8444 4444
Website: www.travelwiseuk.com
Tube: East Finchley or Highgate
Bus: 102, 234
Open: Mon-Sat 9am-6pm

This neighbourhood travel agency has been dispensing low-cost holidays for over twenty years. Specialising in packages to places like Greece, the Balearics and other warm climes, they are ace at putting together inexpensive holidays whether they last two days or two weeks.
Also at: 76 Upper Street N1, Tel: 020 7359 7359

STA Travel
Website: www.statravel.co.uk
Call centre: 0870 160 6070 (Europe & Worldwide). Call this number rather than the individual branches.
STA Travel has over 65 branches in the UK and over 400 branches world-wide. They offer cheap flights to full-time students and those aged under 26. Some airlines have restrictions on the age of students for their reduced flight prices, so mature students will not be eligible for all deals.
Branches at:
33 Bedford Street, Covent Garden WC2
Easy Internet Café, 9-13 Wilton Road, Victoria SW1
37 Eastcheap EC3
24 Ludgate Hill EC4
86 Old Brompton Road SW7
11 Goodge Street W1
117 Euston Road NW1
38 Store Street WC1
University of London Union, Malet Street WC1
Imperial College, Sherfield Building SW7
King's College, Macadam Building WC2
London School of Economics, East Building WC2
Queen Mary and Westfield College, 329 Mile End Road E1
85 Shaftesbury Avenue W1
40 Bernard Street WC1

Top Deck Adventure Travel Centre
135 Earls Court Road, SW5
Tel: 020 7244 6411
Tube: Earls Court
Bus: 74, 328, C1, C3
Open: Mon, Wed-Fri 9am-6pm, Tues 9.30am-6pm, Sat 9.30am-4.30pm
Both branches are a very good source of information and flights to all world-wide destinations. They do not deal in package holidays, but rather create itineraries for travellers who wish to tour areas such as Europe or the Mediterranean.
Also at: 47 Notting Hill Gate W11, Tel: 020 7727 4290

Teletext

Website: www.teletext.co.uk/holidays

Use your TV to find loads of last-minute holiday bargains. From the website, you can access discount flights, accommodation, holidays, ski breaks and cruises.

COURIER FLIGHTS

A cheap way to travel, with a fairly large choice of destinations outside Europe (see BA's list, below). The only real restriction is availability to travel at short notice.

International Association of Air Travel Couriers

Tel: 0800 0746 481

Website: www.aircourier.co.uk

Destinations include New York, Tokyo, Buenos Aires, Miami, Bangkok and Sydney. A return flight to Tokyo can cost as little as £250 or to New York for £160. You have to join the group to qualify for the flights.

BARGAIN TRAVEL WEBSITES

www.bargainholidays.co.uk

Prices get towards rock-bottom within a couple of days of travelling, and the quantity of holidays is impressive. A week in Croatia cost £289. You can also search for flights both scheduled and charter.

www.cheapflights.co.uk

This search engine compares flights from all major carriers to find the best price. You can also search by destination or by low-cost airline. They also deal with holidays, cottages, hotels and short breaks.

www.deckchair.com

Deckchair offer cheap and last-minute flights as well as travel insurance, last-minute holidays, hotels, car hire and ferry tickets.

www.ebookers.com

Another online travel agent booking everything from flights to holidays. The best deals are on last-minute fares. A week in Majorca for £99 per person was a recent deal.

www.expedia.co.uk

Specialises in last-minute bookings for package holidays. Flights and lodging for seven nights in Barbados cost from £467.

www.holidaydeals.co.uk

One of the most basic, but fast, on-line bucket shops, good for last minute deals. Fly to Australia for £479 was a recent offering.

www.lastminute.com

The original and best of the online bucket shops, they now run an online department store, but many bargains are still to be found.

www.opodo.co.uk
An excellent resource for price comparison-shopping for the major airlines. They often have good deals.

www.skydeals.co.uk
Plenty of flight deals to choose from as well as flight search capabilities. Recent deals included Heathrow to Miami for £274.

www.skyscanner.net
Users enter their budget and timeline. Skyscanner tells them where they can afford to go.

www.priceline.co.uk
Originally from the States, Priceline conceived of the novel idea of letting customers name their price for flights, hotels and car rentals. Give it a try.

www.travelocity.co.uk
One of the first and still one of the best. Travelocity searches 95% of the flights or seats available and returns good results. Their "Fare Watcher" will e-mail you with offers on destinations that you can select.

TRAVEL INSURANCE

Getting insurance from your travel agent is convenient, but you often pay well above the market price for that convenience. As with flights and accommodation it's best to phone around and compare prices. If you're travelling light STA offer good rates, otherwise try:

Atlas Direct (www.travel-insurance.co.uk) Tel: 020 7609 5000
Columbus Direct (www.columbusdirect.co.uk) Tel: 0845 330 8518
WorldwideTravel Insurance (www.worldwideinsure.com) Tel: 01892 833 338

Other Useful Addresses:

Air Travel Advisory Bureau (Lupus Travel)
St. Georges House,
14-17 Wells Street, London, W1T 3PD
Tel: 0870 8705540
Website: www.atab.co.uk

Association of British Travel Agents (ABTA)
68-71 Newman Street, W1
Tel: 020 7637 2444
Website: www.abta.com

Association of Independent Tour Operators (AITO)
133A St Margarets Road, Twickenham, TW1 1RG
Tel: 020 8744 9280
Website: www.aito.co.uk

Bargain hunting by Outlet

ARCHITECTURAL SALVAGE

CENTRAL

Lassco
41 Maltby Street,
Bermondsey, SE1
Tel: 020 7394 2103
Website: www.lassco.co.uk
Tube: London Bridge
Bus: 42, 78, 188
Open: Mon-Sat 10am-5pm
This is one of London's largest and best known salvage yards and one of four Lassco outlets. The shop specialises in architectural salvage including a huge selection of interior and exterior doors, ranging in period from Georgian to the 1930s. Among the other things to be found here are lighting, door fittings, room panelling and on a recent visit carousel horses from a long closed fair. A great place to look for unusual bargains.
Also at:
Lassco House & Garden, Mark Street EC2, Tel: 020 7739 0448
Lassco St Michael's, Mark Street EC2, Tel: 020 7749 9944

NORTH

The Architectural Forum
312-314 Essex Road, N1
Tel: 020 7704 0982
Tube: Angel
Bus: 38, 56, 73, 341
Open: Mon-Sat 8.30am-6pm
This established salvage yard is divided into two small yards containing bathroom fittings, radiators, fireplaces, doors, some light fittings, wooden panelling and a large selection of paving stones. Among the bargains on a recent visit was a large, free-standing bath with ornate feet for £280, it needed some attention but was still a bargain given that such baths new are about £500.

The Architectural Forum

Brondesbury Architectural Reclamation
136 Willesden Lane, Brondesbury, NW6
Tel: 020 7328 0820
Rail: Brondesbury Park
Bus: 98, 206
Open: Mon-Sat 10am-6pm
A yard and showroom offering a wide range of antiques, architectural items and smaller artifacts.

SOUTH

Architectural Salvage
83 Haydons Road,
South Wimbledon, SW19
Tel: 020 8543 4450
Tube: South Wimbledon
Bus: 93, 200
Open: Tues-Sat 10am-5pm
This small shop and yard offers a reasonable selection of doors, fire places and sanitary ware.

The House Hospital
9 Ferrier Street, SW18
Tel: 020 8870 8202
Rail: Wandsworth Town
Bus: 28, 44, 37, 39, 77A, 156, 170, 337
Open: Mon-Sat 10am-5pm
A modern industrial warehouse site specialising in reconditioned cast iron radiators, but also offering doors, fireplaces, flooring and bathroom furniture among its stock.

OUT OF TOWN

Architectural Reclaim
Theobalds Park Road,
Crews Hill, Enfield, Middlesex
Tel: 020 8367 7577
Website: www.architecturalreclaim.com
Rail: Drews Hill
Open: Mon-Fri 8am-5pm, Sat-Sun 9am-3pm
This massive three acre site has anything from old telegraph poles and railway sleepers to Victorian garden furniture. Well worth a trip out of town to visit.

AUCTIONS

Auctions have the reputation for being fusty old institutions where fine art is sold to equally fusty old art dealers and dilletantes. The auctions reviewed below are quirky and idiosyncratic places, but tend to have more general goods such as cameras, bikes, household furniture, books, office equipment and much more. There are plenty of bargains to be found at these auctions and they are usually a lot of fun to visit. When visiting an auction it's a good idea to attend the viewing before the sale starts. This gives you time to inspect the lots you are interested in before bidding begins and to set yourself a maximum price for each item – this will hopefully prevent you from losing your head when bidding begins. This chapter also includes car and house auctions for those with more money to spend.

NORTH

Centaur Auctions

Harbet Road, N18
Tel: 020 8803 9796
Fax: 020 8807 7111
Sales: Monthly on the first Sat of every month from 10am
Viewing: Fri 10am-4pm, Sat from 9am
Buyers' premium: 20%
Bidders' returnable deposit: £50

This established auction house deals largely in liquidated stock provided by bailiffs and the Inland Revenue and as such can include anything from office equipment to computers and kitchenware. There are always enough bargains here to justify sacrificing a Saturday morning lie-in.

Hornsey Auctions Ltd

54-56 High Street, N8
Tel: 020 8340 5334/8341 1156
Deliveries arranged (min charge £25)
Sales: Every Wed 6.30pm-9pm
Viewings: Tues 5pm-7pm and Wed 9am until the sale
Buyers' premium: 10%
Bidders' returnable deposit: £0

Hornsey Auctions has a rather grand exterior, but deals mainly with house clearances, probate and insolvency stock. The auction offers a good mix of items from boxes of bric-à-brac for a fiver, to imposing period furniture for over £300. It's a particularly good place to find large ornate mirrors for under £100, one of which takes pride of place in my lounge.

Schools Connect
The Auction House, Pegamoid Road, Edmonton, N18
Tel: 020 8345 6535
Website: www.tagpc.co.uk
Sales: Fortnightly Sats 11am-4pm
Viewing: Sat 9am-11am
Buyers' premium: 10% (+VAT)
Bidders' returnable deposit: £40
This hi-tech auction house has all kinds of equipment going under the hammer including fully operational PCs, printers, keyboards and other accessories. They also sell other items for the office such as photocopiers, telephones and office furniture. A recent sale included about 450 lots, some of which still had the manufacturers' warranty. Those without a warranty are sold with a 90 day guarantee. It's a good idea if you don't know much about computers to bring a technically minded friend with you for guidance.

North London Auctions
8
Lodge House,
9-17 Lodge Lane, N12
Tel: 020 8445 9000
Fax: 020 8446 6068
Sales: Mon from 5pm
Viewing: Sun 9am-1pm, Mon 9am-5pm
Buyers' premium: 15%
Bidders' returnable deposit: £10
A large auction house selling antiques, collectables and general household goods from a variety of sources. The quality of the stock tends to be high, and every 6 to 8 weeks they hold a sale of the classier items.

Southgate Auction Rooms
55 High Street, Southgate, N14
Tel: 020 8886 7888
Fax: 020 8882 4421
Sales: Mondays from 5pm
Viewing: Sat 9am-12pm, Mon 9am-5pm
Buyers' premium: 15%
Bidders' returnable deposit: £30 (cash)
A general household auction, selling items on behalf of individuals. A good place to find basics for the home as well as some reasonably priced antiques.

WEST

Chiswick & West Middlesex Auctions

31 Colville Road, W3
Tel: 020 8992 4442
Fax: 020 8896 0541
Sales: Tues 5pm-7pm for smaller items, 7pm onwards for furniture
Viewing: Sun 12noon-6pm, Mon 10am-6pm, Tues 10am-5pm
Buyer's premium: 15%
Bidders' returnable deposit: £0
This auction house has chandeliers dangling from the ceiling, rugs strewn on the floor and quantities of crockery, porcelain, silverware and furniture in between. The quality of the goods varies from genuine antiques to bric-à-brac.

Francis Smith

107 Lots Road,
Chelsea, SW10
Tel: 020 7349 0011
Fax: 020 7349 0770
Sales: Fortnightly Tues from 6pm
Viewing: Mon 9am-7pm, Tues 9am-6pm
Buyers' premium: 15% (+VAT)
Bidders' returnable deposit: £0
This auction room sells mostly antiques, but usually offers about 50 lots of more modern furniture among the 150 lots which go under the hammer every fortnight.

Lots Road Auctions

73 Lots Road, SW10
Tel: 020 7376 6800
Fax: 020 7376 6899
Website: www.lotsroad.com
Sales: Sun 2pm contemporary goods, 4.30pm antiques
Viewing: Thurs 2pm-7pm, Fri-Sun 10am-4pm
Buyers' premium: 17.02%
Bidders' returnable deposit: £0
As befits its location in the heart of Chelsea, this is a rather smart antiques auction with not much selling for under £50. There are bargains to be found, but this venue is definitely more suited to well-heeled wannabe bargain hunters, rather than those looking for cheap bric-à-brac.

Richmond & Surrey Auctions
Kew Road, Richmond, TW9
Tel: 020 8948 6677
Fax: 020 8948 2021
Sales: Thurs 6pm-8.30pm
Viewing: Wed 4pm-8pm, Thurs 10am-6pm
Buyers' premium: 15%
Bidders' returnable deposit: £0
This weekly auction usually has between 300 and 400 lots offering good quality modern and antique furniture, objets d'art, watches, silverware and paintings. The bidding is brisk at about 160 lots per hour, so don't wander too far from the saleroom.

SOUTH

General Auctions (6)
63-65 Garratt Lane, SW18
Tel: 020 8870 3909
Fax: 020 8877 3583
Website: www.generalauctions.co.uk
Sales: Mon 11am for cycles, 12noon-5pm general goods, (motor vehicles are sold at 2pm)
Viewing: Sat 10am-3pm
Buyers' premium: 12.5%
Bidders' returnable deposit: £50
As the name suggests this auction shifts a gallimaufry of goods, from designer clothing to cars. Many items come from the Inland Revenue, Customs & Excise and liquidators. This is a very good auction for finding quality second-hand bikes.

R.F. Greasby
211 Longley Road, SW17
Tel: 020 8672 2972
Fax: 020 8767 8616
Sales: Tuesdays from 10am
Viewing: Monday 2.30pm-6.30pm, 8.30am-10.30am on day of sale
Buyers' premium: 12.5% (plus VAT)
Bidders' returnable deposit: £100
All sorts of items turn up here as sales are held on behalf of the Metropolitan Police, London Transport, Customs and Excise, and bailiffs. This is an excellent auction for bargain bikes, cameras, electronics, jewellery and office furniture.

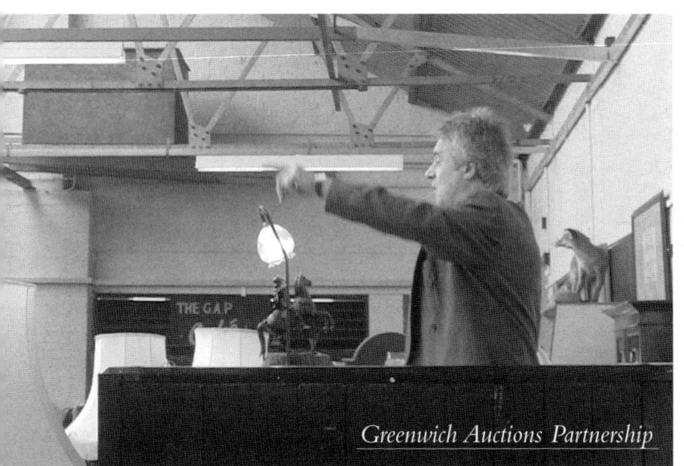

Greenwich Auctions Partnership

Greenwich Auctions Partnership
47 Old Woolwich Road, SE10
Tel: 020 8853 2121
Sales: Sat 11am-3pm
Viewing: Fri 2pm-7pm, Sat 9am-11am
Buyers' premium: 10%
Bidders' returnable deposit: 0%
About 800 lots are sold under the glass roof of this large factory space on a typical auction day. It's a good auction for bargains, because much of the stock derives from house clearances and is therefore sold without a reserve price. Boxes of books go for around £1, and a 1930's bedside table was a mere £15 – you will also find pictures, jewellery, furniture and antiques. There's a caff on site and Greenwich Park is just around the corner if you want a break. If you are going in the winter be sure to wear something warm.

Lloyds International Auction Galleries

Lloyds House, 9 Lydden Road, SW18
Tel: 020 8788 7777
Fax: 020 8874 5390
Website: www.lloyds-auction.co.uk
Rail: Earlsfield
Sales: Alternate Weds 3pm
Viewing: Wed 10.30am-2.45pm
Buyers' premium: 17.5%
Bidders' returnable deposit: £40

This established auction house holds regular sales for bodies such as the Metropolitan Police and Heathrow Airport. At these events you can find all kinds of bargains including bikes, cameras, computers, video recorders and even designer clothes. It's a good idea to get here early to view the lots before bidding. Auction dates are posted on Lloyd's website and you can even download the auction catalogue to prepare yourself in advance.

Rosebery's
74-76 Knight's Hill, SE27
Tel: 020 8761 2522
Fax: 020 8761 2524
E-mail: auctions@roseberys.co.uk
Website: www.roseberys.co.uk
Sales: Fortnightly usually on a Tues 12noon-5pm
Viewing: Sun 2.30pm-5.30pm, Mon 10am-7pm, Tues 9.30am-11.45am
Buyers' premium: 15% (+VAT)
Bidders' returnable deposit: £0
This auction house alternates between a general auction and an antiques auction where the finer items are sold. The general auction is a great place to pick up furniture and things for the home, with plenty of bargains among the 700 or so lots. Rosebery's also hold specialist auctions covering subjects like Modern Design and Toys and Collectables.

EAST

Frank G. Bowen Ltd
73 Sceptre Road, E2
Tel: 020 7790 7272
Fax: 020 7790 7373
E-mail: mail@frankbowen.co.uk
Website: frankbowen.co.uk
Sales: Alternate Thursdays from 11am
Viewing: Wed 12noon-4pm, Thurs 9.30am-11am on the day of sale
Buyers' premium: 10%
Bidders' returnable deposit: £0
This auction deals largely in commercial equipment from the official receiver, insolvency practitioners, bailiffs and the police. Lots can include commercial stock and equipment as well as cars.

OUTER LONDON

Bainbridge's

The Auction Room, Ickenham Road,
Ruislip, Middlesex, HA4
Tel: 01895 621 991
Fax: 01895 623 621
Sales: One Thurs per month from 11am
Viewing: Wed before the sale 1pm-7pm, Thurs 9.30am-11am
Buyers' Premium: 17.5%
Bidders returnable deposit: £0

This company trades in probate clearance and most items sell without a reserve. Sales can vary from valuable antiques to basic household goods, depending on the houses being cleared.

Parkins

18 Malden Road, Cheam, Surrey, SM3
Tel: 020 8644 6633
Fax: 020 8255 4703
Website: www.parkinsauction.co.uk
Sales: 1st Mon of the month 10am (antiques), 2nd & 4th Mons 10am (general sales). Monthly Fri evening sale 7pm (small antiques)
Viewing: (Mon sale) Fri 2pm-4pm, Sat 10am-4pm, Mon 9am-10am, (Fri sale) Fri 2pm-7pm
Buyers' premium: 10% (+ VAT)
Bidders' returnable deposit: £0

There are a number of different sales held at this auction house, with the general sale being of most interest to the bargain hunter. There are all manner of chattels to be found, and one or two bargains among the 200-400 lots.

Rosans & Company

Croydon Auction Rooms,
145-151 London Road, CR0
Tel: 020 8688 1123
Fax: 020 8681 3284
Sales: Sat (fortnightly) 10am-1.30pm
Viewing: Fri 9am-4.45pm, Sat 9am-10am
Buyers' premium: 10%
Bidders' returnable deposit: £20

This company usually deals in bankrupt commercial stock of all kinds. There are generally about 700 lots in each sale, with vehicles being sold at midday. The sales are occasionally held at the site of a bankrupt company, so get details before visiting.

BOOK AUCTIONS

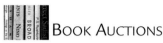

Bloomsbury Book Auctions
3-4 Hardwick Street, EC1
Tel: 020 7636 1945
Fax: 020 7833 3954
Sales: Thurs 1pm usually twice a month
Viewings: Tues 9.30am-5.30pm, Wed 9.30am-8pm,
Thurs 9.30am-1pm before the sale
Buyers' premium: 17.5%
Bidders' returnable deposit: £0

This auction is strictly for the collector, and those with an interest in books as objects as well as things to be read. The catalogue is the size of a novella and contains arcane descriptions like 'original decorative roan, gilt, uncut, some joints split'. A far cry from the usual 'box of books' seen in most auction catalogues. The prices are equally rarefied with most lots selling for over £50, and a commission of 17.5% on top of the hammer price. It's a great place to visit for an insight into the book world, but only an expert would be able to spot a bargain.

CAR AUCTIONS

As long as you're careful and put in a bit of effort, car auctions can be a good place to buy a second-hand car. It's important to choose the type of vehicle you want in advance, bearing in mind factors like the insurance group of the car, fuel consumption, reliability and repair bills. Monthly publications like Parker's Car Price Guide are a useful reference point for the general public, giving lots of important information as well as market prices for all makes and models.

Once you've determined the car you're looking for, and set yourself a budget, you can begin the hunt. If you're after a popular model, it may be worth looking out for a fleet car. These have been regularly serviced and the mileage is always genuine. The auctioneer will use the word 'direct' to describe any lot originating from this source. Many auctions use windscreen sheets and these should be studied carefully for details of the car's history. Above all, avoid any car sold without warranty. The warranty allows you an hour to try the car out and return it if something is wrong. If you have any problems contact the Motor Industry Federation (01788 576 465), although they can only help if the auction is a member. Provided you keep your head, and remain patient the auctions listed below may be the place to find a four-wheel bargain. Good luck!

BCA Auctions
620 Great Cambridge Road, EN1
Tel: 020 8366 1144

Manheim Motor Auctions
Waterside Way,
Plough Lane, SW17
Tel: 020 8944 2000

Dingwall Motor Auctions
Beddington Farm Road,
Croydon, Surrey, CRO
Tel: 020 8684 0138

Thameside Motor Auctions
Wandsworth Bridge Road, SW6
Tel: 020 7736 0086

PROPERTY AUCTIONS

If you're interested in buying a property by auction the companies listed below will send you details and a catalogue of their next sale. It is essential that you view the property and have valuations done before bidding. You'll need a 10% deposit on the day of the sale, and the financial ability to finalise the contract within 28 days. For those willing to do the leg work, there are incredible bargains to be found.

Allsop
100 Knightsbridge, SW1
Tel: 020 7494 3686
Website: www.allsop.co.uk

Andrews & Robertson
27 Camberwell Green, SE5
Tel: 020 7703 2662
Website: www.a-r.co.uk

Barnard Marcus
Commercial House,
64-66 Glenthorne Road, W6
Tel: 020 8741 9990/9001

Clive Emson Property Auctioneers
8 Cavendish Way,
Bearsted, Maidstone,
Kent, ME15
Tel: 01622 630 033
Website: www.cliveemson.co.uk

Countrywide Property Auctions
144 New London Road,
Chelmsford, CM2
Tel: 0870 240 1140

Drivers Norris
407-409 Holloway Road, N7
Tel: 020 7607 5001
Website: www.drivers.co.uk

Edwin Evans
253 Lavender Hill, SW11
Tel: 020 7228 5864
Website: www.edwinevansproperty.co.uk

FPD Savills
139 Sloane Street, SW1
Tel: 020 7824 9091
Website: www.fpdsavills.co.uk

Willmotts
12 Blacks Road, W6
Tel: 020 8748 6644
Website: www.willmotts.com

CHARITY SHOPS

Note: some charities, notably the Notting Hill Housing Trust, Relief Fund for Romania and the YMCA, are given free accommodation for some of their shops in empty stores whose owners are in the process of trying to sell them. This means that a small number of the shops listed here may not still be there when you visit them. We have indicated which shops are temporary. In the case of Relief Fund for Romania and YMCA, they are very likely to have relocated to a nearby shop. The law has now changed to prevent charity shops from selling used electrical goods without them having been checked by a qualified electrician. We have indicated all shops that have checking procedures and still sell electrical goods.

COVENT GARDEN WC2

Tube: Covent Garden
Bus: 1, 8, 14, 19, 24, 25, 29, 38, 55, 98, 176, 242

Oxfam

23 Drury Lane
Tel: 020 7240 3769
Open: Mon-Sat 11am-6pm
This tidy, well laid out shop reflects its prestigious Covent Garden location. The local luvvies and trendies ensure the stock is above average charity shop fare. As well as the rails of men's and women's wear, there is a well stocked designer rail.

Oxfam Original

22 Earlham Street
Tel: 020 7836 9666
Open: Mon-Sat 11am-6pm
This busy, central store specialises in clothes aimed at a young, trendy crowd. Designer labels and retro gear are mixed in with stuff hand-picked to appeal to London's clubbers and hipsters. As well as second-hand clothes, some new and nearly-new batches of jeans occasionally hit the rails. The shop is situated next to Earlham Market which is a good place to find new fashionable clothing.

SOHO W1

Tube: Oxford Circus/Piccadilly Circus
Bus: 3, 6, 9, 12, 13, 14, 15, 19, 22, 23, 38, 53, 88, 94, 139. 159

Oxfam Original

26 Ganton Street
Tel: 020 7437 7338
Open: Mon-Sat 11am-6pm
Run by young staff who know their Gabicci from their Benetton, this well-placed store is a haven of retro cool among the tourist trash of Carnaby Street. The prices, although higher than other Oxfam's, are still better than many of the exorbitant vintage clothing stores in this area.

Salvation Army Charity Shop/Cloud 9

9 Princes Street
Tel: 020 7495 3958
Open: Mon-Fri 10.30am-6pm,
Sat 11.30am-5.30pm
The downstairs section of this Salvation Army shop has the usual charity shop clothes, books and bric-à-brac, but the accent is on quality. Upstairs is the more interesting part, housing a small but carefully selected and organised range of vintage and retro clothing, accessories and bits and bobs. The prices are low, especially compared with nearby Regent Street.

Marylebone W1

Tube: Baker Street/Bond St/Marylebone
Bus: 2, 3, 13, 25, 30, 53, 55, 74, 82, 113, 139, 189, 176, 274

Cancer Research UK
24 Marylebone High Street
Tel: 020 7487 4986
Open: Mon-Fri 10am-6pm, Sat 10am-5pm, Sun 12noon-5pm
The emphasis in this shop is on quality and the tone of the clothes is fairly formal. Menswear consists mainly of suits, jackets and slacks, while the women's rails contain lots of flowery frocks, long skirts and satin blouses.

Oxfam Books and Music
91 Marylebone High Street
Tel: 020 7487 3570
Open: Mon-Sat 10am-6pm, Sun 11am-5pm
The question asked by every dedicated charity-shopper in search of books must be, 'Why do most charity shops have an average ratio of fifty Mills & Boon to one orange Penguin?' The answer is partly explained by this recently refurbished store that now specialises in records, books and prints. Clearly all the decent books donated to Oxfam wind up here, which makes for an exemplary well-priced bookshop with not a Mills & Boon in sight. A new feature is the on site Oxfam fair trade coffee shop, providing comfy couches for the weary bargain hunter to relax with their recent purchases.

Other charity shops in this area include:

Geranium Shop for the Blind
4 George Street
Tel: 020 7935 1790
Open: Mon-Fri 10am-5pm, Sat 10am-4pm

Oxfam
76 Marylebone Lane
Tel: 020 7487 3852
Open: Mon-Sat 10am-5pm

Sue Ryder
2 Crawford Street
Tel: 020 7935 8758
Open: Mon-Sat 10am-5pm

Victoria SW1

Tube/Rail: Victoria
Bus: 8, 11, 16, 24, 38, 52, 73, 82, 185, 211, 239, C1, C10

Crusaid
19 Churton Street, SW1
Tel: 020 7233 8736
Open: Mon-Sat 10.30am-5pm
This large, well organised shop is a real gem. The clothes include lots of quality high street names as well as designer labels and prices are not expensive. They also have a selection of books, CDs and bric-à-brac.

Fara
40 Tachbrook Street
Tel: 020 7630 7406
Open: Mon-Sat 11am-7pm, Sun 11am-5pm
A delightfully crammed shop, with a lively, friendly atmosphere. Unusual bric-à-brac fills several shelves, and odd items constantly crop up.

Oxfam
15 Warwick Way
Tel: 020 7821 1952
Open: Mon-Sat 10am-5pm
Two floors of quality stuff, with clothes on the ground floor and a basement full of books, records and bric-à-brac.

Oxfam Books & Music
34 Strutton Ground
Tel: 020 7233 3908
Open: Mon-Fri 10.30am-5pm, Sat 11am-3pm
This Oxfam store is dedicated to books and music. Everything is carefully priced and categorised with an entire room given over to books on arts and literature. Great finds included a 1st

Chelsea Oxfam Shop

edition volume of Edmond Spencer poetry and a modern 1st edition Martin Amis.

Other charity shops in this area include:

Fara
14 Upper Tachbrook Street
Tel: 020 7630 1774
Open: Mon-Sat 10am-6pm, Sun 11am-5pm

Sue Ryder
35 Warwick Way
Tel: 020 7630 0812
Open: Mon-Sat 10am-5pm

Trinity Hospice
85 Wilton Road
Tel: 020 7931 7191
Open: Mon-Sat 10.30am-5.30pm (closes Mon 4.45pm)

GOODGE STREET W1

Tube: Goodge Street
Bus: 10, 24, 29, 73, 134

Oxfam
52 Goodge Street
Tel: 020 7636 7311
Open: Mon-Fri 10.30am-6pm, Sat 11am-5.30pm
A particularly good Oxfam, with lots of designer labels dotted among the cardies and slacks upstairs. The basement holds bric-à-brac, books and toys.

YMCA
22 Goodge Street
Open: Mon-Thurs 9.30am-6.30pm, Fri 9.30am-6pm, Sat 11am-6pm
This central London charity shop is well stocked with clothes, books, records and bric-à-brac. The shop is large and cluttered, but more fun to potter around as a result.

Other charity shops in this area include:

Notting Hill Housing Trust
24 Goodge Street
Tel: 020 7636 4201
Open: Mon-Sat 10am-6pm

OLD STREET EC1

Tube: Old Street
Bus: 43, 55, 76, 141, 214, 243, 271

Age Concern
53 Leather Lane
Open: Mon-Fri 10am-3pm
This is a traditional charity shop staffed by a friendly team of regulars and with a good mixed stock of clothing, shoes, books and toys. On a recent visit there was a pair of D&G jeans for only £4. They usually have a discounted rail with garments reduced to clear for £1. A great little charity shop.

NORTH LONDON

ISLINGTON N1

Tube: Angel/Highbury & Islington
Bus: 4, 19, 30, 38, 56, 73, 153, 214, 274, 341

Cancer Research UK
34 Upper Street
Tel: 020 7226 8951
Open: Mon-Sat 10am-6pm, Sun 11am-5pm
Prices are a bit steep for a charity shop, but the clothes have clearly been hand-picked for quality and condition. There is also a fairly impressive bookshelf and a good selection of CDs.

Oxfam
29 Islington High Street
Tel: 020 7837 2394
Open: Mon & Sat 10.30am-5.30pm, Tues-Fri 10am-5.30pm, Sun 11am-5pm
Despite the tiny shop front, this is a sizeable store, usually with a worthwhile selection of books, clothing and household goods.

Salvation Army Charity Shop

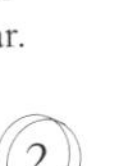

284 Upper Street
Tel: 020 7359 9865
Open: Mon-Fri 10am-4pm, Sat 10am-5pm
One of the best charity shops in the capital amid the trendy boutiques of Upper Street. As well as clothes, there is a plentiful selection of household goods, records and toys. There is usually a good mix of books and records outside the shop reduced to clear.

Sue Ryder

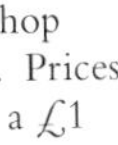

72 Essex Road
Tel: 020 7354 9050
Open: Mon-Sat 9.30am-5.30pm

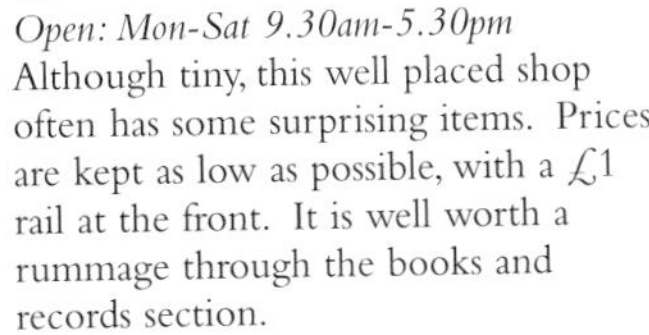

Although tiny, this well placed shop often has some surprising items. Prices are kept as low as possible, with a £1 rail at the front. It is well worth a rummage through the books and records section.

Other charity shops in this area include:

Marie Curie Cancer Care

318-320 St Paul's Road
Tel: 020 7226 0565
Open: Mon-Sat 9am-5.30pm

STOKE NEWINGTON N16

Rail: Stoke Newington
Bus: 67, 73, 76, 149, 243, 106

Bosnia Herzegovina Community Biblioteka
7 Cazenove Road
Open: Mon-Sat 10.30am-6.30pm
A small shop crammed to bursting point with clothes of all types at rock-bottom prices. The section at the back has a constantly replenished supply of shoes, bric-à-brac and books. Well worth a visit.

Other charity shops in this area include:

All Aboard
2A Regent Parade, Amhurst Park, N16
Tel: 020 8880 2458
Open: Mon-Fri 9.30am-5.30pm, Sun 10am-4.00pm

Scope
236 Stamford Hill
Tel: 020 8809 1306
Open: Mon-Sat 9am-5pm

FINCHLEY N3

Tube: Finchley Central
Bus: 82, 125, 260

Fara

13 Ballards Lane
Tel: 020 8346 7375
Open: Mon-Sat 9.30am-5.30pm, Sun 10am-4pm
The generally cheap prices and simple layout make this a pleasant shop to browse in. There are a lot of men's and ladies' clothes, with several trendy labels among the M&S jumpers.

Cancer Research UK

69 Ballards Lane
Tel: 020 8349 4962
Open: Mon-Sat 9am-5.30pm
A very tidy and well-organised shop with a preponderance of women's clothes. There is also a good selection bric-à-brac and a few new products imported especially for the charity.

The ORT Shop

80 Ballards Lane
Tel: 020 8349 4554
Open: Mon-Fri 9.30am-4pm
A huge store packed with bargains and oddities. Tons of bric-à-brac is clustered around the till, with some furniture at the back and an entire shelf display dedicated to board games. Clothes of every shape and size fill the rails, with prices for every budget. Well worth the trek to north London.

Other charity shops in this area include:

Norwood Ravenswood

66 Ballards Lane, N3
Tel: 020 8371 0006
Open: Mon-Fri 10am-5pm

Oxfam

55 Ballards Lane
Tel: 020 8346 3870
Open: Mon-Sat 10am-5pm

NORTH FINCHLEY N12

Tube: Woodside Park
Rail: North Finchley
Bus: 82, 125, 134, 221, 260, 263, 383

Cancer Research UK

775 High Road
Tel: 020 8446 8289
Open: Mon-Sat 9am-5pm
A very well-stocked and well-organised shop, with a small rack of new scarves, prints and candles made for the ICR. This store has a sale of antique clothing, some of it quite rare, every six weeks on a Tuesday. Check the window for details of the next sale. There is also an ongoing half-price sale of items which have not been sold after 4 weeks.

Relief Fund for Romania

824 High Road
Tel: 020 8445 9351
Open: Mon-Sat 10am-5.30pm
The cheapest shop in the area, and one of the best for the dedicated rummager. Fixed price rails for blouses, all at £2.50, and skirts at £2. Women's clothes outnumber menswear, but there are plenty of both, as well as lots of kids' clothes. A £1 rail is near the door.

Other charity shops in this area include:

Barnardos

802 High Road
Tel: 020 8445 5433
Open: Mon-Sat 9am-5.30pm

British Heart Foundation

718 High Road
Tel: 020 8446 0840
Open: Mon-Sat 9.30am-5pm

North London Hospice

839 High Road
Tel: 020 8343 8841
Open: Mon-Sat 9.30am-5pm

GOLDERS GREEN NW11

Tube: Golders Green
Bus: 13, 82, 83, 102, 183, 210, 226, 240, 245, 260, 268, 328

All Aboard

125 Golders Green Road
Tel: 020 8455 3184
Open: Mon-Fri 9.30am-5.30pm, Sun 10.30am-5.30pm
A bit of a trek down Golders Green Road if you've come by tube, but worth it, as the prices here are low, the quantity and quality high. Loads of clothes, bric-à-brac and books, as well as records and toys.

All Aboard

616 Finchley Road
Tel: 020 8458 1733
Open: Mon-Fri 10am-6pm, Sun 10am-3pm
A busy, well-stocked shop with plenty of records and books, as well as clothes.

All Aboard
1111 Finchley Road,
Temple Fortune
Tel: 020 8458 7078
Open: Mon-Fri 9.30am-5.30pm (Tues till 6.30pm), Sun 11am-3pm
This busy shop is crammed with clothes. Men's jackets go for around £10, but they're good quality. Heaps of hats, and plenty for the kids, including sale rails with constant additions.

Jami

89 Golders Green Road
Tel: 020 8201 8074
Open: Mon-Thurs 9.30am-5pm, Fri & Sun 9.30-4.30pm
This unusual shop is big on books, all fairly cheap. Men's suits were a bargain at £12, women's dresses all £7-£12. Some elegant evening wear has its own rail. There is sometimes a £1 rail of unsold stock.

Norwood Ravenswood

84 and 87 Golders Green Road
Tel: 020 8209 0041
Open: Mon-Fri, Sun 10am-5pm
The first branch at no. 87 has a large selection of menswear, mainly traditional suits, shirts and ties, all at reasonable prices. Across the road at no. 84 you'll find some very nice ceramics, as well as more upmarket ladies' wear.

Oxfam

1049 Finchley Road,
Temple Fortune
Tel: 020 8455 3830
Open: Mon-Sat 10am-5pm
An excellent selection of quality books, all at 59p. There is also plenty of bric-à-brac, such as 4 cocktail glasses for £2.

Other charity shops in this area include:

Cancer Research UK

871 Finchley Road
Tel: 020 8458 6914
Open: Mon-Fri 10am-6pm,
Sat 9.30am-5.30pm, Sun 11am-4pm

HIGHGATE N6

Tube: Highgate
Bus: 43, 134, 263

Cancer Research UK

72 Highgate High Street
Tel: 020 8341 6330
Open: Mon-Sat 9.30am-5.30pm, Sun 11am-5pm

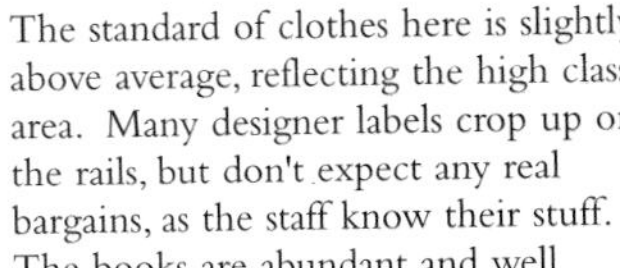

The standard of clothes here is slightly above average, reflecting the high class area. Many designer labels crop up on the rails, but don't expect any real bargains, as the staff know their stuff. The books are abundant and well worth sifting through.

Other charity shops in this area include:

Oxfam

80 Highgate High Street
Tel: 020 8340 3888
Open: Mon-Sat 10am-5pm,
Sun 11am-3pm

HOLLOWAY N7

Tube: Holloway Road
Bus: 4, 10, 17, 41, 43, 271, 143, 263

Scope

46 Seven Sisters Road
Tel: 020 7607 7779
Open: Mon-Sat 9am-4.45pm

Traid

375 Holloway Road
Tel: 020 7700 0087
Open: Mon-Sat 10am-6pm &
Sun 11am-5pm

MUSWELL HILL N10

Bus: 43, 102, 134, 144, 234, 299, W3

Cancer Research UK

85 Muswell Hill Broadway
Tel: 020 8365 3788
Open: Mon-Sat 9.30am-5.30pm, Sun 11am-4.30pm
There is a good selection of clothes in this shop and often more unusual items turn-up among the rails of high street labels.

North London Hospice

44 Fortis Green Road
Tel: 020 8444 8131
Open: Mon-Sat 9.30am-5pm

A traditional charity shop with lots of clothes and a particularly good selection of books and bric-à-brac.

Sue Ryder
129 Muswell Hill Broadway
Tel: 020 8444 6061
Open: Mon-Sat 9.30am-5pm
This shop tends to be a little cheaper than some of the charity shops in the area and offers a particularly good selection of clothes.

Other charity shops in this area include:

Cancer Research UK
161 Muswell Hill Broadway
Tel: 020 8444 6688
Open: Mon-Sat 9.30am-5.30pm, Sun 10am-5pm

Oxfam
233 Muswell Hill Broadway
Tel: 020 8883 2532
Open: Mon-Sat 10am-5.30pm

WOOD GREEN N22

Tube: Wood Green
Bus: 29, 67, 121, 123, 141, 144, 184, 221, 230, 232, 243, 329, W3

Cancer Research UK
7 High Road
Tel: 020 8365 7876
Open: Mon-Sat 9am-5pm
The accent here is on quality and respectability, so don't expect to find any frilly underwear or skintight leather trousers. Prices are in keeping with the good condition of most of the clothes, and some interesting books turn up.

North London Hospice
212 High Road
Tel: 020 8365 8622
Open: Mon-Sat 9.30am-4.45pm
Like all its branches, the NLH offers competitive prices for their splendid collection of clothes, bric-à-brac and books. We found a copy of John Updike's Rabbit trilogy for only £1.

Oxfam
12a The Broadway
Tel: 020 8881 6044
Open: Mon-Sat 10am-5.30pm
This shop has a young, trendy feel about it, and you can often find interesting CDs. Bargains include CD for as little as 50p.

CAMDEN NW1

Tube/Rail: Camden Town
Bus: 24, 27, 29, 88, 134, 168, 214, 253

All Aboard
59 Camden High Street
Tel: 020 7387 0500
Open: Mon-Wed 9.30am-5.30pm, Thurs 9.30am-7pm, Fri 9.30am-5.30pn, Sun 11am-5.30pm
A large shop which has resisted the temptation to modernise and is all the better for it. There is a good selection of clothes and bric-à-brac, and a few rails of discounted garments.

Books for Amnesty
241 Eversholt Street, NW1
Tel: 020 7388 0070
Open: Mon-Sat 10am-6pm
A charity shop specialising in books. The stock is extensive and carefully displayed by subject. Among the bargains was a hardback copy of Don De Lillo's 'Underworld' which was originally £18, but on sale here for only £3.50. Keen bargain hunters will also find a reasonable selection of books reduced to clear for only 50p.

Mind in Camden

20 Camden Road
Tel: 020 7916 0158
Open: Mon-Sat 10am-6pm

This is an eccentric little charity shop offering a mix of clothes, CDs and records, books and bric-à-brac. There is always something of interest to be found here which on a recent visit included a good condition Olympus camera for only £40.

Scope
73 Camden High Street
Tel: 020 7380 1455
Open: Mon-Sat 10am-6pm
This busy, well-organised shop offers a wide selection of clothes and books and is particularly good for kids' clothing.

Other charity shops in this area include:

Help the Aged

63 Camden High Street
Open: Mon-Sat 9am-5pm

Cancer Research UK
81 Camden High Street
Tel: 020 7383 5910
Open: Mon-Sat 9am-5pm, Sun 11am-5pm

Oxfam
89 Camden High Street
Tel: 020 7387 4354
Open: Mon-Thurs 10am-5.30pm, Fri-Sat 10am-5pm

Sue Ryder
103-105 Parkway
Tel: 020 7424 0225
Open: Mon-Sat 9.30am-5.30pm

Sue Ryder
19 Hampstead Road, Euston
Tel: 020 7387 1691
Open: Mon-Sat 9.30am-5.30pm

KENTISH TOWN NW5

Tube: Kentish Town
Rail: Kentish Town West
Bus: 46, 134, 214, C2

Help the Aged
247 Kentish Town Road
Tel: 020 7485 9245
Open: Mon-Sat 9am-5.30pm
A good selection of clothes, shoes and books.

Other charity shops in this area include:

Oxfam
166 Kentish Town Road
Tel: 020 7267 3560
Open: Mon-Sat 10am-5pm

Pdsa
249 Kentish Town Road
Tel: 020 7485 6153
Open: Mon-Sat 9am-5pm

CRICKLEWOOD NW2

Tube: Colindale
Bus: 32, 142, 204, 292, 303

Bosnia Herzegovina Community Charity Shop
129 Cricklewood Broadway
Tel: 020 8450 5392
Open: Mon-Sat 9am-7pm, Sun 10am-4pm
This cramped charity shop has a great selection of clothes, bags, books and accessories. The pricing policy is simple with all bags going for £1.50, and tops for only £1 each. A great little charity shop, well worth a visit.

WEST HAMPSTEAD NW6

Tube/Rail: West Hampstead
Bus: 139, 328, C11

All Aboard
224 West End Lane
Tel: 020 7794 3404
Open: Mon-Fri 10am-6pm (Thurs until 7pm), closed Saturday, Sun 10am-4pm
One of the best charity shops in town with a large selection of clothing, books and bric-à-brac. The clothes are

well displayed with designer ware meriting its own rail, and plenty of discounted items.

Other charity shops in this area include:

Cancer Research UK

234 West End Lane
Tel: 020 7433 1962
Open: Mon-Sat 10am-5pm, Sun 11am-4pm

The Community Charity Shop

92 Mill Lane
Tel: 020 7431 5250
Open: Mon-Fri 11am-5pm, Sat 9am-5pm

Oxfam

246 West End Lane
Tel: 020 7435 8628
Open: Mon-Sat 10am-6pm, Sun 12noon-4.30pm

Scope Charity Shop

214 West End Lane
Tel: 020 7431 5531
Open: Mon-Sat 9.30am-5.30pm

Scope

139 Kilburn High Road
Tel: 020 7624 7798
Open: Mon-Sat 9am-5pm
Plenty of footwear for men and women as well as clothes, shoes, toys and videos.

KILBURN NW6

Tube: Kilburn Park
Rail: Kilburn High Road
Bus: 16, 32, 98, 189, 206, 316

Traid

69-71 Kilburn High Street
Tel: 020 7328 1453
Open: Mon-Sat 10am-6pm
This well-organised charity shop is the size of a supermarket and offers great value clothes, shoes, bags, curtains and accessories. The clothes are not all second-hand with a fair amount of new men's shirts (probably last season's surplus stock) for between £5.99 and £7.99. One of the capital's largest and most popular charity shops.

Oxfam
152 Kilburn High Road
Tel: 020 7624 6697
Open: Mon-Sat 10am-6pm, Sun 11am-5pm
One of Oxfam's budget shops with a uniform pricing system; all jackets £2.99, all tops and trousers £1.99 and all bags £1.29. They have a particularly large selection of book.

Other charity shops in this area include:

Cancer Research UK

187 Kilburn High Road
Open: Mon-Sat 9.30am-5.30pm

Pdsa
198 Kilburn High Road
Tel: 020 7328 9632
Open: Mon-Sat 9.30am-5.30pm

Relief Fund for Romania

231 Kilburn High Road
Open: Mon-Sat 10am-5pm, Sun 11am-4pm

WEMBLEY HA9

Tube: Wembley Central
Bus: 18, 79, 83, 92, 182, 204, 233, 297

Oxfam
405 High Road
Tel: 020 8900 8482
Open: Mon-Sat 9.30am-5.30pm

Traid
Unit 12, 13 Central Square
Tel: 020 8900 1317
Open: Mon-Sat 10am-6pm, Sun 11am-5pm

WEST LONDON

CHELSEA SW10

Tube: Sloane Square
Bus: 11, 19, 22, 137, 211, 360, C1

Cancer Research UK
393 King's Road
Tel: 020 7352 4769
Open: Mon-Sat 9.30am-5.30pm, Sun 11.30-4.30pm
This is one of the best charity shops in London with a wide selection of books, clothes, bric-à-brac, shoes and records. The shop is cluttered with stock and has managed to avoid the plain and rather antiseptic atmosphere of many contemporary charity shops. The staff are young and very involved in the running of the shop.

Oxfam
432 King's Road
Tel: 020 7351 6863
Open: Mon-Sat 10am-6pm, Sun 12noon-5pm
This shop was refurbished in June 2002, but is still quirky and distinctive with an exceptionally high quality of goods from the surrounding salubrious neighbourhood. They have a particularly strong selection of designer clothes which included on a recent visit a Prada dress for £49.99. Another distinctive thing about this shop is the range of bric-à-brac and valuables which are displayed in glass cabinets on the wall and include jewellery and used cameras. There is also a large stock of books and records.

Oxfam
123A Shawfield Street, King's Road
Tel: 020 7351 7979
Open: Mon-Sat 10am-6pm
Specialising in accessories this modern Oxfam store manages to stand out amid the chain-stores clustered around it. Clothing with a good label or enough street cred hits the rails but in the main the store is dedicated to the world of accessories – hats, handbags, belts, shoes, scarves and jewellery.

Other charity shops in this area include:

Notting Hill Housing Trust
303 King's Road
Tel: 020 7352 8606
Open: Mon-Sat 10am-6pm, Sun 1pm-6pm

Trinity Hospice

389 King's Road
Tel: 020 7352 8507
Open: Mon-Sat 10am-4.45pm

FULHAM SW6

Tube: Fulham Broadway/Parsons Green
Bus: 11, 14, 22, 28, 295, 391, 424

Fara
841 Fulham Road
Tel: 020 7371 0141
Open: Mon-Sat 10am-6pm, Sun 11.30am-5.30pm
This charity shop is the most likely repository for the designer cast-offs from the wealthy local neighbourhoods. A recent visit unearthed several hand-made shirts for under a tenner.

Fara
325 North End Road
Tel: 020 7385 4949
Open: Mon-Fri 9.30am-5.30pm, Sat 10am-6pm, Sun 11am-4pm
Nicely laid-out displays and friendly staff make this a pleasant place for a serious rummage. The clothes are good quality and priced fairly. Books are all £1 for hardbacks and 50p for paperbacks.

Notting Hill Housing Trust
309 Fulham Road, SW10
Tel: 020 7352 7986
Tube: South Kensington
Bus: 14, 345
Open: Mon-Sat 10am-6pm,
Sun 12noon-4pm
This charity shop has a fair amount of designer labels among the more usual high street names. There is a high turn-over of stock which makes the place worth regular visits.

Other charity shops in this area include:

Cancer Research UK
350 North End Road
Tel: 020 7381 8458
Open: Mon-Sat 9.30am-6pm,
Sun 11am-5pm

Cancer Research UK
387 North End Road
Tel: 020 7381 0497
Open: Mon-Sat 9am-5.30pm,
Sun 10am-3pm

Fara
297 New King's Road
Tel: 020 7736 2833
Open: Mon-Sat 10am-6pm,
Sun 11am-5pm

Geranium Shop for the Blind
817 Fulham Road
Tel: 020 7610 6986
Open: Mon-Sat 10am-5pm

Notting Hill Housing Trust
654a Fulham Road
Tel: 020 7384 9663
Open: Mon-Sat 10am-6pm &
Sun 12noon-5pm

Sue Ryder

341 North End Road
Tel: 020 7385 5644
Open: Mon-Sat 9.30am-5.30pm

KENSINGTON W8

Tube: High Street Kensington & Notting Hill Gate
Bus: 9, 10, 27, 28, 49, 52, 70, 328, C1

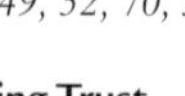

Notting Hill Housing Trust

57 Kensington Church Street
Tel: 020 7937 5274
Open: Mon-Sat 10am-6pm,
Sun 12noon-5pm
This small charity shop is crammed with good quality clothes and many designer labels. They also have an excellent stock of books and CDs which are kept at the back of the store.

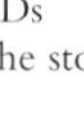

Trinity Hospice
31 Kensington Church Street
Tel: 020 7376 1098
Open: Mon-Sat 10.30am-5.30pm,
Sun 11am-4pm
This long established old-fashioned charity shop always has an interesting mix of books, clothing and bric-à-brac. Prices can occasionally be on the high side, but there are enough bargains to make it worth a visit.

Other charity shops in this area include

Geranium
8A Earl's Court Road
Tel: 020 7795 6166
Open: Mon-Sat 10am-5pm

Notting Hill Housing Trust
266 High Street Kensington
Tel: 020 7602 6043
Open: Mon-Sat 10am-6pm, Sun 1pm-6pm

Oxfam
202B Kensington High Street
Tel: 020 7937 6683
Open: Mon-Sat 10am-5.30pm,
Sun 12noon-5pm

BAYSWATER/PADDINGTON W2

Tube: Bayswater/Queensway
Bus: 7, 12, 23, 27, 70, 94, 148

Notting Hill Housing Trust
178 Queensway
Tel: 020 7221 8582
Open: Mon-Sat 10am-6pm, Sun 1pm-6pm
A small but well organised and stocked branch with a particularly good selection of paperback fiction.

Trinity Hospice
158 Queensway
Tel: 020 7229 8291
Open: Mon-Sat 10am-5pm, Sun 11am-5pm
A traditional charity shop with lots of clothing, shoes, books and bric-à-brac. The store is probably the largest charity shop in the area and is always busy with locals sifting through the stock for bargains.

Other charity shops in this area include:

All Aboard
3 Porchester Road
Tel: 020 7229 0048
Open: Mon-Fri 9am-5pm, Sun 10am-4pm (closed Saturday)

All Aboard
12 Spring Street
Tel: 020 7262 5955
Open: Mon-Fri 10am-5.30pm, Sun 12noon-4pm (closed Saturday)

Sue Ryder
27 Praed Street
Tel: 020 7262 6108
Open: Mon-Sat 10am-5pm

Traid
61 Westbourne Grove, W2
Tel: 020 7221 2421
Open: Mon-Sat 10am-6pm & Sun 11am-5pm

NOTTING HILL W11

Tube: Notting Hill Gate
Bus: 12, 27, 28, 31, 52, 70, 94, 148, 328

Notting Hill Housing Trust

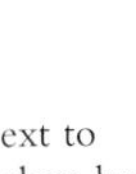

59 Notting Hill Gate
Tel: 020 7229 1476
Open: Mon-Sat 10am-7pm, Sun 1pm-6pm
With a prime location right next to Notting Hill tube station, this shop has a fast turnover, with new stuff constantly being added to the rails, making it well worth a visit.

Trinity Hospice
20 Notting Hill Gate
Tel: 020 7792 2582
Open: Mon, Thurs-Sun 10.30am-8pm, Tues & Wed 10.30am-6pm
This charity shop is a great place to find all kinds of clothing, books, records and CDs as well as bric-à-brac. As befits one of the smartest areas in town the quality of donations is very high.

Other charity shops in this area include:

Marie Curie
114 Ladbroke Grove, W10
Tel: 020 7229 9512
Open: Mon-Sat 9am-4.30pm

Oxfam

144 Notting Hill Gate
Tel: 020 7792 0037
Open: Mon-Sat 10am-5.30pm

Oxfam
245 Westbourne Grove
Tel: 020 7229 5000
Open: Mon-Sat 9.30am-5.30pm (Thursday open until 7.30pm)

SHEPHERD'S BUSH W12

Tube: Shepherd's Bush
Bus: 49, 72, 95, 207, 220, 237, 260, 272, 283

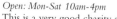

Age Concern
110 Uxbridge Road
Tel: 020 8749 9888
Open: Mon-Sat 10am-4pm

This is a very good charity shop and one of the few to stock small items of furniture as well as the usual mix of books, clothes, CDs and bric-à-brac.

Fara
84 Uxbridge Road
Tel: 020 8743 7799
Open: Mon-Sat 10am-6pm, Sun 11am-4pm
With an underwear section near the counter, this small store is clearly trying to extend the boundaries of what people are prepared to wear second-hand. The books are also well worth a rummage and the record section regularly turns up some unusual offerings.

Traid
164 Uxbridge Road
Tel: 020 8749 1437
Open: Mon-Sat 10am-6pm, Sun 11am-5pm
This large store is a bit on the sparse side, quantity-wise, but they often have £1 rails with anything from suits to mini-skirts. The sale prices quoted in the window can be misleading, as many items are not included.

Other charity shops in this area include:

Notting Hill Housing Trust
76 Askew Road
Tel: 020 8740 4878
Open: Mon-Sat 10am-6pm

HAMMERSMITH W6

Tube: Hammersmith
Bus: 9, 10, 27, 33, 72, 190, 209, 211, 220, 266, 267, 283, 295, 391, 419, H91

Books for Amnesty
139 King Street
Tel: 020 8746 3172
Open: Mon-Fri 10am-6pm, Sat 10am-4pm

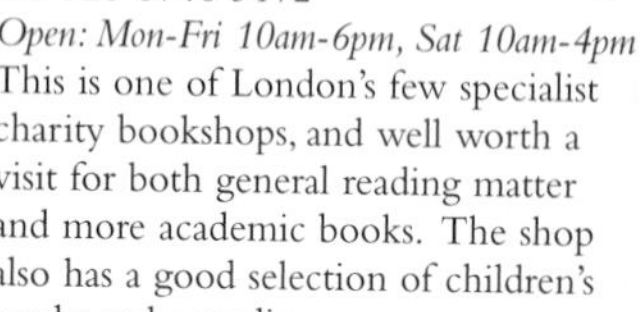

This is one of London's few specialist charity bookshops, and well worth a visit for both general reading matter and more academic books. The shop also has a good selection of children's books and a reading area so you can try before you buy.

Cancer Research UK
108 King Street
Tel: 020 8746 3215
Open: Mon-Sat 9.30am-5.30pm, Sun 11am-3pm
Targeting the younger crowd, this store has put all the trendy gear on special rails, with a heavy accent on 70s retro. Packed to the hilt, the ordinary rails are also worth looking through for bargains, of which there are many.

The Red Cross Shop
152 Shepherd's Bush Road
Tel: 020 7602 3534
Open: Mon-Sat 9.30am-5.30pm
With its dedicated team of volunteers, this little shop is constantly being improved and added to. Well worth a visit, especially if trawling charity shops in both Hammersmith and Shepherd's Bush, as this is the one that links them.

Traid
119 King Street
Tel: 020 8748 5946
Open: Mon-Sat 10am-6pm & Sun 11am-5pm
Another trendy charity shop with a great selection of clothing and books. The stuff is well displayed and anything that doesn't shift is sold at a discount.

Other charity shops in this area include:

British Heart Foundation

127 King Street
Tel: 020 8563 8851
Open: Mon-Sat 9.30am-5pm

Cancer Research UK
123A King Street
Tel: 020 8563 0440
Open: Mon-Sat 9.30am-5.30pm & Sun 11am-5pm

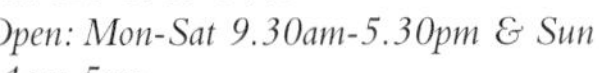

Oxfam

87 King Street
Tel: 020 8846 9276
Open: Mon-Sat 9.30am-5pm

Chiswick W4

Tube: Turnham Green
Bus: 27, 190, 237, 267, 391, E3, H91

Barnardos
72 Turnham Green Terrace
Tel: 020 8994 9931
Open: Mon-Sat 9am-5pm
The speciality here is children's clothes and toys, although there are a fair few clothes for adults.

Cancer Research UK
392 Chiswick High Road
Tel: 020 8994 4391
Open: Mon-Sat 9.30am-5.30pm & Sun 12noon-5pm
The staff know their stuff here, so don't expect any super finds. That said, the gear is all of such high quality that browsing is a pleasure, and everyone is sure to find something new and exciting for their wardrobe. Good leather jackets were all priced around £30, and there was a good selection of classic vintage dresses.

Cancer Research UK
278 Chiswick High Road
Tel: 020 8742 2501
Open: Mon-Sat 9.30am-5.30pm & Sun 11am-4pm
The clothes here are the usual dispiriting blend of frumpy blouses and woolly cardies, with a few pairs of jeans to break the pattern, but the real incentive for coming into this little shop is the books and the music. Contemporary fiction figures heavily on the bookshelves, all of it moderately priced at around 75p. The records feature many now-revived 70s classics such as Abba and Roxy Music, and there are cassettes for only 75p each.

Notting Hill Housing Trust
46 Turnham Green Terrace
Tel: 020 8995 8864
Open: Mon-Sat 10am-6pm & Sun 1pm-6pm
There is an emphasis on new stock such as candles, throws and cushions at this store. There is a reasonable selection of second-hand gear but it is concentrated at the back.

Oxfam
190 Chiswick High Road
Tel: 020 8994 4888
Open: Mon-Sat 10am-5pm & Sun 12noon-4pm
This tidy, Tardis-like store is well worth a browse. A good selection of hats, some of them brand-new, were priced at £3-£4. There's an excellent book department at the back of the shop, with all books arranged neatly in alphabetical order, with separate sections for travel, biography etc.

Trinity Hospice
25 Turnham Green Terrace
Tel: 020 8742 3036
Open: Mon-Sat 10am-5pm
Definitely the best charity shop in Chiswick, this one has very good and cheap clothes upstairs, including much designer and vintage stuff. Downstairs you will find nice men's coats, and plenty of them, priced around £15.

Ealing W5

Tube: Ealing Broadway
Bus: 83, 207, 65, 112, 297, 607, E1, E7, E8, E9, E10, E11

Oxfam Books
1 The Green
Tel: 020 8567 2152
Open: Mon-Sat 9.30am-6pm (Wed 10am-6pm), Sun 12noon-5pm
An eclectic, well-organised selection of titles, with prices ranging from £1.50 upwards.

Oxfam Music
11 The Green
Tel: 020 8840 8465
Open: Mon-Sat 10am-6pm (closes Thurs at 2pm)
Here's where all the interesting records end up, if you ever wondered why you only ever find Mantovani and James Last in regular Oxfam shops. This is the only London Oxfam shop entirely dedicated to music, and stocks a wide range of vinyls, CDs, cassettes and sheet music.

YMCA
16 Bond Street
Tel: 020 8832 1638
Open: Mon-Sat 10am-5pm
With its lively staff and quick turnover, this shop is a must for any bargain hunter.

Other charity shops in this area include:

Cancer Research UK
66 The Mall, Ealing Broadway
Tel: 020 8840 1197
Open: Mon-Sat 9.30am-6pm & Sun 11am-5pm

Notting Hill Housing Trust
40 High Street
Tel: 020 8567 8003
Open: Mon-Sat 10am-6pm, Sun noon-5pm

Oxfam
34 New Broadway
Tel: 020 8579 6532
Open: Mon-Sat 9.30am-5.30pm, Sun 11am-4pm

Sue Ryder
2 Bond Street
Tel: 020 8840 0570
Open: Mon-Sat 9.30am-5.30pm

South London

Brixton SW2

Tube/Rail: Brixton
Bus: 2, 3, 35, 37, 59, 109, 118, 133, 159, 196, 250, 322, 345, 355, P4

Barnardos
414 Brixton Road, SW9
Tel: 020 7274 4165
Open: Mon-Sat 9am-5pm
This large store offers a great selection of clothing, toys, books, records and CDs. The stock is well priced and there are always discount rails with items reduced to clear.

Traid
2 Acre Lane
Tel: 020 7326 4330
Open: Mon-Sat 10am-6pm, Sun 11am-5pm
This Brixton branch of Traid stocks an eclectic mix of retro, casual clothing and designerwear, enabling the imaginative shopper to put together an outfit for under £20.

PUTNEY SW15

Tube: East Putney
Rail: Putney
Bus: 14, 22, 39, 74, 85, 93, 220, 265

British Heart Foundation
65 Putney High Street
Tel: 020 8780 5611
Open: Mon-Sat 9.30am-5pm
The clothes in this small shop are nothing to write home about, but the unusual books near the till are worth looking through.

Oxfam
149 Putney High Street
Tel: 020 8789 3235
Open: Mon-Sat 9.30am-5.30pm, Sun 11am-5pm
Larger than it looks from outside, this shop has the usual Oxam fare at the front, the exception being some wedding dresses for around £30 each. At the back is an extensive book section, as well as records.

Other charity shops in this area include:

Cancer Research UK
127 Putney High Street
Tel: 020 8788 9305
Open: Mon-Sat 9.30am-5.30pm, Sun 11am-4pm

Notting Hill Housing Trust
288 Upper Richmond Road
Tel: 020 8788 5763
Open: Mon-Sat 10am-6pm

Trinity Hospice
147 Putney High Street
Tel: 020 8780 0737
Open: Mon-Sat 9.30am-5.30pm (Fri closes 4.30pm), Sun 11am-5pm

WANDSWORTH/SOUTHFIELDS SW1

Tube: Southfields
Rail: Wandsworth Town
Bus: 28, 37, 39, 44, 77A, 156, 170, 220, 337

Salvation Army Charity Shop
209 Wandsworth High Street
Tel: 020 8871 1812
Open: Mon-Fri 10.30am-5.30pm, Sat 11am-5pm
A little out of the way from Wandsworth's shopping hub, but worth the trek, as the prices are within anyone's budget, and the free-for-all nature of the displays ensure bargain hunters are very likely to succeed.

Other charity shops in this area include:

Oxfam
4 Replingham Road
Tel: 020 8870 2676
Open: Mon-Sat 10am-4.30pm

Fara
551 Garratt Lane
Tel: 020 8947 8308

CLAPHAM SW11

Open: Mon-Sat 10am-6pm, Sun 11am-5pm
Rail: Clapham Junction
Bus: 35, 37, 39, 77A, 156, 170, 219, 295, 344, 337, C3

Ace of Clubs
53 St John's Road
Tel: 020 7978 6318
Open: Mon-Fri 10am-5pm, Sat 9am-5pm
The first of a cluster of charity shops just across from Clapham Junction railway station, this is a nice, cheap shop with constantly updated stock. Clothes are a mixed bag, and the toys and bric-à-brac around the window are difficult to resist a rummage through.

Fara
19 Northcote Road
Tel: 020 7924 4477
Open: Mon-Sat 10am-5.30pm & Sun 11am-5pm
A good, busy little shop on a road with an excellent fruit & veg market. Many bargains are to be had when rummaging through the packed rails. The selection of records, books and toys in the window also merit a look at as well.

Scope
69 St John's Road
Tel: 020 7801 0746
Open: Mon-Sat 9.30am-5.30pm
Just across the road from Ace of Clubs, this is an altogether more upmarket, and therefore more expensive, charity shop. Nonetheless it contains an excellent variety of clothes, especially coat.

Trinity Hospice
40 Northcote Road
Tel: 020 7924 2927
Open: Mon-Sat 10am-5pm
Known locally for its outlandish window displays during most public holidays, the clothes often reflect the young, trendy volunteers. This is one of the nicest charity shops in the area.

Other charity shops in this area include:

British Heart Foundation
62 St John's Road
Tel: 020 7978 4237
Mon-Sat 9.30am-5pm

Cancer Research UK
83 St John's Road
Tel: 020 7223 5349
Open: Mon-Sat 9am-5pm, Sun 10am-4pm

Fara
254 Battersea Park Road
Tel: 020 7924 5575
Mon-Tues & Thurs-Fri 9.30am-5.30pm, Wed & Sat 10am-7pm, Sun 11am-5pm

BALHAM SW12

Tube/Rail: Balham
Bus: 155, 219, 249, 315, 355, 319

British Heart Foundation
184 Balham High Road
Tel: 020 8675 5401
Open: Mon-Sat 9.30am-5pm

Salvation Army Charity Shop
38 Balham High Road
Tel: 020 8675 3809
Open: Mon-Fri 10am-4pm
(Thursday closes 12noon)

Sue Ryder
87 Balham High Road
Tel: 020 8675 8208
Open: Mon-Sat 9.30am-4.30pm

STREATHAM SW16

Rail: Streatham
Bus: 50, 60, 118, 159, P13

Oxfam
23 Streatham High Road
Tel: 020 8769 1291
Open: Mon-Sat 10am-5.30pm
This Oxfam shop specialises in furniture and electrical goods. They have two qualified electricians to check the quality and safety of all electrical goods including computers. The selection of furniture is also extensive, with anything from a 60s coffee table to a three-piece suite.

Other charity shops in this area include:

All Aboard
83 Streatham High Road
Tel: 020 8769 9410
Open: Mon-Fri 10am-6pm & Sun 10am-4pm

Cancer Research UK
65 Streatham High Road
Tel: 020 8677 3940
Open: Mon-Sat 9am-5pm

Oxfam
7 Astoria Parade, High Road
Tel: 020 8769 0515
Open: Mon-Sat 9.30am-4.30pm

EAST LONDON

WHITECHAPEL E1

Tube: Aldgate East/Liverpool Street/Whitechapel
Bus: 15, 25, 67, 115, 205, 253

Muslim Care Charity Shop (11)
208 Brick Lane
Tel: 020 7613 0772
Open: Mon-Fri 10am-5pm, Sun 10am-2pm
This large shop takes some browsing, with large quantities of clothes packed tightly on countless rails. There is a whole rail for leather jackets, priced £10-£20. A good place to pop into while doing Brick Lane market.

Spitalfields Crypt Trust Shop
26-28 Toynbee Street
Tel: 020 7377 9893
Open: Mon-Fri & Sun 10am-5pm (closed Saturday)
A stone's throw from Spitalfields Market, and worth seeking out, this friendly little shop has a fascinating variety of stuff. A whole rail of men's tweed jackets were only £5 each. Designer ware has its own rail and is reasonably priced with women's designer gear hanging from the ceiling.

Spitalfields Crypt Trust Shop
34-36 Watney Market
Tel: 020 7791 0200
Open: Mon-Sat 10am-5pm
Located just off Commercial Road, this is a sister branch to the above, and well worth checking out.

DALSTON E8

Rail: Dalston Kingsland
Bus: 67, 149, 242, 243

Oxfam
570-572 Kingsland Road
Tel: 020 7923 1532
Bus: 149 from Liverpool Street tube, bus 76 from Waterloo
Open: Mon-Sat 9.15am-5.15pm
The biggest Oxfam in London, with the lowest prices. Stock turnover is huge, with new items being added daily. Everything is priced by rail or box, to avoid confusion, so all records are 69p, all books (with an excellent selection of every type) 49p. Menswear boasts several rails of suits, trousers and shirts, while womenswear spreads itself all over the shop on a multitude of rails and in a bewildering amount of colours and styles.

HACKNEY E8 & E9

Rail: Hackney Central
Bus: 30, 38, 236, 242, 276, 277, W15

Community of Reconciliation and Fellowship
407 Mare Street, E8
Tel: 020 8985 7356
Open: Mon-Fri 9.30am-4.30pm
This charity shop is large and well stocked with a good mix of clothing, toys, video tapes, books and household goods. The pricing is cheaper than you will find in charity shops in smarter areas – on a recent visit a nearly new pair of Levi jeans was only £2.50.

Other charity shops in this area include:

Salvation Army Charity Shop
Cambridge Heath, 70 Mare Street, E8
Tel: 020 8985 4410
Open: Mon-Fri 10am-4pm, Sat 11am-2pm

Scope
4 Morning Lane, E9
Tel: 020 8985 5825
Open: Mon-Sat 9.30am-5.30pm

BETHNAL GREEN E3

Tube: Bethnal Green
Bus: 8, 106, 253, D3

Sudana
51 Roman Road
Tel: 020 8981 1225
Open: Tues-Fri 12am-6pm, Sat 12noon-5.30pm (closed Sunday and Monday)
Attached to the Buddhist centre next door, this packed little shop never fails to produce some cracking bargains, if you rummage long enough.

OUTER LONDON

RICHMOND TW9

Tube/Rail: Richmond
Bus: 33, 190, 337, 371, 391, 419, 485, 490, H22, R68, R70

Cancer Research UK
1 Hill Street
Tel: 020 8940 4581
Open: Mon-Sat 9.30am-5.30pm, Sun 10.30am-4.30pm
The best in the area for modern, stylish clothes at moderate prices. A collection of nice little handbags, some vintage, ranged from £2-£3. The occasional cashmere sweater makes an appearance on the women's rails, priced around £8. In menswear, a good as new Gap pull-over was only £5.

Marie Curie
1 Lichfield Terrace (on Sheen Road)
Tel: 020 8940 1800
Open: Mon-Sat 9.30am-5.30pm
A little out of the way of the other charity shops in this area, but its prices offer good competition. Packed with clothes for both sexes, many of them veer towards the smart or formal.

Oxfam
6 The Quadrant
Tel: 020 8948 7381
Open: Mon-Sat 9.30am-6pm (open Sundays depending on staff availability)
A fairly recent type of Oxfam, containing all new stuff. Styles and prices seem about right for young home-owners. All the wares are from around the world, and though similar to what you'll see in other High Street stores, at least you can be sure the money is going back to the communities who produced the stuff.

TWICKENHAM TW9

Rail: Twickenham
Bus: 33, 110, 267, 281, 290, 490, H22, R70

The Mind Shop
386 Richmond Road
Tel: 020 8891 2295
Open: Mon-Sat 9.30am-5pm

Notting Hill Housing Trust
394 Richmond Road
Tel: 020 8891 6819
Open: Mon-Sat 10am-6pm, Sun 12.30pm-5.30pm

Oxfam
46 King Street
Tel: 020 8892 4605
Open: Mon-Sat 10am-4.30pm

Discount Outlets

Below are reviews of shops in and around London that claim to sell goods at discounted prices. Some are distinctly old-fashioned, with service to match, which makes them a pleasure to shop in, others sell clearance lines or bulk bought goods at rock-bottom prices with a fast turnover and little in the way of salesmanship. It is worth comparing prices with places like Argos, where you choose from a huge catalogue in their stores, IKEA which imports furniture and housewares from Sweden, and B&Q for gardening equipment, bathrooms and DIY. Bear in mind that 'discount' isn't always synonymous with 'quality'. It is worth checking that what you're buying isn't damaged or won't fall apart before you get it home. Also see the section on Basic Clothing and Curtains.

Central

Alexander Furnishings
51-61 Wigmore Street, W1
Tel: 020 7935 2624
Open: Mon-Sat 9am-6pm (Thurs-7pm)
See main entry in the Curtains section on page 101.

David Richards & Sons
10 New Cavendish Street, W1
Tel: 020 7935 3206
Tube: Baker Street/Bond Street
Bus: 88, 453, C2
Open: Mon-Fri 9.30am-5.30pm
Established 33 years ago this well-established shop sells silverware direct to the public at wholesale prices. Silver photo frames start from £20. Miniature silver animals are one of their best sellers and are priced from £40-£2000, silver wine coasters cost £65 each, silver mounted decanters from £80. A great place to search for gifts and wedding presents. They offer a repair service which includes getting rid of 'chips' in glasswear, and they will engrave anything you buy.

Reject China Shops
71 Regent Street, W1
Tel: 020 7734 4915
Tube: Piccadilly Circus
Bus: 3, 6, 12, 13, 15, 23, 88, 94, 139, 159, 453
Open: Mon-Sat 9am-6pm, Thurs until 8pm, Sun 11am-5pm
Reject China Shops offer substantial discounts year-round on famous brands of tableware, glassware, cutlery and giftware. Each branch carries different lines and offers special promotions and even bigger discounts at sale time in January and June/July. Manufacturers include Royal Worcester, Royal Doulton, Wedgwood, Minton, Portmeirion and Spode. Look out for reasonably priced 'seconds'.
Branches at: The Piazza, Covent Garden WC2, and 183 Brompton Rd SW3

G. Thornfield Ltd
321 Gray's Inn Road, WC1
Tel: 020 7837 2996
Tube: King's Cross
Bus: 10, 17, 45, 46, 63, 259
Open: Mon-Fri 8am-6pm, Sat 9am-2pm
This shop opened in 1953 so they know all about old-fashioned service. Up to 20% discounts are offered on current wallpapers and fabrics. They don't hold stock so you choose from the 200 catalogues and samples on display, which include top designers. Orders are dispatched within 48 hours. The bigger the quantity, the bigger the discount. They will mix Dulux paints, offer a bespoke framing service and also have a print and poster gallery.

Wallers
21-24 Newport Court, Charing Cross Road, WC2
Tel: 020 7437 1665
Tube: Leicester Square
Bus: 24, 29, 176
Open: Mon-Fri 9am-5.30pm, Sat 10am-5pm
Rabbit warren of a place behind Chinatown with three floors of men's clothing at savings of up to 40% on High Street prices. Over 20,000 items are in stock at any one time, many of them end of ranges, cancelled orders and samples. A family business since 1925 they hope to import a member of the fourth generation soon. Famous for supplying clothes for TV programmes (Only Fools & Horses, Yes, Minister, Inspector Morse) and many West End plays, they are perhaps best known for their suits (lots of Continental brands and formal evening wear) and have a tailor on the premises. Old-fashioned service plus a good supply of braces and cufflinks.

NORTH

The Catalogue Bargain Shop

252 Green Lanes, N15
Tel: 020 8886 9532
Website: www.bargaincrazy.com
Tube: Wood Green   Rail: Palmers Green
Bus: 67, 123, 141, 144, 230, 243, W3
Open: Mon-Sat 9am-5.30pm, Sun 10am-4pm

This is a High Street outlet selling surplus stock and returns from mail order firms including Kays, Choice and Argos. Much of the stock is clothing for women, men and children starting at under £5 and including names such as Miss Sixty, D&G, Burberry, Levi's and Lambretta. There is also a good selection of electrical goods (with hi-fi's starting from £85 and 21" colour TVs for the same price) as well as china, luggage and furniture. Prices are about half those of the catalogue and many items are not seconds, but simply surplus stock from the current catalogue. Everything comes with a year's guarantee.

The Curtain Factory Outlet

269 Ballards Lane,
North Finchley, N12
Tel: 020 8492 0093
Tube: West Finchley
Bus: 82, 125, 134, 221, 260, 263, 383
Open: Mon-Sat 9am-6pm, Sun 10am-4pm

A curtain wholesalers and exporters offering over half a million metres of fabric from top designers in a large converted house and warehouse (next to Waitrose). A warren of rooms is piled high with rolls of fabric, for upholstery as well as curtains. Prices are all under £6.99 (plus VAT) a metre, regardless of the retail price, which could be £50 a metre upwards. There are fabrics of every description from heavy calicoes to vibrant floaty voiles and a making-up service on the spot. At the back is a trade warehouse which the public are allowed into when the shop is quiet. The staff are attentive and very helpful.

Direct Dance Wear

Lancaster House, Dollis Hill Estate,
105 Brook Road, NW2
Tel: 020 8450 2456
Website: www.directdancewear.com
Tube: Dollis Hill
Bus: 52, 98, 226, 260, 266, 302
Open: Mon-Thurs 9.30am-5.30pm, Fri 10am-1.30pm, Sun 10am-1.30pm

This small retail outlet on the second floor of an uninspiring office block offers dancewear for adults and children at discount prices. They sell their own label to dance shops but you can buy from them direct. Children's leotards start from £8, children's ballet shoes from £6.50. They also stock jazz shoes, tights and anything else you might need for dance classes.

Fatto in Italia
16a Pratt Street, NW1
Tube: Camden Town, Mornington Crescent
Bus: 24, 27, 29, 88, 134, 168, 214, 253
Open: Mon-Sat 10.30am-7pm
A tiny shop offering good discounts (up to 40%) off Italian labels, including Dolce & Gabbana and Versace for men and women, as well as accessories. The Italian owner regularly travels to Italy and brings back bargains, especially in knitwear. Nothing hangs around for long and there is a quick turnover in stock.

Matalan
279 Edgware Road, Cricklewood, NE2
Tel: 020 8450 5667
Website: www.matalan.co.uk
Tube: Kilburn
Bus: 16, 32, 89, 316
Open: Mon-Fri 9am-6pm, Sat 9am-6pm, Sun 11am-5pm
Matalan are a large chain of discount stores offering very low prices on a wide range of fashion and homeware. The stores cater for the whole family and offer brand names such as Farah, Wolsey, Playtex, Gossard and Jeffrey Rogers at up to 50% off the usual High Street price. They also offer a great choice of jeans with top names like Wrangler, Lee Cooper and Falmers found on their rails at well below the usual price. It costs £1 for lifetime membership and this means you are sent information about current offers. The number of stores has expanded hugely in recent years, below are the main London branches – refer to the website for a full listing or call 0845 300 1199.
Beckton Alps Retail Park E6, Tel: 020 7473 9780
Bugsby Way, Charlton SE7, Tel: 020 8269 4290
The Brand Centre, Enfield EN3, Tel: 020 8344 9620
Pump Lane, Hayes, Middlesex UB3, Tel: 020 8606 6700
Thurston Road, Lewisham SE13, Tel: 020 8463 9830
High Road, Leytonstone E11, Tel: 020 8988 8630
Great Western Industrial Retail Park, Southall UB2, Tel: 020 8574 0660
Lakeside Retail Park, West Thurrock RM16, Tel: 01708 864 350

S & M Myers
100-106 Mackenzie Road, N7
Tel: 020 7609 0091
Website: www.myerscarpets.co.uk
Tube: Caledonian Road
Bus: 17, 91, 259, 274
Open: Mon, Wed, Fri 10-5.30pm, Tues & Thurs 10am-5pm, Sat 9.30am-2pm
This family business started in 1819 and still offers good quality new carpets and a wide range of remnants at very competitive prices. Among the bargains an 80% wool mix carpet was only £13.50 a square metre and seagrass started from as little as £8.99 a square metre. The remnants are displayed on a board and labelled with the dimensions and price, making it easy to choose what you want. A 2.9m x 4m 80% wool remnant was found here for only £128. The East End Road branch has a wider range of rugs, but all remnants can be cut and the edges sewn at very little cost to make a bespoke rug. Probably the best budget carpet outlet in the capital.
Also at:
81-85 East End Road N2, Tel: 020 8444 3457
Open: Mon-Fri 8am-5.30pm, Sat 9.30am-5pm

S & M Myers

Poundstretcher
Tel: 01132 406 406
Shops at: Kilburn NW6, Cricklewood NW2, Hackney E8, Leyton E10, Walthamstow E17, Wandsworth SW18, Acton W3, Ealing W7
Open: Mon-Sat 9am-5.30pm, Sun 10am-4pm
These discount shops sell everything for the family from garden furniture to shoes, kitchenware to toys and toiletries at very low prices. While you never know what they are going to have in stock, their most popular items are kitchen pan sets, schoolwear, gardening tools and Christmas decorations. There are definite bargains to be had. At the time of going to press they were 'streamlining' their range to offer 'more quality goods'.

Soviet Carpet and Art Centre
303-305 Cricklewood Broadway, NW2
Tel: 020 8452 2445
Rail: Cricklewood Broadway
Bus: 16, 32, 245, 266, 316
Open: Sundays only 10.30am-5.30pm (ring the bell)
Now here's an interesting place; a warehouse (just south of Matalan) that is a wholesale outlet for handmade rugs, from Eastern Europe, China and Pakistan. Established some 15 years ago, they only admit the public on Sundays. Ring the bell and you will be escorted around the 20,000 square foot premises strewn with piles of rugs of all sizes sorted by country. Upstairs there are fabulous silk creations and rooms stacked with paintings (many unframed) and wall hangings from Russian artists. 100% wool rugs from Eastern Europe that retail at over £300 in shops here were £150. A signed lithograph by a listed artist was on sale for £30 (retails at £150). Forget about haggling for carpets on your holidays – head for Cricklewood, you are unlikely to see a bigger collection anywhere.

Swimgear
11 Station Road, Finchley, N3
Tel: 020 8346 6106
Website: www.swimgear.co.uk
Tube: Finchley Central
Bus: 82, 125, 260
Open: Mon-Fri 9.30am-5pm
Tony Godfrey the owner of this mail order company which also sells direct to the public at wholesale prices, invented the Mark One goggles worn by Ian Thorpe in the last Olympics. The shop opened in the sixties and although old-fashioned, offers the latest in swimwear. Situated next to Finchley Central station they sell their own brand to

swimming clubs and schools and well-known brands at a discount. Their navy or black plain costumes (similar to Olympic Speedo) cost £11.50 or £13.50 depending on the size. They have Lycra men's shorts for £17.99 and U-back costumes start from £8. As well as a large range of goggles they also sell hats, leisurewear and swimming gear for children and babies.

TK Maxx
Wood Green Shopping Centre N22,
Tel: 020 8 888 8803
See entry in West London (following page) for full details.

Top Value Drug Store
23 Temple Fortune Parade,
Finchley Road, NW11
Tel: 020 8905 5448
Tube: Golders Green
Bus: 82, 102, 260
Open: Mon-Sat 8.30am-6pm, Sun 9.30am-1.30pm
Small family-run business just north of Golders Green, which regularly undercuts neighbouring supermarkets and chemists on some, but not all, brands of toiletries and household goods including sunscreens, haircare products, film, cleaning materials, bakeware, nappies and babyfood.

WEST

The Curtain Fabric Factory
236a North End Road, W14
Tel: 020 7381 1777
Tube: Brompton Road or West Kensington
Bus: 28, 391
Open: Mon-Sat 9.30am-5.30pm
Large importers of furnishing fabrics with a massive warehouse behind a busy shop near the market. Up to 1500 rolls of fabric to choose from supplied direct from manufacturers and offered at discounts of up to 40%. Some seconds and samples but most is regular stock supplied in bulk and on sale from £2.99 to £20 a metre. They do their own printing and if what you want is not in stock they will order it in. Made to measure service for curtains and blinds plus tracks and fitting.
Also see entry in Curtains (page 104).

TK Maxx
45-63 King Street, Hammersmith, W6
Tel: 020 8563 9200
Website: www.tkmaxx.com
Tube: Hammersmith LU
Bus: 9, 10, 33, 209, 211, 419
Open: Mon-Fri 8am-9pm, Sat 9am-7pm, Sun 11am-5pm

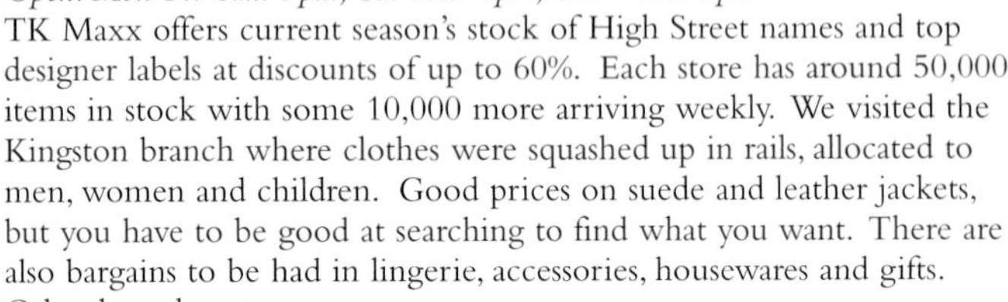

TK Maxx offers current season's stock of High Street names and top designer labels at discounts of up to 60%. Each store has around 50,000 items in stock with some 10,000 more arriving weekly. We visited the Kingston branch where clothes were squashed up in rails, allocated to men, women and children. Good prices on suede and leather jackets, but you have to be good at searching to find what you want. There are also bargains to be had in lingerie, accessories, housewares and gifts.

Other branches at:
The Galleria, Hatfield, Tel: 01707 260 066
Wood Green Shopping Centre N22, Tel: 020 8888 8803
Kingston, KT1, 2 Clarence Street, Tel: 020 8974 6296
Ealing, W5, The Arcadia Centre, The Broadway, Tel: 020 8566 0447
Croydon, The Drummond Centre, Tel: 020 8686 9753

SOUTH

Bucks Warehouse
125 Evelyn Street, SE8
Tel: 020 8692 4447
Tube: Surrey Quays
Bus: 47, 199, 188
Open: Mon-Fri 10am-7pm, Sat 10am-5pm, Sun 10am-4pm
Trailer loads of good quality furniture arrives weekly at this large warehouse in Surrey Quays where you can pick up a solid oak dining room set for £675 (6 chairs and an extending table) and all sorts of furniture bargains. Three quarters of the stock is from a well-known store famous for its undies. Some of it is ex-photo shoot, slightly scratched, end of range or from former shop floor displays. There's a huge selection of beds (doubles from £140), sofa beds (from £420) plus upholstered furniture. Almost everything is discounted by between 45% and 55%.

P&Q Home Depot
Unit 4, Surrey Quays Road,
Surrey Quays, SE16
Tel: 020 7252 1441
Tube: Surrey Quays
Bus: 47, 188, 199, 225, 381
Open: Mon-Sat 9am-5.30pm, Sun 10am-4pm

Huge, 27,000 square foot warehouse opposite Canary Wharf selling household goods, bathroom fittings, garden furniture, microwaves, pots and pans and gifts at prices discounted by around 15%. Much of the stock is ends of lines and clearance. Prices range from four cans of Coke for £1 to £800 for a garden furniture set which would retail at £1000.

OUT OF LONDON

Bicester Village

50 Pingle Drive, Bicester, Oxon
Tel: 01869 323 200
Website: www.bicestervillage.com
Car: 2 miles from Junction 9 M40
Rail: Bicester Town (from Oxford) Bicester North (London-Birmingham); courtesy shuttle bus Thurs-Sun
Open: Daily 10am-6pm (until 7pm in early summer)
Huge discount village with 90 stores offering savings of up to 60% on the previous season's branded goods, so don't expect to find the very latest fashions. Bargains nevertheless to be had in all number of stores depending on the time of year and what they happen to have in stock. Expect to find at least 25% discount on regular prices and often a lot more. Outlets include: Escada, Penhaligon's, Reebok, Versace, Aquascutum, Clarks, Ted Baker, Karen Millen, Tod's, Burberry, Paul Smith, Diesel and Petit Bateau. The centre can get packed at weekends, especially between 1pm and 3pm. There's a huge Pret a Manger and a Starbucks plus a restaurant. When the car park's full they offer a park and ride at a local school.

The Galleria Outlet Centre

Comet Way, Hatfield
Website: www.galleriaoutletcentre.co.uk
Car: A1(M) between junctions 3/4
Rail: Hatfield, then local buses (10 mins)
Open: Mon-Fri 10am-8pm, Sat 10am-6pm, Sun 11am-5pm
A huge aircraft hanger straddling the A1 motorway, The Galleria is a shopping discount outlet with around 80 stores in separate units. Shops are constantly changing but all offer discounts of up to 50%. The emphasis is on fashion but there are also furniture and homeware stores. Newest outlets include Marks and Spencer and Reebok. Others include Tog 24, TK Maxx, Choice, Designer Room, Mexx, and Donnay. Much is this season's surplus stock or end of product lines. There are also some regular stores like Waterstones, Superdrug, Body Shop and Oasis. On weekends and Bank Holidays, which get pretty crowded, there are children's activities, including a trampoline. There is also a UCI cinema and for those who get impatient with partners, numerous cafés and restaurants.

Kenton Warehouse Superstore

2A Charlton Road, Kenton, Middlesex, HA3
Tel: 020 8732 2525
Tube: Kenton
Bus: 114, 183, 223, H10, H18
Open: Mon-Sat 9.30am-5.30pm

Shop and huge warehouse selling discounted carpets, beds, laminated flooring and ready-made curtains and blinds. Special promotions offer half-price carpets and beds including Relyon, Cumfilux, Nestledown, and Sealy. Hundreds of rolls of carpets in stock in the 10,000 square foot warehouse with good prices for ends of rolls. They offer free underlay on most of the carpets they sell.

TK Maxx

Flagship store: The Galleria, Hatfield
Tel: 01707 260 066 or 020 8686 9753
Website: www.tkmaxx.com
Rail: East Croydon
Open: Mon-Sat 9am-6pm; Fri 9am-7pm; Sun 11am-5pm

'No frills' stores based on an American concept offering famous label womenswear, menswear, childrenswear, gifts and homewear all at up to 60% less than recommended retail prices. Each store has around 50,000 items in stock with up to 1,000 new items arriving by the week. Expect to find huge savings for all the family if you're prepared to search through rail upon rail of clothes. For further information log on to their website. See page 218 for a list of other London branches.

Tog 24 Outlet

Unit 52, The Galleria, Hatfield
Tel: 020 8785 3565
Website: www.tog24.com

Adventure clothing and 'active' fashion for all the family at prices discounted by 30% and more from their other retail outlets. Combat trousers from £29, Gortex jackets cost £170 (retail at £250), Windstoppers cost £50 (retail at £100). They have a great selection of discounted skiiwear with prices up to 70% off, particularly at the end of the season in April and May. You can have a look at their range on their website.

Wheelhouse

9-21 Bell Road, Hounslow, Middlesex
Tel: 020 8570 3501
Tube: Hounslow Central
Bus: 81, 120, 203, 222, H20, H22, H28
Open: Mon-Sat 8.30am-5.30pm, Sun 10am-4.30pm

Large shop in busy shopping area on two floors offering keen prices on housewares, gardening equipment, DIY, lighting, furniture, paint, ceramics and electrical goods. Ever changing clearance stock from numerous manufacturers means you may or not get a bargain.

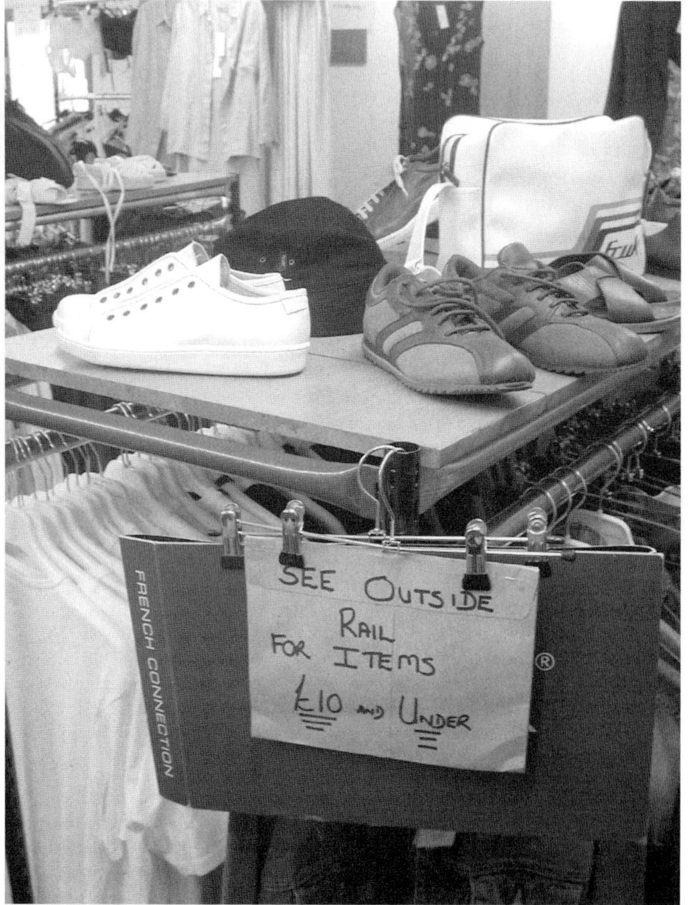

French Connection/Nicole Farhi Outlet Shop

FACTORY SHOPS

The term factory shop has become synonymous with good value and for that reason quite a number of outlets describe themselves as such without actually having any link with a factory or particular manufacturer. The factory shops featured below are all in one way or another the genuine article and more importantly all offer good quality at below High Street prices.

ACCESSORIES

James & Alden plc

Hanover House
385 Edgware Road, NW2
Tel: 020 8830 8008
Rail: Cricklewood
Bus: 16, 32, 245, 266, 316
Open: Mon & Thurs Fri 8am-4.45pm, Fri 8am-2pm

This wholesalers and manufacturers is the best place in London to buy bags, belts and wallets. Unfortunately, the company has moved further out of town and it is now quite a trek for most people to visit, but it is still well worth a visit as long as you don't object to the rather industrial atmosphere of the place. Among the bargains were a 1 inch belt for only £3.40, leather wallets for £6 and great quality cow hide shoulder bags for only £39.50. Strongly recommended to those looking for cheap leather goods.

CLOTHING

The Burberry Factory Outlet

29-53 Chatham Place, E9
Tel: 020 8985 3344
Rail: Hackney Central
Tube: Bethnal Green
Bus: 30, 236, 276, W15
Open: Mon-Fri 11am-6pm, Sat 10am-5pm, Sun 11am-5pm

This large factory shop sells top quality Burberry clothing, shoes, jewellery and accessories at considerable savings from department store prices. The space is massive and there is a large showroom to the left of the entrance that is easily missed, but worth exploring. Among the bargains on a recent visit were men's shirts reduced to £10, sports tops that were slight seconds for £11.95 and £20 off all leather garments over £150. The shop is a magnet to Japanese tourists who comprised about half the customers when I last visited.

Clarks Factory Shop

See main entry in the Shoes, Boots and Bags section on page 48.

French Connection/Nicole Farhi Outlet Shop

3 Hancock Road, E3
Tel: 020 7399 7125
Tube: Bromley by Bow
Bus: 8, 108, S2
Open: Mon-Wed & Sat 10am-3pm, Thurs 11am-6.30pm, Fri 10am-5.30pm
In fact a small portakabin by the warehouse, this factory shop is nevertheless jam-packed with clothes for men and women. Massive discounts on previous season's stock, samples and seconds. It's pot luck as to what you'll find, but a £200 dress could be anything from £20 to £150 depending on its condition (check carefully for damage before you buy). They also sell accessories.

IC Companys

6

100 Garratt Lane, SW18
Tel: 020 8871 2155
Rail: Wandsworth Town
Tube: Southfields
Bus: 44, 270
Open: Mon-Sat 10am-5.30pm, Sun 11am-5pm
The name has changed in recent years (it used to be called In-Wear), but the discounts on quality clothing remain the same. The garments come from cancelled orders, samples and surplus stock from their warehouse in Holland. Own brands include Matinique, Part Two Men and Women, Jackpot and Cottonfield. Discounts range from 10% to 75% on suiting, casual wear, underwear and accessories but it won't be current stock.

Timothy Everest

Bespoke tailor by appointment only
32 Elder Street, Spitalfields, E1
Tel: 020 7377 5770
Website: www.timothyeverest.co.uk
Tube: Liverpool Street
Bus: 67
Open: Mon-Fri 9am-6pm, Sat (telephone appointment)
Timothy Everest create garments that are traditional with a contemporary twist. Their quality bespoke men's suits are cut from a pattern made to the customer's measurements and are then hand sewn and finished. They sell their suits for about half the price of big name Savile Row equivalents, with a two piece starting from around £1,498.

Household Goods

Alma Home

12-14 Greatorex Street, E1
Tel: 020 7377 0762
Tube: Aldgate East
Bus: 25, 67, 205, 253
Open: Mon-Fri 9am-6pm, Sat-Sun 10.30am-4pm

A 60 year old leather company that branched out into making trendy leather and suede home furnishings six years ago. The retail showroom is next to the factory. Enterprising and imaginative in their use of a huge variety of skins, they supply major stores like Liberty, the Conran Shop and Harrods with console tables, cushions, bean-filled stools and cubes and are currently working on producing suede blinds. Mongolian sheepskin rugs cost from £100; seating from £125. They offer regular special promotions at discounts of between 20% and 30% when they have surplus skins to use up. They have just opened a flagship store at 8 Vigo Street, W1, but for the major discounts visit the Greatorex Street branch.

Big Table Furniture Co-op Ltd

56 Great Western Road, W9
Tel: 020 7221 5058
Tube: Westbourne Park
Bus: 23, 28, 31, 328
Open: Mon-Sat 10am-6pm, Thurs 10am-10pm, Sun 12noon-5pm

Although they started off making tables about 18 years ago, the Big Table Furniture Co-op soon found bed frames and mattresses more profitable. They manufacture everything themselves on the premises using Swedish pine with a range of finishes and natural fillings for the mattresses. Prices for single beds start from around £220 (including mattress) with doubles from £325. They can offer lengths of up to 7ft and widths of 6ft. They also make under bed storage units. Brochure available.

Chomette

307 Merton Road, SW18
Tel: 020 8877 7000
Website: www.chomette.co.uk
Tube: Southfields
Bus: 39, 156
Open: Tues-Fri 10am-5pm

This factory outlet next to the main Chomette warehouse is small but well stocked with a wide range of porcelain cookware and tableware, cutlery, glass, non-stick cookware and kitchen knives. The company supplies quality names such as Pillivuyt porcelain and SKK cookware to hotel and retail outlets and sells direct to the public at considerable discounts. Slight seconds and discontinued lines are sold at even greater discounts and they have regular seasonal sales. The shop is not far from Villeroy & Boch and well worth visiting.

The Curtain Fabric Factory

See main entry in Curtains on page 104.

Poetstyle Ltd

Unit 1 Bayford Street Industrial Units,
Bayford Street, Hackney, E8
Tel: 020 8533 0915
Tube: Bethnal Green
Bus: 26, 48, 55, 106, 253, 277, D6
Open: Mon-Fri 8am-5.30pm, Sat 10am-5pm, Sun 10am-2.30pm

Jack Cohen's grandfather started this family upholstery business in the late 19th century. The showroom is in the middle of the factory where, as bespoke upholsterers, they manufacture their own sofas, sofa beds and armchairs. You can specify your own dimensions and supply your own fabric and they also offer a refurbishment service. Sofa beds from £560. A price list and brochure illustrating their thirty or so designs is available.

Price's Patent Candle Co
100 York Road, SW11
Tel: 020 7924 6336
Rail: Clapham Junction
Bus: 44, 49, 295, 319, 344, 345, C3
Open: Mon-Sat 9.30pm-5.30pm, Sun 11am-5pm
This famous candlemaker's has been going for a hundred years and although the Bicester-based firm has several factory shops, this is the only London one, with overstock and end of lines discounted by up to 75 per cent. As well as church candles, fragrance candles, floating candles and outdoor candles, the shop sells accessories such as bowls and lamps.

Taurus Beds
242 Kilburn High Road, NW6
Tel: 020 7624 3024
Website: www.tauruspinebeds.co.uk
Tube: Kilburn
Bus: 16, 32, 189, 316

& 167A Finchley Road, NW6
Tel: 020 7372 1166
Tube: Finchley Road
Bus: 13, 82, 113, 187, 268

Open: Mon-Sat 10am-6pm, Sun 11am-4pm
Taurus have a reputation for great value pine beds, which they have been manufacturing now for over 20 years. A single bed and mattress costs from £198, a double with orthopaedic mattress from £294. Most beds are guaranteed for 5 years. They produce a free colour brochure.

Villeroy & Boch
267 Merton Road, SW18
Tel: 020 8875 6006
Tube: Southfields
Bus: 39, 156
Open: Daily 10am-5pm

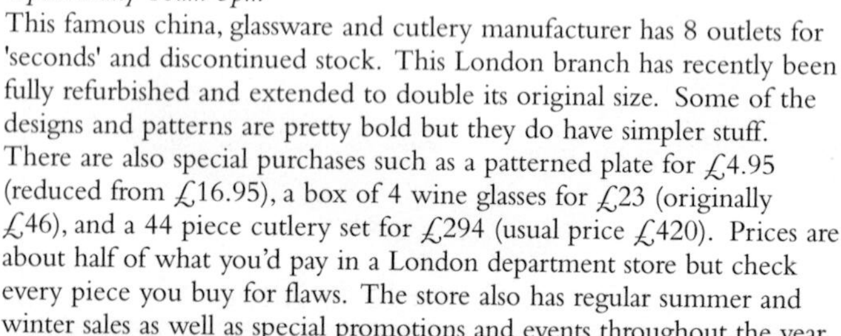

This famous china, glassware and cutlery manufacturer has 8 outlets for 'seconds' and discontinued stock. This London branch has recently been fully refurbished and extended to double its original size. Some of the designs and patterns are pretty bold but they do have simpler stuff. There are also special purchases such as a patterned plate for £4.95 (reduced from £16.95), a box of 4 wine glasses for £23 (originally £46), and a 44 piece cutlery set for £294 (usual price £420). Prices are about half of what you'd pay in a London department store but check every piece you buy for flaws. The store also has regular summer and winter sales as well as special promotions and events throughout the year. *Also at The Galleria, Hatfield (see page 219).*

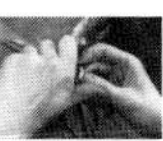

INDEPENDENT DESIGNERS & MANUFACTURERS

FASHION AND TEXTILES

Dragana Perisic
Studio M, 52 Florida Street, E2
E-mail: info@draganaperisic.com
Website: www.draganaperisic.com
Open: 11am-4pm first Sunday of every month, other times by appointment
London based designer Dragana Perisic's work has appeared in fashion magazines from the Guardian, and Elle to BBC television. As well as selling to London's leading boutiques such as Hub (Stoke Newington), Sublime (Victoria Park) and Clusaz (Islington), Dragana hosts open days once a month, selling her collection at reduced prices. Her collection is an eclectic mixture of contemporary cuts and sophisticated fabrics including fine silk dresses, swirling cotton skirts, beautifully tailored jackets and trousers, and individually designed shirts, hand-painted, and accessorised with tiny beads and embroidery. Her studio is within walking distance from Columbia Road and Spitalfields markets, so ideal for a Sunday fashion splurge.

SINE
Cockpit Yard, Northington Street, WC1
Tel: 020 7916 8916
Fax: 020 7916 2455
E-mail: sine@sine-london.co.uk
Website: www.sine-london.co.uk
Open: By appointment
This small workshop makes children's knitwear (ages 0-5 years) from 100% natural fibres: cashmere, camel hair, silk and cotton. All garments are made to order, so you can choose the yarn and design. Prices start at £20 and go up to as much as £150, but given the quality of the clothes and the prices charged for similar items in smart boutiques, this is still great value. Phone in advance to book an appointment.

PICTURE FRAMERS

John Hinds
Clapham, SW8
Tel: 020 7978 2350
Mob: 07958 737242
E-mail: j.rathore@btopenworld.com
Open: By appointment
John Hinds makes quality frames at considerably less than High Street prices. For example, a large oak frame (24" x 20") can be bought from his workshop for only £40.

CERAMICS

Caroline Bousfield Gregory
Workshop, 77A Lauriston Road, E9
Tel: 020 8986 9585
E-mail: caro@carolinebousfield.co.uk
Website: www.carolinebousfield.co.uk
Open: Tues-Wed, Fri-Sat 10.30am-5.30pm, and by appointment
Caroline has been making and selling her own unique stoneware pots, plates, cups and other more unusual items since 1975. Her work has a matt or semi-matt finish and can be used in the oven and dishwasher. Prices start from £5 and go up to £100 for larger more elaborate pieces, with things like a hand-made tea pot for as little as £20.

Kate Malone
Balls Pond Studio,
8B Culford Mews, N1
Tel/Fax: 020 7254 4037
E-mail: kmaloneceramics@clara.co.uk
Open: By appointment
Kate Malone is a highly acclaimed ceramic artist and her work is intricate and colourful. Prices start from £38 for pots and objects in the form of giant fruit and go up to thousands for large public works. Visitors to her studio can purchase items for 10%-20% off the gallery price.

LIGHTING

Extraordinary Design Ltd

311 Chase Road, Southgate, N14
Tel: 020 8886 9020
E-mail: extraordinarydesign@btconnect.com
Website: www.extraordinarydesign.com
Mail Order Service

Extraordinary Design create contemporary lighting products. Their range includes colourful knitted pendant shades, simple printed organza shades and funky chandeliers created from layered transparent acetate. They also do a selection of fun shades including animal pendants suitable for kids' rooms. Their products can be found in independent shops and stores such as John Lewis and Heals with prices ranging from £20 to £235 but visitors to their annual open studio (call/e-mail for details) can purchase discontinued lines and seconds at up to 50% off the retail price. Visitors welcome at other times by appointment.

Helen Rawlinson

The Chocolate Factory,
Unit 5, First Floor, Farleigh Place, N16
Tel/Fax: 020 7503 5839
E-mail: helen_rawlinson@yahoo.co.uk
Website: www.helenrawlinson.com
Open: By appointment
Mail Order

Helen Rawlinson designs and makes fantastic lamps with beech wood stems and hand printed shades in a variety of sizes, colours and designs. Her lamps sell in a number of smart stores, but can be purchased by mail order from her workshop at a discount. Lamps start at £48.

FURNITURE

Alison Cooke

12 The Old Police Station, Commercial Street, Spitalfields, E1
Tel/Fax: 020 7613 3063
Website: www.alisoncooke.co.uk
Open: By appointment

This workshop offers contemporary upholstered furniture and beanbags at about two-thirds of the retail price. Prices start at £150 for a large beanbag and go up to £400. Great value for those looking for contemporary and original furniture.

Moss Brothers Metal Designs

26 Sunbury Workshops,
Swanfield Street, E2
Tel: 020 7739 2361
E-mail: mossbed@dircon.co.uk
Website: www.mossbed.co.uk
Open: By appointment

This company has been producing hand-made steel beds for years and although one of the Moss brothers has moved on, Oliver Moss continues to offer a good range of established designs as well as a bespoke service. A hand-made, solid steel, single bed can be bought here for £325 with kingsize beds starting from only £455. Phone in advance to get a copy of the latest catalogue, or view the beds on the website.

Unto This Last

230 Brick Lane, E2
E-mail: unto@untothislast.co.uk
Website: www.untothislast.co.uk
Open: Sun 10am-6pm or by appointment

Housed in a converted Victorian pub, this Brick Lane workshop makes original, contemporary furniture from birch ply and sells directly to the public at a fraction of the High Street price. Prices start at £35 for an original shelf unit, while the trendy coffee table is also terrific value for £85. All business is conducted via e-mail. Visit the workshop on a Sunday to see their fantastic furniture in the flesh.

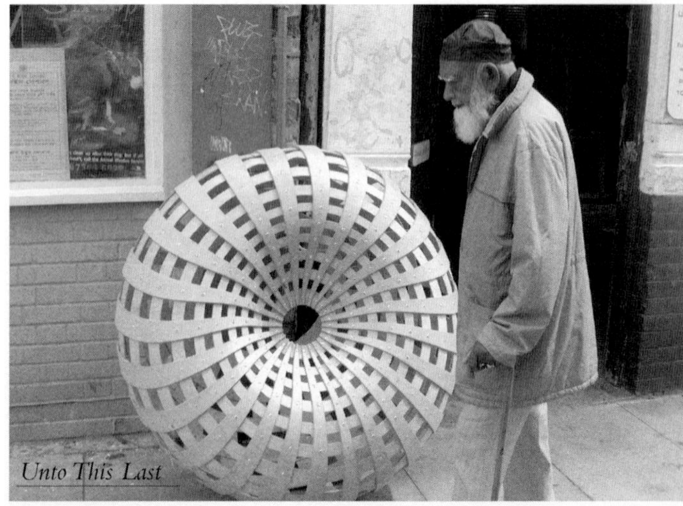

Unto This Last

Clocks

Russell Callow
7 Sunbury Workshops,
Swanfield Street, Shoreditch, E2
Tel/Fax: 020 7729 1211
E-mail: info@russellcallowclocks.com
Website: www.russellcallowclocks.com
Open: By appointment
Russell Callow restores and sells 20th century clocks. There's a wonderful range of unusual timepieces at his workshop; from the kind found on railway platforms, to 70s designs and massive industrial clocks. His clocks are often used by fashion or interior design stylists so there is a possibility you have seen some of his stock within the pages of the glossy style mags. Despite the authentic exteriors, all clocks are fitted with quartz mechanisms which are guaranteed for two years. Prices start from only £25.

Accessories

Janice Derrick
Studio 18, Pennybank Chambers,
33-35 St John's Square, EC1
Tel: 020 7253 1649
E-mail: info@janicederrick.com
Website: www.janicederrick.com
Open: By appointment
Product: Jewellery
Janice designs and makes a wide range of jewellery in silver and gold for both men and women. There is a discount for those who buy directly from the studio with prices ranging from £20 to £2000.

Kate Hodgson
Studio 23, Pennybank Chambers,
33-35 St John's Square, EC1
Tel: 020 7251 1185
Website: www.katehodgson.co.uk
Open: By appointment
Product: Jewellery
Kate designs and makes abstract precious metal jewellery which sells to smart stores like Jess James, Gill Wing and Barneys in New York. Prices start from £26 and go up to as much as £3000. There is a discount for those who buy directly from the studio. Contact Kate about her most recent collections or view her website.

Melissa

Business Centre, Gor-Ray House,
758 Great Cambridge Road, Enfield, EN1
E-mail: melissa@melissa.uk.com
Website: www.melissa.uk.com
Open: Mon-Fri 10.30am-6pm
Product: Handbags, briefcases, leather accessories

Melissa's collection of hand-made leather briefcases, handbags and accessories are both simple and contemporary, ranging from bridle leather bags edged with colour to casual bags using the softest, tactile leathers. Visitors to the workshop can not only see how the bags are made, but have the opportunity to purchase samples and seconds at up to 50% discount and receive a 10% discount on the current collection. Prices range from £28 to £500.

Noa Phillips – Framed

Studio W6, Cockpit Arts, Northington Street, WC12
Tel: 020 7813 4415
E-mail: framed2000@hotmail.com
Tube: Holburn, Chancery Lane
Bus: 38, 55, 45
Product: Eyewear and accessories

Noa makes made to measure luxury eyewear. Her range includes individually designed, hand-made gold and silver glass frames – her recent collection incorporated precious stones and coloured lenses. Visitors to the studio receive a 10%-20% discount and a chance to buy samples and end of lines at up to 50% discount. Noa also designs and sells glasses cases and accessories. Well worth a visit for unique and individual eyewear.

Susse Collection Ltd

Studio 2, 124 Southgate Road, N1
Tel: 020 7249 9094
Website: www.susse.co.uk
E-mail:susse@susse.co.uk
Open: By appointment

Susse Andersen makes a fantastic range of bags and purses. All her products are made with great attention to detail and have a variety of distinctive embroidered patterns. One of her bags is used to illustrate the cover of this book. Susse exhibits at the East London Design Sale, but you can arrange to visit her workshop and get a discount of 30% on the retail price. Susse also offers a bespoke service.

INDEPENDENT WORKSHOP OPEN DAYS

401½ Workshops

401 Wandsworth Road, SW8
Tel: 01865 358832
Website: www.401art.co.uk
Rail: Wandsworth Road
Bus: 77, 77A, 322
Open: Mid-November

This group of workshops holds an annual open weekend in November, showcasing the clothing, jewellery, ceramics, glass and metalwork produced by the thirty artisans occupying the site. Lamps, paintings, furniture and beautifully crafted sculptural vessels and enamelled gold bowls are amongst some of the objects to peruse. It's not exactly prime bargain hunting territory, but the items on sale are unusual and beautiful with some work available at trade prices.

Archway Ceramics Open Studios

410 Haven Mews, 23 St Paul's Way, E3
Tel: 020 8983 1323
Tube: Mile End
Bus: 8, 277, 339, D6, D7
Open: 2nd weekend of December & July, 11am-4pm
Admission Free

Featuring the work of its resident artists and designers, this twice yearly open studio is dedicated entirely to the world of ceramics ranging from contemporary, functional homeware to more figurative, sculptural pieces with prices starting at around £10. Visitors can purchase discontinued lines, samples and seconds at up to 60% off the retail price.

Artists at Home

Various artists' studios in Chiswick,
Hammersmith and Shepherd's Bush, W4, W6, W12
Contact: Joanna Brendon
Tel: 020 8743 5030 Fax: 020 8749 4034
E-mail: aah@joannabrendon.net
Website: www.chiswickw4.com/aah
Tube: Hammersmith, Shepherd's Bush
Bus: 49, 72, 95, 207, 220, 237, 260, 272, 283, 295, 607
Open: Mid-June
Admission Free

An annual artistic highlight in West London attracting visitors from far and wide. AAH is a great opportunity to browse for and purchase original art and design at studio prices and to meet the artists. There are over

40 artists and craftsmen including painters, potters, photographers, textile designers, sculptors and jewellers with prices ranging from a few pounds to several thousand or more! Although AAH is only once a year, individual artists can be contacted at any time.

The Chocolate Factory
Farleigh Place, Stoke Newington, N16
Tel: 020 7503 5839 / 020 7503 7896
Website: www.chocolatefactory.org.uk
Rail: Rectory Road
Bus: 67, 76, 149, 243
Open: November-December and June
This north London studio collective opens its doors to the public twice a year. Within its walls can be found painting, sculpture, ceramics, lighting and fashion. Most items are sold for 20% below the retail price and there are usually quite a few end of lines, and slight seconds for much larger discounts.

Cockpit Arts
Cockpit Yard, Northington Street, WC1
Tel: 020 7419 1959
E-mail: info@cockpitarts.com
Website: www.cockpitarts.com
Tube: Chancery Lane
Bus: 19, 38, 55, 243
Open: 2 open events per year (end of June and November)
The Cockpit is home to over 100 of London's finest and most imaginative artisans representing just about every applied art discipline from furniture-making to textile design, ceramics to jewellery. Doors open to the public twice a year, in the summer and just before Christmas. At these events most items are good value, but there are also samples and end of lines at incredibly low prices. The dates vary from year to year, so contact the central office for the details.

East London Design Show
Tel: 020 8510 9069
Website: www.eastlondondesignshow.co.uk
Now a major biannual event in June and December, the East London Design Show profiles the best of contemporary interior and product design alongside fashion, jewellery and artists' editions. Many designers use the show to launch products and it is a great opportunity to buy direct from the maker. The venue, dates and a full list of exhibitors can be seen on the website.

East London Design Fair

Great Western Open Studios
Lost Goods Building, Great Western Road, W9
Tel: 020 7221 0100
Fax: 020 7221 0200
Tube: Westbourne Park
Bus: 7, 23, 52, 70
E-mail: office@greatwesternstudios.com
Open: Twice yearly, 1st weekend of June and December
Previously a British Rail lost property store, the aptly named Lost Goods Building now houses around 160 fine and applied artists and designers including ceramicists, painters, furniture makers, jewellery and textile designers, to name just a few. These twice yearly open studio events provide the opportunity for visitors to check out what's on offer from some of london's most talented artists and designers – some selling to outlets such as Heals and Habitat – and pick up a bargain among the sample sales, seconds, and end of lines available.

Iliffe Yard & Peacock Yard Open Studios
Iliffe Yard, Crampton Street
& Peacock Yard, Iliffe Street, SE17
Tube: Elephant & Castle
Bus: 1, 53, 63, 172, 188
Open: First weekend of December

Once a year the workshops of Iliffe and Peacock Yards open to the public, with jewellery, designer mirrors, crockery, glassware, furniture, photography and textiles on offer at a fraction of their shop price. This Christmas Fair is a festive event with lashings of mulled wine and mince pies all round.

Made in Clerkenwell

Pennybank Chambers,
33-35 St John's Square, EC1
& Cornwell House, 21 Clerkenwell Green, EC1
Tel: 020 7251 0276
E-mail: info@cga.org.uk
Tube: Farringdon
Bus: 55, 153, 243
Open: Bi-annual weekend event held in June and December
Admission Free

These open weekends are a great opportunity to meet some of the artisans of Clerkenwell in their studios and buy or commission work from them. With around 40 designers and makers participating, visitors to the studio can expect to see a diverse range of work from cutting edge designs, using new techniques and technologies to more traditional, craft methods of production. Ceramics, fashion, jewellery, silversmithing, lighting and textiles are among some of the disciplines represented. Prices range from £10-£300.

Mazorca Projects 'Hidden Art'

Shoreditch Stables, 138 Kingsland Road, E2
Tel: 020 7729 3301
E-mail: info@hiddenart.co.uk
Website: www.hiddenart.com
Tube: Old Street
Bus: 67, 149, 242, 243
Open: Nov/Dec (held over two weekends)
Admission Free

Established in 1994 representing just 13 Hackney based designer makers Mazorca Projects now represent over a 1000 designer-makers in the East London area. Once a year the Hidden Art Event celebrates this rich seam of art and design with open studios and a design fair held in two pavilions at Mile End Park. Call or e-mail for more information about the event including a free map revealing the whereabouts of studios that are normally only open by appointment.

JUNK SHOPS

NORTH

Mr All Sorts

191 Northchurch Road, N1
Tel: 020 7359 1791
Tube: Highbury & Islington
Bus: 38, 56, 73, 341, 476
Open: Mon-Sat 10am-6.30pm

Mr All Sorts has been trading from this small rather run-down shop, just off Essex Road for over 30 years. The stock is a mix of furniture, pictures, mirrors, bric-à-brac and a small selection of books. On a recent visit a simple wooden fireplace was £150 and a modern sink with pedestal was £75. On fine days the stock extends onto the pavement where the owner can often be found sunning himself. A little further along towards Islington there is a small architectural salvage yard which is worth a visit (see The Architectural Forum on page 178).

Cliford's Antiques

8

15 Long Lane, N3
Tel: 020 8343 0084
Tube: Finchley Central
Bus: 82, 125, 260
Open: Mon-Fri 9.30am-4pm, Sat 9am-1pm (ring in advance before visiting)

A quirky, cluttered shop with a reasonable range of furniture, glassware and knick-knacks. It's a fun shop to potter around, but the opening times are irregular to say the least and it is best to phone before making the effort to visit.

Cobwebs

73 Prince of Wales Road, NW5
Tel: 020 4785 1119
Rail: Kentish Town West
Bus: 46, 134, 214, C2
Open: Mon-Sat 11am-6pm

Maureen has been running this little junk shop for over 5 years now, and manages to get her hands on some very attractive items. Among the stock recently was a fine bathroom chest with marble top for £240, a large set of modern bookshelves for £25 and small items like an espresso machine for £4 and a limited selection of books from 50p. The large solid wood chest for £125 was a good buy. Although the stock is not large, there is a fairly fast turnover, so it always pays to have a look around if you're passing.

D & A Binder
101 Holloway Road, N7
Tel: 020 7609 6300
Tube/Rail: Highbury & Islington
Bus: 43, 153, 271
Open: Tues-Sat 10am-5pm

This shop specialises in traditional shop fittings, some of which can look good in the home. Most of the stock consists of traditional glass display cabinets – the sort you find in ancient gentleman's outfitters – but they occasionally sell more practical items of furniture such as desks and picture frames. If you visit the shop don't miss the large back room where many of the larger items are kept.
Also at: 34 Church Street NW8, Tel: 020 7723 0542

Emporium Gallery
6-7 The Mansion, 33 Mill Lane, NW2
Tel: 020 7435 7215
Tube: Kilburn
Bus: 139, 328, C11
Open: Mon-Sat 10am-7.30pm, Sun 2am-8pm
A quirky junk shop which still has some of the fixtures and fittings of the Mexican restaurant that used to occupy this site. There is a good selection of bric-à-brac and pictures to sift through, although opening times are erratic.

Furnishers Ltd
107 Holloway Road, N7
Tube/Rail: Highbury & Islington
Bus: 43, 153, 271
Open: Mon-Sat 11am-7pm
This shop has a limited mix of furniture, books and records, but is particularly good for sofas with about 10 in stock at any time. On a recent visit there was a very nice green velvet three-piece suite for only £150, the other sofas were pretty dire, but for this one suite it was worth a visit. The books and records are great value at 50p and £1 respectively.

Holloway Furniture
141-143 Holloway Road, N7
Tel: 020 7609 0455
Tube/Rail: Highbury & Islington
Bus: 43, 153, 271
Open: Mon-Sat 9am-5pm
This junk shop extends over two shop fronts and on fine days takes up most of the pavement outside. It's probably the cheapest shop in the area with a mixed bag of goods and a fair amount of cheap and tacky furniture as well as the occasional gem. Among the better deals on a recent visit were kids' school chairs for £5, kids' desks for £15 and a few reasonable gas cookers for £85. Always worth a visit and next door to the smarter Ooh-La-La! (see the following page).

Junk
372 Caledonian Road, N1
Tel: 020 7700 3168
Tube: Caledonian Road
Bus: 17, 91, 259, 274
Open: Mon-Sat 9am-6pm
This is a great junk shop with all kinds of things on offer including glassware, furniture, fridges, washing machines and other electrical goods (all with a 6 month guarantee). Bargains on a recent visit included a 1950s Formica kitchen table for £20, filing cabinets from £20, a glass fronted bookcase for £35 and two exercise bikes for £25 each. The smaller items of bric-à-brac are piled in boxes and range in price from 50p to £5. The shop is not large, but the stock spreads out onto the pavement on all sides even on rainy days, making an impressive display for passing traffic.

Junk and Disorderly
129 Stoke Newington Church Street, N16
Tel: 020 7275 7007
Rail: Stoke Newington
Bus: 67, 73, 76, 149, 243
Open: Mon-Sat 10.30am-6pm, Sun 11.30am-6pm
This Stokey institution has undergone some changes in recent years with hardly any furniture now for sale, and a greater concentration on smaller gift items and bric-à-brac. The shop is still well worth a visit with lots of second-hand and slight seconds to sift through. A recent visit unearthed a large sea grass rug (a slight second) for only £10, a large wooden chess-board also for £10, and a box of ethnic cushion covers for £2.50 each. The day of visiting was unusually hot, so the large Chinese fans for only 50p each came in very useful. The shop also sells a reasonable selection of paperback books for around £1 each. A great little shop.

The Junk Yard
121 Marton Road, N16
Tel: 020 7254 9941
Rail: Stoke Newington
Bus: 67, 73, 76, 149, 243
Open: Daily 10.30am-5pm
This ramshackle junk yard offers furniture, electrical goods and bric-à-brac and is a firm favourite with many of the Stokey locals. On fine days the larger items of furniture and the occasional washing machine or fridge are put out on the pavement to encourage passersby. The old school desks stacked-up in the yard for £15-£20 were a good buy. A great shop, well worth a visit if you're in the area.

Olde Hoxton Curios
192 Hoxton Street, N1
Tube/Rail: Old Street
Bus: 67, 149, 242, 243
Open: Tues-Fri 12noon-4.30pm, Sat 10am-4.30pm
This shop offers a well chosen selection of bric-à-brac, pictures, mirrors, books and smaller items of furniture. All the stock is well priced, and although you probably won't find all the things in this eclectic mix to your liking, there is usually something of interest. On a recent visit there was an original dark wood corner unit for only £35, an attractive Chinese style glazed bowl for £6 and a six volume set of the writings of Winston Churchill for a mere £18. Well worth a visit if you're in the area.

Ooh-La-La!
147 Holloway Road, N7
Tel: 020 7609 6021
Tube/Rail: Highbury & Islington
Bus: 43, 153, 271
Open: Mon-Sat 11am-6pm
This shop has undergone something of a transformation in recent years. It still sells quality second-hand and collectable furniture, but has diversified into retro clothing and a small selection of books. The change is a welcome one and gives visitors to the store a lot more to entertain them than the handful of select items of furniture that were once the shop's speciality. Among the bargains on a recent visit were a fantastic, 1970, Scandinavian leather sofa for a reasonable £350, a stylish 1960s office chest made from grey steel and glass for only £45 and a 70s teak coffee table for £35. The clothes and books are kept at the back of the store in a neat area dedicated to their display. The clothes are reasonably priced and there are always garments reduced to clear.

Pandora's Box

358 High Road, Kilburn, NW2
Tube: Kilburn
Bus: 16, 32, 189, 316
Open: Mon-Sat 10am-5pm

This little junk shop offers a limited mix of furniture, clothes and knick-knacks. There is little attempt to prepare or present the stock which is reflected in the cheap prices with things like a scruffy but generally sound chest of drawers for only £20.

Past Caring

76 Essex Road, N1
Tube: Angel
Rail: Essex Road
Bus: 38, 56, 73, 341
Open: Mon-Sat 12am-6pm

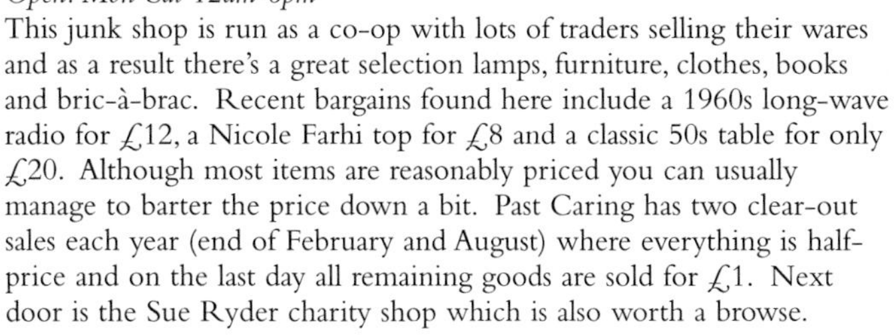

This junk shop is run as a co-op with lots of traders selling their wares and as a result there's a great selection lamps, furniture, clothes, books and bric-à-brac. Recent bargains found here include a 1960s long-wave radio for £12, a Nicole Farhi top for £8 and a classic 50s table for only £20. Although most items are reasonably priced you can usually manage to barter the price down a bit. Past Caring has two clear-out sales each year (end of February and August) where everything is half-price and on the last day all remaining goods are sold for £1. Next door is the Sue Ryder charity shop which is also worth a browse.

D.A. Thompsons

189 Cricklewood Broadway, NW2
Tel: 020 8452 2614
Tube: Kilburn
Bus: 16, 32, 245, 266, 316
Open: Tues-Fri 10am-4pm, Sat 10am-1pm

This junk shop has been around for years. It was once a jewellers and has not only kept the name, but also all the fixtures and fittings which are now used to display bedding, cutlery, bric-à-brac, toys and clothes. The atmosphere inside is a little dark, with the stock piled high, but the staff are friendly and helpful and there are always locals coming in for a chat. In the narrow entrance where once couples would look for engagement rings, stand smaller items of furniture looking for a new home.

Past Caring

WEST

L.H. Cook Furnishers

289 Portobello Road, W10
Tel: 020 8969 3458
Tube: Ladbroke Grove
Bus: 7, 23, 52, 70
Open: Mon-Sat 10am-6pm

This established shop sells a mix of new and modern used furniture as well as second-hand fridges and washing machines. The pine bookshelf found here recently for £29 was good value as was the Samsung fridge freezer for £98.

The Furniture Exchange

3

42 Shepherd's Bush Road, W6
Tel: 020 7602 7865
Tube: Hammersmith, Shepherd's Bush
Bus: 72, 220, 283, 295
Open: Mon-Sat 9am-6pm

There is not, in fact, very much furniture at this shop, but they do have a good choice of second-hand fridges, cookers and washing machines. On a recent visit they had a top quality AEG Lavamat washing machine for only £150. Electrical goods come with a 1 month guarantee.

Golborne Furniture

99 Golborne Road, W10
Tel: 020 8969 8399
Tube: Ladbroke Grove
Bus: 7, 23, 52, 70, 295
Open: Mon-Sat 9am-5.30pm

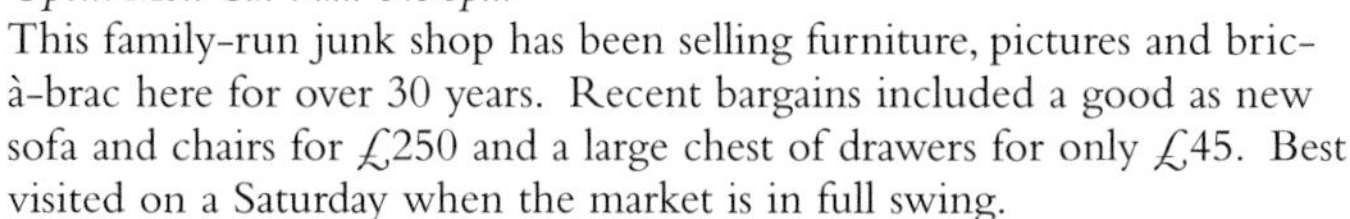

This family-run junk shop has been selling furniture, pictures and bric-à-brac here for over 30 years. Recent bargains included a good as new sofa and chairs for £250 and a large chest of drawers for only £45. Best visited on a Saturday when the market is in full swing.

Great Expectations

115 Shepherd's Bush Road, W6
Tel: 020 7603 2376
Tube: Hammersmith, Shepherd's Bush
Bus: 72, 220, 283, 295
Open: Daily 11am-6pm

This family-run, Hammersmith institution is easily the best junk shop in the area and is always busy with locals popping in for a chat and to have a look around. Among the stock you will find furniture, bric-à-brac, pictures, electrical goods, CDs, vinyl and videos. The bright red chest was a good buy for only £25 and behind the piles of smaller items was concealed a large pine kitchen table for a mere £90. The café next door is an ideal place to inspect your latest purchase and enjoy a bacon butty.

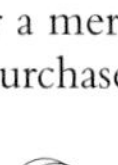

Ollies

69 Golborne Road, W10
Tel: 07768 790 725
Tube: Westbourne Park
Bus: 7, 23, 28, 31, 52, 70, 295, 328
Open: Tues-Sat 9am-5pm

This shop sells more designer retro than junk, but is still worth having a look around when you're in the area. The furniture is very well chosen and sold at a reasonable rather than a bargain price.

Les Couilles du Chien

65 Golborne Road, W10
Tel: 020 8968 0099
Tube: Westbourne Park
Bus: 7, 23, 28, 31, 52, 70, 295, 328
Open: Mon-Thurs 9am-5.30pm, Fri 8am-5.30pm, Sat 9.30am-5.30pm

This funky shop offers a good range of 20th century furniture, ornaments and lighting. The stock is very collectable and therefore prices are a good deal higher than the genuine junk shop, but still great value when you compare with smarter design shops.

South

Bambino's
32 Church Road, Crystal Palace, SE19
Tel: 020 8653 9250
Rail: Crystal Palace
Bus: 2, 3, 63, 122, 157, 202, 227, 249, 322, 358
Open: Thurs-Sat 12noon-6pm
This traditional junk shop offers a real mix of things from vintage leather jackets to funky retro furniture and smaller items of bric-à-brac. Among the interesting things uncovered on a recent visit was a leather desk chair for only £65 and two large chrome frame leather chairs for £100 the pair – which was great value even though they needed some attention. If you have a more limited budget they have lots of smaller knick-knacks to sift through for as little as £1. A great shop and just down the road from Enigma and Renaissance Bookshops (see bookshop section on page 154).

Cosmic Gaze
148 Maple Road, Penge, SE20
Rail: Penge West
Bus: 176, 227, 312, 351
Open: 10.30m-4.30pm, Sat 10am-5pm (closed Wed)
This shop doesn't have a sign, but is easy to spot with its regular pavement displays of furniture, chandeliers and bric-à-brac. One of the best junk shops in the capital and worth making an effort to visit given that Maple Road boasts several other junk shops, a car boot sale on Saturdays and a market on most days.

The Junk Box
151 Trafalgar Road, Greenwich SE10
Tel: 020 8293 5715
Rail/DLR: Greenwich
Bus: 177, 180, 188, 286, 386
Open: Mon-Wed, Fri 10am-5pm, Thurs 11.30am-5pm,
Sat-Sun 11am-5pm
This unusually tidy and well-ordered little shop offers all kinds of furniture, pictures, ornaments and glassware for the home. The shop belongs to the nearby Greenwich Auction Rooms and it is the auction that provides the stock. Most of the goods are keenly priced with very few items for over a tenner. A great place to rummage for bargains in the heart of Greenwich.

The Junk Shop
9 Greenwich South Street, SE10
Tel: 020 8305 1666 ext 25
Website: www.spreadeagle.org
Rail/DLR: Greenwich
Bus: 180, 199
Open: Daily 10am-5pm
This shop has a good mix of furniture, pictures and other decorative items. In addition they also have a large yard of larger architectural and antique items – things like old paving, railings and antique garden furniture. They pride themselves on being very competitively priced with a high turn-over of stock, making it worth a regular visit.

EAST

Arch 31
Arch 31, Grimsby Street, E1
Tel: 07747 122 515
Tube: Shoreditch
Bus: 8, 67, 388
Open: Wed and Sat 12noon-7pm, Sun 8am-7pm
This junk shop occupies two large railway arches just off Brick Lane. It specialises in furniture and has over 50 items at any time. Among the stock recently were five large 1960s kitchen cupboards for about £90 each, a massive ancient wooden chest for £150, and a selection of large filing cabinets for £35. This is one of the largest second-hand furniture outlets in London and they offer free local delivery. The old damp railway arches are under constant threat from developers, let's hope this shop manages to stick around.

Bacon Street Junk Shop

14 Bacon Street, E1
Tube: Shoreditch
Bus: 8, 67, 388
Open: Daily 9am-5pm

This large junk shop has all kinds of things for sale from its dark railway arch lock-up, just off Brick Lane. Among the bargains were a vast selection of cast-iron casserole dishes for £10 each, gas cookers (with 6 month guarantee) for £95, LPs for £1 and paperback books for only 50p. This is a great place to potter around and well worth a visit if you're in the area.

Beedell Coram Antiques

7 Lamb Street, Spitalfields, E1
Tel: 020 7377 1195
Tube: Liverpool Street
Bus: 67
Open: Wed-Fri 12noon-4.30pm, Sun 9am-5.30pm

Situated in Spitalfields Market this shop has its fair share of antiques, but there is enough bric-à-brac to justify its inclusion this section. Recent bargains unearthed included a box of old pictures of London from 50p each, an old carpenter's saw for only £3 and a rather ornate mirror for £60. This is a great shop for pottering around and there is a basement and several tables outside selling second-hand books (see books section for more details). On a recent visit they were playing an album from The Incredible String Band, which gives some indication of the quirky nature of the place.

Dublin Jim

64 Sclater Street, E1
Tel: 07973 742 585
Tube: Liverpool Street
Bus: 8, 67, 388
Open: Mon-Fri 7.30am-6pm, Sun 5.30am-4.30pm

This shop is located smack in the middle of Brick Lane Market and is probably best visited when the market is in full flow on a Sunday. It is open during the week if you're in the area and has a reasonable selection of all kinds of furniture and office equipment. Among the bargains on a recent visit were monitors for £10, carpet tiles for 50p each and office chairs for between £10 and £20.

Evil Cathedral (11)
24 Grimsby Street, E1
Tel: 07932 439 050
Tube: Shoreditch
Bus: 67, 388
Open: Wed-Fri 1.30pm-6.30pm, Sat-Sun 9am-8pm
This huge railway arch has the best name of any junk shop, but unfortunately it isn't on the entrance. The stock on a recent visit included LPs for £2-£10, jeans for £5-£60 and a few bikes including a very good Brompton for £250. There were also some very unusual items such as an old rocket from a merry-go-round and several large plastic Burger King signs. The interior is very dark and damp, but it's still a fun place to wonder around.

Lazy Days
21 Mare Street, E8
Tel: 07816 323 848 (Charlie), 07957 984 611 (Paul)
Tube: Bethnal Green
Bus: 26, 48, 55, 106, 253, D6
Open: Mon-Fri 9am-5pm, Sat 9am-2pm
This junk shop has been going for over 14 years, and is a great place to find all kinds of furniture for the home and office. Among the bargains on a recent visit were a large chest of drawers for £25, 4 drawer filing cabinets for £30 and a set of golf clubs and bag for a mere £30. The shop is best visited on fine days when the stock is displayed on the wide pavement outside.

New & Second Hand Furniture
24/26 Amhurst Road, E8
Tel: 020 8533 1102
Rail: Hackney Central
Bus: D6, W15
Open: Mon-Sat 9am-6pm
This is an unassuming junk shop with a fair amount of cheap and tacky furniture, but also the occasional quality item and a reasonable selection of cookers for £100-£150. A recent visit unearthed a large angle-poise lamp for only £12. Worth visiting if you are in the area, particularly if you're looking for good value cooker.

Markets

Alfies Antique Market, W2
13-25 Church Street, Marylebone
Tube: Edgware Road
Bus: 6, 16, 98, 139, 189
Open: Tues-Sat 10am-6pm
Alfies is the UK's largest indoor antique market with over five floors of antique, vintage and retro goods supplied by nearly 100 dealers. There are enough bargains here to make it worth a visit and there is a roof-top restaurant should you feel peckish.

Bermondsey, SE1
Bermondsey Square, (between Abbey Street, Bermondsey Street and Tower Bridge Street)
Tube: Borough/London Bridge
Rail: London Bridge
Bus: 42, 78, 188 (Tower Bridge Street); 1, 78 (Grange Road)
Open: Fridays 5am-1pm
Bermondsey Market is the largest antiques market in the capital and attracts antique dealers from across Europe. Members of the public are welcome, but you should be prepared to get there before dawn to see the market in full swing. Most of the dealers know the value of their stock and you are unlikely to find fine antiques at a huge discount, savings are more likely on the lower value bric-à-brac to be found here. If you do go early, take a torch.

Brick Lane, E1& E2

Brick Lane (north of the railway bridge), Bethnal Green Road (from Brick Lane to Commercial Street), Cheshire and Sclater Street (see map, page 269 for details)
Tube: Aldgate East, Liverpool Street, Old Street, and Shoreditch
Bus: 8, 25, 67, 205, 253, 388
Open: Sunday 6am-1pm

Brick Lane Market is always changing and at the moment the building development on Sclater Street has forced even more of the itinerant traders onto the narrow pavement on Bethnal Green Road. It is here that lots of the bargains in bric-à-brac, bikes, books, clothing and electrical goods can be found. Everything here is cheap and it's just a matter of sorting through the piles of stuff to unearth something of interest. If this part of the market hasn't exhausted you then walk east along Sclater and Cheshire Street. Both streets are packed with stalls selling new clothes, tools, fruit and veg and shoes, but there are lots of courtyards and archways along the route which feature more unusual used goods. The Bagel Bakery at the top of Brick Lane is always popular for refreshments as is Coffee @ Brick Lane which is just a few doors down.

Brixton, SW9

Brixton Station Road, Pope's Road, Atlantic Road,
Electric Road and Electric Avenue
Tube/Rail: Brixton
Bus: 109, 118, 196, 250, 355, P4
Open: Mon-Sat 8am-5.30pm, Wed 8am-1pm

For those more interested in bargain hunting than food shopping Brixton Station Road is the most rewarding part of this market, which gets interesting after the junction with Pope's Road, where all the second-hand stalls are located.

Camden, NW1 (1)

Camden High Street
(North of Camden Town tube)
Tube: Camden Town, Chalk Farm
Bus: 24, 27, 29, 31, 46, 88, 134, 168, 214, 253, C2
Open: Sat-Sun 9am-5pm (all parts of the market),
Thurs-Fri 9am-5pm (about half the market)

Camden is not just one market but several, each with different opening hours and each specialising in different merchandise. The market opposite Inverness Street is called Camden Market and is a good place to find cheap new and used clothes, it is also open on Thursday and Friday if you want to avoid the weekend crush. Camden Lock is another major part of the market and has stalls selling anything from books to designer and retro clothing. Prices can be high, but if you hunt around you can usually find some interesting things for less than you might expect. The most interesting part of the market for the determined bargain hunter is the Stables Market which is situated in the most northerly part of the market but regrettably is only open at the weekends. It is here that the majority of the junky second-hand stuff is sold. If you want to avoid the crowds use Chalk Farm tube station and walk south.

Camden Passage, N1

On the junction of Essex Road and Upper Street, opposite Islington Green, N1
Tube: Angel
Bus: 38, 56, 73, 341 (Essex Road); 4, 19, 33, 43 (Upper Street)
Open: Wed 7am-2pm, Sat 8am-4pm (Antiques)
Thursdays 10am-4.30pm (Books), Sunday 10am-2pm (Farmers' Market)

This market is not in Camden, but Islington. The antiques market is not as cheap as Bermondsey Market, but it's usually possible to pick a few bargains. The best place to look is along the passage outside the Camden Head pub, where traders sell bric-à-brac on the pavement. The book market on Thursdays is small with just a few regular stalls, but lots of bargains.

Greenwich, SE10

Greenwich Church Street, Stockwell Street, Greenwich High Road
Rail/DLR: Greenwich
Bus: 177,180, 188, 199, 286, 386
Open: Sat-Sun 9.30am-5pm
Wed-Fri 9am-5pm (Crafts Market within the Charter Market)
Thurs 9.30am-5pm (Collectables Market within the Charter Market)

Greenwich is a huge market and one of the best for books, furniture, fashion and bric-à-brac. It is not as fashionable or as busy as Camden and for that reason it's generally a little cheaper than its north London rival. The best parts of the market are the Antiques Market on Greenwich High Road and the Central Market on Stockwell Road both of which are good for second-hand things.

Kingsland Waste, E8

Kingsland Waste, Kingsland Road (between Forest and Middleton Road)
Rail: Dalston Kingsland
Bus: 67, 149, 242, 243
Open: Sat 9am-5pm

This market is a bit rough and ready with lots of junk, used electrical goods and books sold on an unprepossessing stretch of Kingsland Road. Despite the lack of scenery, this is good bargain hunting terrain.

Leather Lane, EC1
Leather Lane between Clerkenwell Road and Greville Street
Tube: Chancery Lane, Farringdon
Bus: 55, 243, (Clerkenwell); 17, 45, 46, 341 (Gray's Inn Road)
Open: Mon-Fri 10.30am-2pm
Leather Lane is one of London's lunch-time markets, much frequented by the office workers of Clerkenwell. There are no second-hand goods sold here, but lots of contemporary smart and street fashion at below shop prices. If you can, visit in the morning before it gets too busy.

Merton Abbey Mills, SW19
Off Merantun Way, behind the Savacentre, South Wimbledon
Tube: Colliers Wood
Bus: 57, 152, 155, 200, 219
Open: Sat-Sun 10am-5pm, Thurs 6am-12pm (antiques and collectables)
This weekend market is a pleasant place to visit with the river Wandle flowing by and a good few places to eat and drink. Besides the entertainment value there are also quite a few independent designers who sell their clothing or jewellery here at below the usual price. If you're looking for antiques, visit on a Thursday when the market is given over to antiques and collectables.

Petticoat Lane, E1
Middlesex Street and Wentworth Street, and adjacent streets and lanes
Tube: Aldgate, Aldgate East, Liverpool Street
Bus: 42, 78, 100, 205 (Houndsditch Minories)
8, 26, 35, 43, 47, 48, 78, 149, 242, 388 (Liverpool Station)
Open: All streets Sun 9am-2pm
Petticoat Lane is a vast market, but doesn't sell any used goods which makes it less interesting than nearby Spitalfields and Brick Lane markets. Still if you're on the hunt for new street fashion, shoes, bags or leather goods this is a useful place to visit.

Portobello, W11

Portobello Road (from and including Golborne Road to Chepstow Villas)
Tube: Ladbroke Grove, Notting Hill Gate
Bus: 12, 70, 94, 148 (Notting Hill Gate); 31, 27, 28, 31, 328 (Pembridge Road); 70, 7 (Westbourne Park Road); 7, 23, 52, 70 (Ladbroke Grove)
Open: Sat 8am-5.30pm (Antiques), Mon-Sat 9am-5pm (General Market), Sun 9am-1pm (Car Boot Sale)

Portobello Road is at its most crowded and generally most expensive south of the Westway as most tourists approach it from Notting Hill tube station. To avoid the worst of the crowds and find the best bargains try approaching the market from Ladbroke Grove station. The best of the bric-à-brac, used clothing and second-hand books can be found on the narrow streets running alongside the Westway and under the canopy at the junction with Portobello Road. If you still have the energy walk north along Portobello Road to Golborne Road where there are lots of junk shops (see Junk Shops section on pages 242-43) and more stalls selling bric-à-brac.

Roman Road, E3

Roman Road (from St Stephen's Road to Parnell Road)
Tube: Mile End
Bus: 8, D6 (Roman Road); 277, 339, D6 (Grove Road)
Open: Tues, Thurs and Sat 8.30am-5.30pm

Roman Road is a great value East End market which is at its busiest and best on a Saturday. Look out for the stall at the far end of the market which specialises in slight seconds from established labels like French Connection.

Spitalfields Market, E1

West side of Commercial Street between Folgate and Brushfield Street
Tube: Liverpool Street
Bus: 67, 242, 388 (Commercial Street);
8, 26, 35, 43, 47, 48, 78, 149 (Liverpool Station)
Open: Sun 11am-3pm (main Sunday market)

The back part of this market is being redeveloped, but the front part is still a massive indoor space housed in an atmospheric purpose-built Victorian iron building. There's a wide range of bargains to be found here, from designer and vintage clothing, to furniture and bric-à-brac. Sunday is the best time to visit, when the market is in full swing.

Car Boot Sales

Battersea, SW8
New Covent Garden Market, Nine Elms Lane, Battersea
Sundays 8am-2.30pm (set up 7am)
Cars from £7, Vans from £10
250 pitches
Contact: Bray Associates
Tel: 01895 639912/637269

Battersea Technology Centre, SW8
Battersea Park Road
Every Sunday 1.30pm-5pm
Cars £8, Vans £10
Tel: 07941 383 588

Bounds Green, N22
Nightingale School, Bounds Green Rd
Sundays 7am-1pm (6am set up)
Cars £9, Vans £15
250 pitches
Contact: Red Arrows
Tel: 020 8889 9017

Brunswick Indoor Market, SW6
St Thomas's Way, Fulham
Tube: Fulham Broadway
Every Saturday 8am till 3pm (set up from 6.30am)
Large table £12, own table £10
Booking requested and advised
Free phone: 0800 389 9634 or
Contact: Paula 0773 9145 149

Chiswick, W4
Chiswick Community School, Burlington Lane
First Sunday of month (except Jan), 7am-1pm (set up from 7am)
Cars £8, Vans £15
200 pitches
Tel: 020 8995 4063

Colney Hatch, N10
Skate Attack Field, Opposite Tesco (A406)
Alternate Sundays 2pm-6pm (also Bank Holidays 1pm-5pm)
Cars £9, Vans £15
200 pitches
Contact: Red Arrows
Tel: 020 8889 9017

Greenford, Middlesex, UB6
Ravenor School, Rosedene Avenue
One Saturday per month, 12am-2pm
Cars £8, Vans £10
100 pitches
Tel: 020 8578 6169

Hackney Wick, E15
Hackney Wick Greyhound Stadium, Waterden Road
Every Sunday from 6am-2pm
Cars from £10
(Just turn-up on the day)
500 pitches

Hayes, Middlesex, UB3
Hayes FC, Church Road
Every Wednesday & Friday 8am-2pm (set up 7am)
Cars £15, No Vans
70 pitches
Tel: 01494 520 513

Holloway, N7
Seven Sisters Rd (behind McDonalds)
Saturdays 8am-4pm, Sundays 10am-2.30pm
Cars from £8
100 pitches
Tel: 01992 717198

Hounslow, Middlesex
Hounslow West Station Car Park
Sunday 7.30am-2pm (set up 7am)
Cars from £7, Vans from £10
75 pitches
Contact: Bray Associates
Tel: 01895 639912/637269

Hounslow, Middlesex
Hounslow Heath Garden Centre, Staines Road
Sundays & Bank Holidays, 6am-approx 1pm
Cars £8, small trailers £2, small vans £9, transit vans £10, large vans £15
250 pitches
Tel: 020 8890 3485

Kilburn, NW6
St Augustine's School, Oxford Road
Saturdays 11am-4pm, (set up 8am)
Cars £9, Vans £16
100 pitches
Tel: 020 8442 0082

The Lee Valley Market Site, N18
Harbet Road, Edmonton
Every Sunday 6am-1pm
Cars £9, Vans £15
Tel: 01992 638664

Penge and Crystal Palace, SE20
Maple Road, Penge
Saturdays 9am-3pm (set up 8am)
Cars £9, Vans £12
100 pitches
Tel: 020 7263 6010

Portobello Road, W11
Under the Westway canopy on Portobello Road
Every Sunday 9am-4pm (set up 8am)
Cars and vans from £12
200 pitches
Contact: Country Wide
Tel: 01562 777 877

Ruislip, Middlesex
Queensmead Sports Centre, Victoria Road South
Saturdays 7am-2pm (May-Sept)
Cars £10, Vans £12
300 pitches
Contact: Irene Calver
Tel: 020 8561 4517

Seven Sisters, N15
Earlsmead School, Broad Lane
Saturdays 7am-1pm (set up 6am)
Cars £9, Vans £15
150 pitches
Contact: Red Arrows
Tel: 020 8889 9017

Shepherd's Bush, W12
BBC Overflow Car Park, Wood Lane
Saturdays & Sundays 11am-4pm (set up 9am)
Cars £10, Vans from £12
100 pitches
Contact: Heather 020 7724 1109

Tottenham, N17
Tottenham Community Sports Centre, Tottenham High Road
Thursdays from 7am
Cars £8, Vans £10
40 pitches
Contact: Countryside Promotions
Tel: 01992 468 619
www.countrysidepromotions.co.uk

Tottenham, N15
Earls Mead School, Broad Lane
Saturdays 7am-1pm (set up 6am)
Cars £9, Vans £15
150 pitches
Contact: Red Arrows
Tel: 020 8889 9017

Wood Green, N22
New River Sports Centre, White Hart Lane
Fridays from 6am
Cars £9, Vans £11
60 pitches
Contact: Countryside Promotions
Tel: 01992 468619
www.countrysidepromotions.co.uk

Woolwich, SE18
Beresford Square, Woolwich Town Centre
Sundays 9am-2pm (set up 7am)
Cars £10, Vans £12
250 pitches
Tel: 020 7263 6010

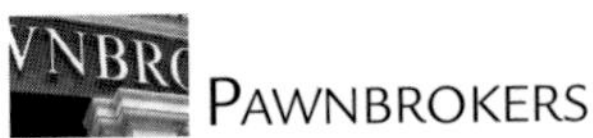

PAWNBROKERS

Cash Converters

Branches at:

286-292 Camberwell Road, SE5
Tel: 020 7277 4424

141-145 Kentish Town Road, NW1
Tel: 020 7482 2000 1

127 Fore Street, N18
Tel: 020 8345 5900

238-240 North End Road, SW6
Tel: 020 7381 6046 7

292-294 Lewisham High St, SE13
Tel: 020 8690 9800

159 High Street, Penge, SE20
Tel: 020 8776 5544

797-801 High Road, Leyton, E10
Tel: 020 8558 7776

363-365 Green Lanes, N13
Tel: 020 8886 4566

12-14 St James St, Walthamstow, E17
Tel: 020 8521 5550

33-35 Hare Street, Woolwich, SE18
Tel: 020 8316 0989

Open: Times vary, most branches are open Mon-Sat 10am-5.30pm
Cash Converter stores are run on a franchise basis and therefore the style of the shop, the range of second-hand goods on offer and the guarantee varies from store to store. Most shops offer a reasonable range of second-hand cameras, electronic goods, sports equipment and bikes.

Cash Exchange

352 Holloway Road, N7
Tel: 020 7609 2022
Tube: Holloway Road
Bus: 43, 153, 271
Open: Mon-Sat 10am-5.45pm
This large shop offers a wide variety of second-hand valuables at very competitive prices. Items on offer include hi-fi's, bikes, musical instruments, computers, camcorders, mobile phones and cameras. All goods come with a two month guarantee.

Cash Express

140-144 Uxbridge Road, W13
Tel: 020 8840 1400
Tube: Northfield or Ealing Broadway
Bus: 65, 112, 297, E1, E7-10, PR1
Open: Mon-Sat 10am-5.30pm
Formerly a branch of Cash Converters, this shop offers a good selection of hi-fi's, TVs, bikes, cameras and much more.

Cash XChange

303 Kilburn High Road, NW6
Tel: 020 7625 1298
Tube: Kilburn
Bus: 16, 32, 189, 316
Open: Mon-Sat 10.30am-6.30pm

This is one of the best pawnbrokers in London to find all manner of cameras, computers, hi-fi separates, TVs, videos and power tools. Among the bargains on a recent visit was a Goldstar video recorder for only £35 and a Technics tape player for £45. They also have a large collection of CDs with an offer of 2 CDs for £5 and 6 CDs for only £10. A great shop for second-hand bargains.

The Enfield Stock Exchange

9-10 Savoy Parade,
Southbury Road,
Enfield, EN1
Tel: 020 8366 5520
Rail: Enfield Town
Bus: 329, 377, W8, W9
Open: Mon-Sat 9.30am-5.30pm

This shop offers a good selection of bikes all of which are slight factory seconds, computers and computer games, hi-fi's, cameras, TVs and musical instruments. The shop also loans money on goods and offers a cheque cashing facility for a charge of 4%-6%.

Price Co.

130 Uxbridge Road,
Shepherd's Bush Green, W12
Tel: 020 8746 1309
Tube: Shepherd's Bush
Bus: 49, 95, 207, 237, 260, 272, 607
Open: Mon-Sat 10am-7pm, Sun 1-7pm

This pawnbrokers offers a wide selection of electronic goods, bikes, sports gear, videos and CDs, books and clothes. The place is always busy and all items are very competitively priced with regular promotions. Recently they had a 21" colour TV for only £60 and were offering any three items of clothing for £5. Smaller items such as mobile phones, walkmans, cameras and watches are all displayed in the window with mobile phones starting from as little as £20. A great shop for bargain hunting.

Shopping Areas

1. Camden
2. Islington
3. Hammersmith & Shepherd's Bush
4. Portobello
5. Kensington Church Street
6. Wandsworth & Putney
7. Fulham
8. Finchley
9. Golders Green
10. Kilburn
11. Brick Lane

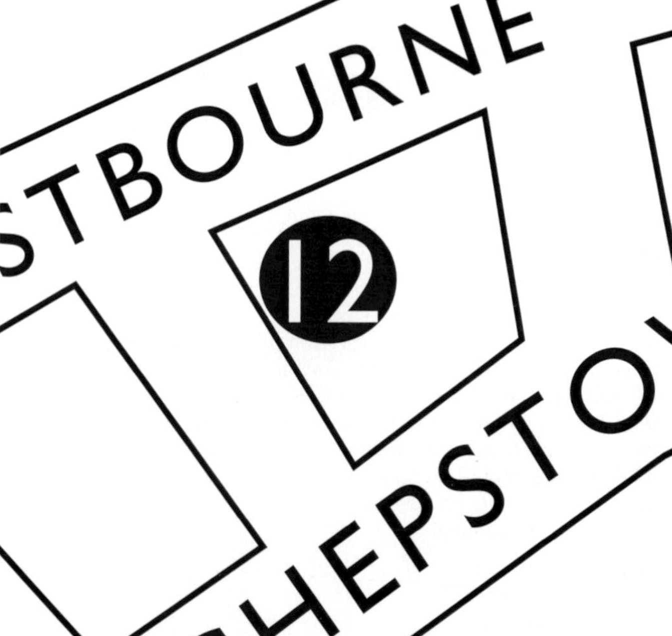

1. CAMDEN

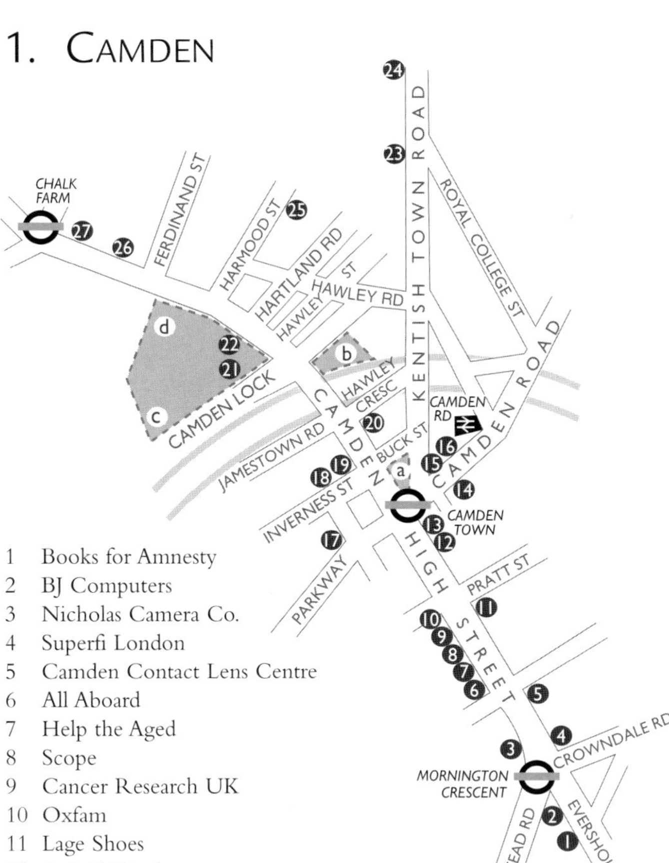

1 Books for Amnesty
2 BJ Computers
3 Nicholas Camera Co.
4 Superfi London
5 Camden Contact Lens Centre
6 All Aboard
7 Help the Aged
8 Scope
9 Cancer Research UK
10 Oxfam
11 Lage Shoes
12 A & K Warehouse
13 Atlantic Clothing
14 Mind
15 Supersport Shoe Warehouse
16 Leyland Paint
17 Camden Camera Centre
18 Out On The Floor
19 Rokit
20 Music and Video Exchange
21 Henry & Daughter
22 Up the Video Junction
23 Cash Converters
24 Oxfam
25 Walden Books
26 Reject Pot Shop
27 Modern Age Vintage Clothing
(a) Camden Market
(b) Canal Market
(c) Camden Lock Market
(d) Stables Market

2. Islington

1 Dress for Less
2 Oxfam
3 Cancer Research UK
4 Blue Audio Visual
5 Reckless Records
6 Bargain Centre
7 Seconda Mano
8 Salvation Army Charity Shop
9 Flashback
10 Sue Ryder
11 Past Caring
12 Sew Fantastic
13 Comfort & Joy
14 Haggle Vinyl
15 Computer Precision
16 Beller's
17 Marie Curie Cancer Research
(a) Chapel Market
(b) Camden Passage

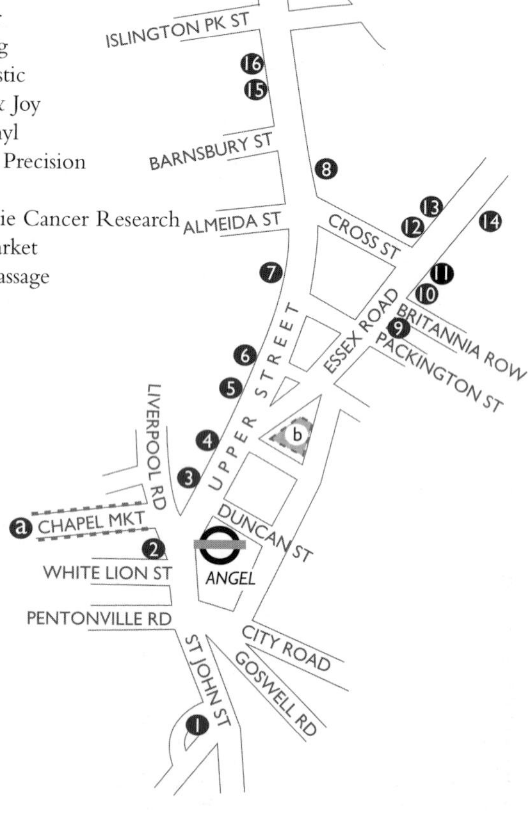

3. HAMMERSMITH & SHEPHERD'S BUSH

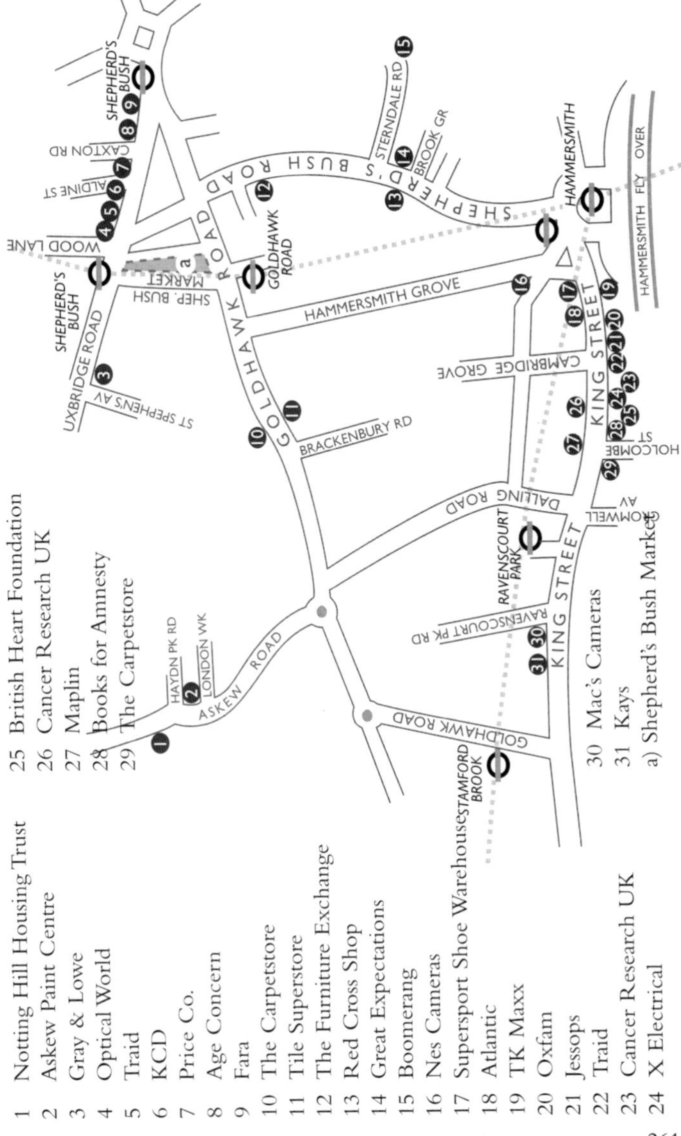

1 Notting Hill Housing Trust
2 Askew Paint Centre
3 Gray & Lowe
4 Optical World
5 Traid
6 KCD
7 Price Co.
8 Age Concern
9 Fara
10 The Carpetstore
11 Tile Superstore
12 The Furniture Exchange
13 Red Cross Shop
14 Great Expectations
15 Boomerang
16 Nes Cameras
17 Supersport Shoe Warehouse
18 Atlantic
19 TK Maxx
20 Oxfam
21 Jessops
22 Traid
23 Cancer Research UK
24 X Electrical
25 British Heart Foundation
26 Cancer Research UK
27 Maplin
28 Books for Amnesty
29 The Carpetstore
30 Mac's Cameras
31 Kays
a) Shepherd's Bush Market
SHEPHERD'S BUSH
CAXTON RD
ALDINE ST
WOOD LANE
SHEP. BUSH MARKET
UXBRIDGE ROAD
ST STEPHEN'S AV
SHEPHERD'S BUSH ROAD
STERNDALE RD
BROOK GR
GOLDHAWK ROAD
HAMMERSMITH GROVE
HAMMERSMITH
HAMMERSMITH FLY OVER
GOLDHAWK ROAD
BRACKENBURY RD
CAMBRIDGE GROVE
KING STREET
HOLCOMBE ST
DALLING ROAD
CROMWELL AV
RAVENSCOURT PARK
RAVENSCOURT PK RD
KING STREET
HAYDN PK RD
LONDON WK
ASKEW ROAD
GOLDHAWK ROAD
STAMFORD BROOK

4. PORTOBELLO

1. WaMa Computer Services Ltd
2. Traid
3. Oxfam
4. Boo's Closet
5. Film Plus
6. Nu-Line
7. Marie Curie Cancer Research
8. Buyers & Sellers
9. Crazy Clothes Connection
10. Bedstock@Puppy
11. L.H. Cook Furnishers
12. Honest Jon's Records
13. The Cloth Shop
14. Golborne Furniture
15. Portobello Bookshop
16. London Camera Repair
17. Ollies
18. Les Couilles du Chien
19. Hot & Cold

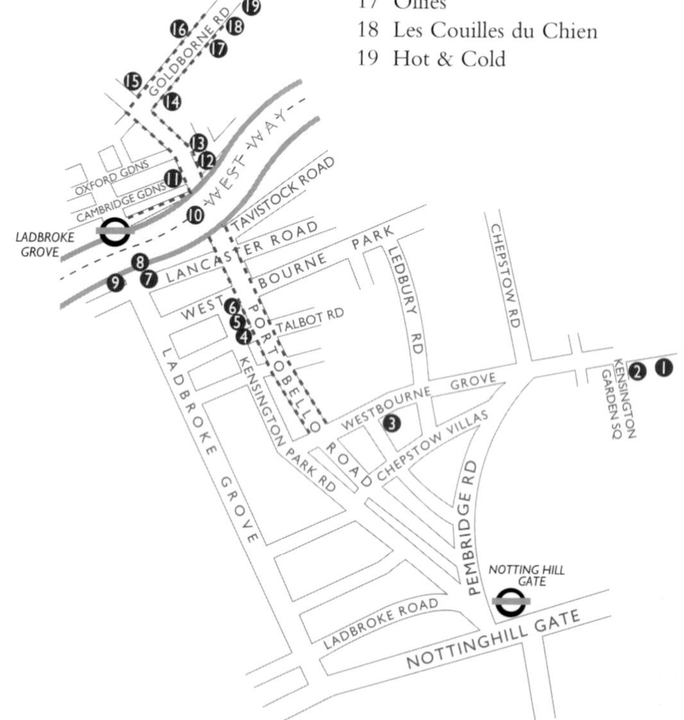

5. Kensington Church Street

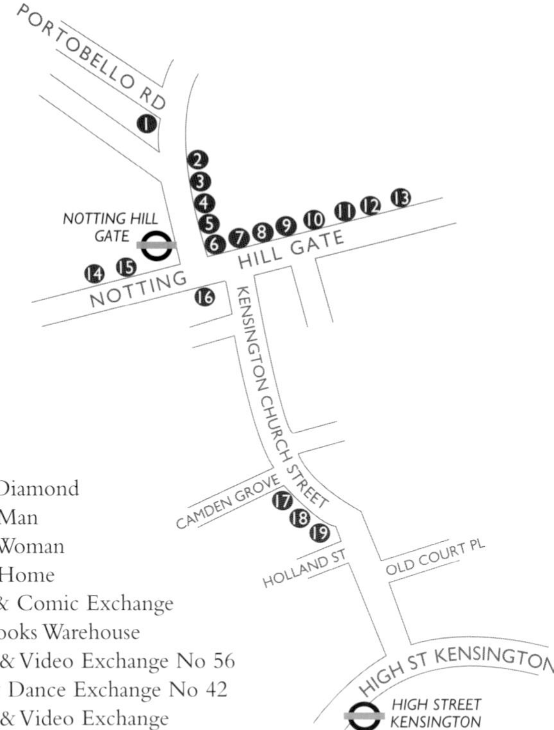

1 Dolly Diamond
2 Retro Man
3 Retro Woman
4 Retro Home
5 Book & Comic Exchange
6 The Books Warehouse
7 Music & Video Exchange No 56
8 Soul & Dance Exchange No 42
9 Music & Video Exchange (Singles & Memorabilia) No 40
10 Music & Video Exchange No 38
11 Classical Music Exchange No 36
12 Stage and Screen
13 Trinity Hospice Shop
14 Oxfam
15 Futon Company
16 Notting Hill Housing Trust
17 Notting Hill Housing Trust
18 Trinity Hospice Shop
19 Designer Bargains

6. WANDSWORTH & PUTNEY

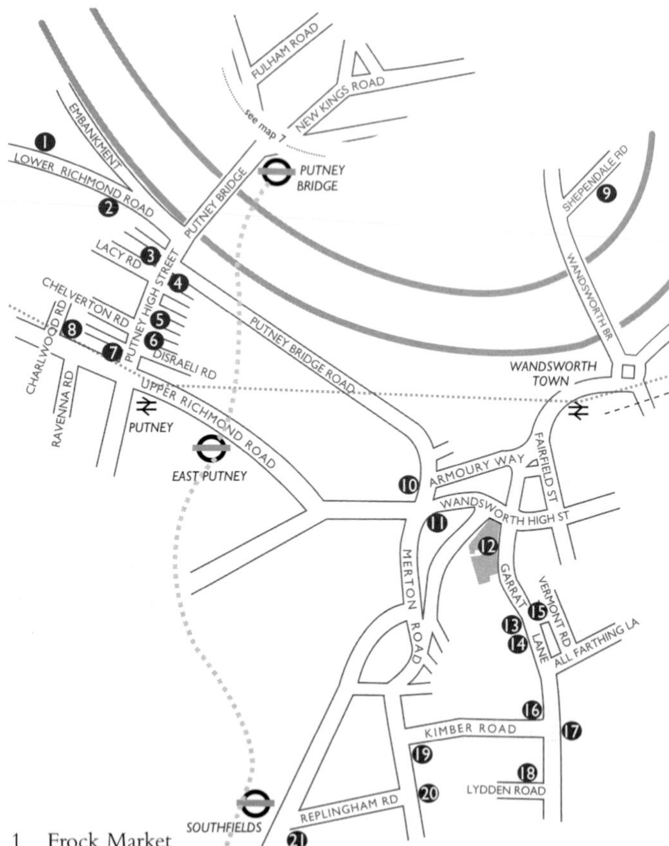

1 Frock Market
2 Butterfly Dress Agency
3 Putney Flight Centre
4 British Heart Foundation
5 Cancer Research UK
6 Oxfam
7 Trinity Hospice
8 Notting Hill Housing Trust
9 The Curtain Exchange
10 The Carpetman
11 Salvation Army
12 Shoe Zone
13 IC Companys
14 Tile Superstore
15 General Auctions
16 A. Gatto & Son
17 331
18 Lloyds International Auction
19 Villeroy and Boch
20 Chomette
21 Oxfam

7. FULHAM

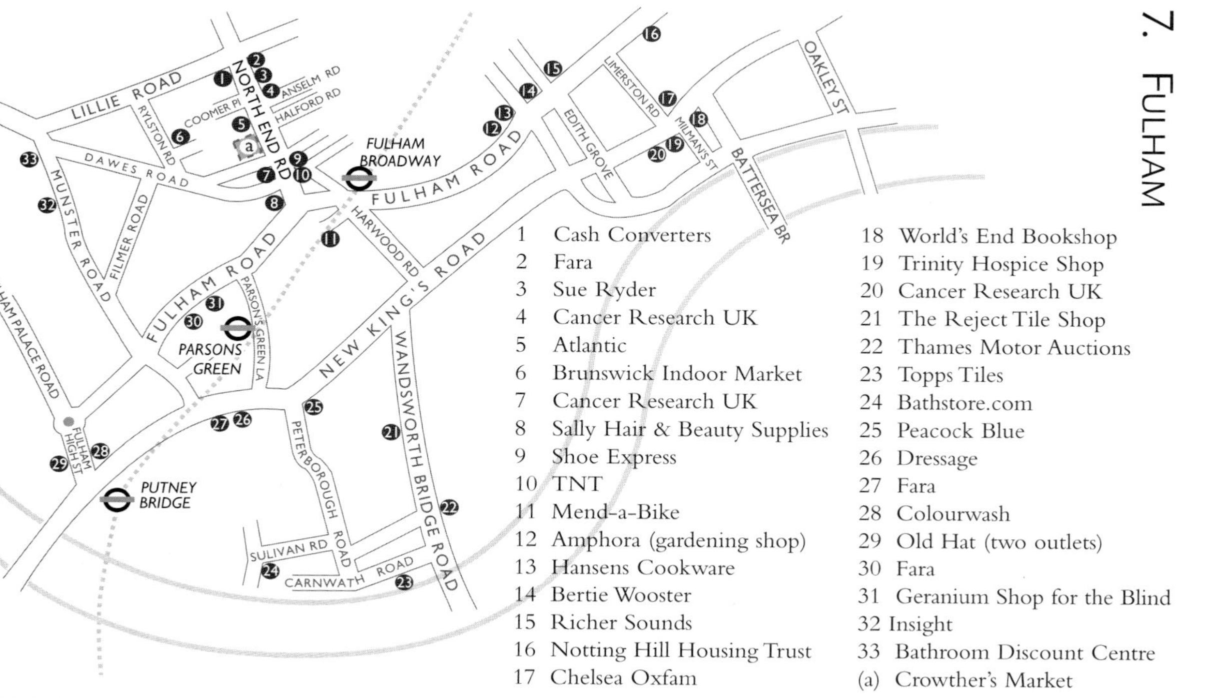

1 Cash Converters
2 Fara
3 Sue Ryder
4 Cancer Research UK
5 Atlantic
6 Brunswick Indoor Market
7 Cancer Research UK
8 Sally Hair & Beauty Supplies
9 Shoe Express
10 TNT
11 Mend-a-Bike
12 Amphora (gardening shop)
13 Hansens Cookware
14 Bertie Wooster
15 Richer Sounds
16 Notting Hill Housing Trust
17 Chelsea Oxfam
18 World's End Bookshop
19 Trinity Hospice Shop
20 Cancer Research UK
21 The Reject Tile Shop
22 Thames Motor Auctions
23 Topps Tiles
24 Bathstore.com
25 Peacock Blue
26 Dressage
27 Fara
28 Colourwash
29 Old Hat (two outlets)
30 Fara
31 Geranium Shop for the Blind
32 Insight
33 Bathroom Discount Centre
(a) Crowther's Market

8. FINCHLEY ROAD

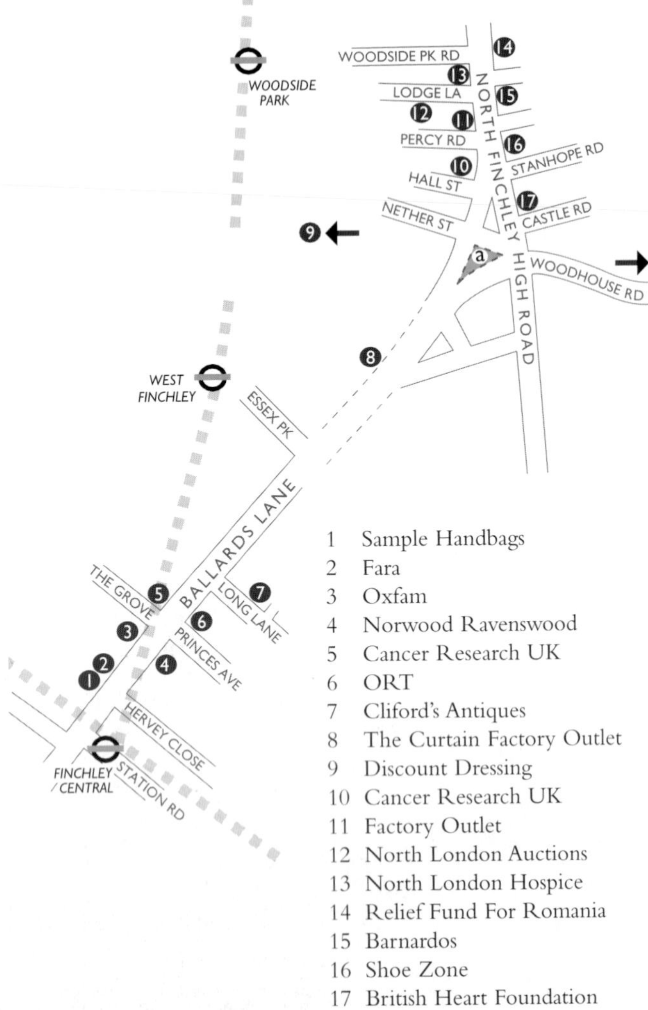

1 Sample Handbags
2 Fara
3 Oxfam
4 Norwood Ravenswood
5 Cancer Research UK
6 ORT
7 Cliford's Antiques
8 The Curtain Factory Outlet
9 Discount Dressing
10 Cancer Research UK
11 Factory Outlet
12 North London Auctions
13 North London Hospice
14 Relief Fund For Romania
15 Barnardos
16 Shoe Zone
17 British Heart Foundation
18 Carpet Tile Centre
(a) Finchley Market Fri-Sat 9am-4pm

9. GOLDERS GREEN

1 All Aboard
2 Cancer Research UK
3 The Flight Centre
4 Sally
5 Next To Choice
6 Le Pop 2
7 Norwood Ravenswood no.87
8 Norwood Ravenswood no.84
9 Jami
10 Golds Factory Outlet
11 All Aboard
12 Blooms
13 Oxfam
14 All Aboard
15 Top Value Drug Store
16 Jo Jo Maman Bébé

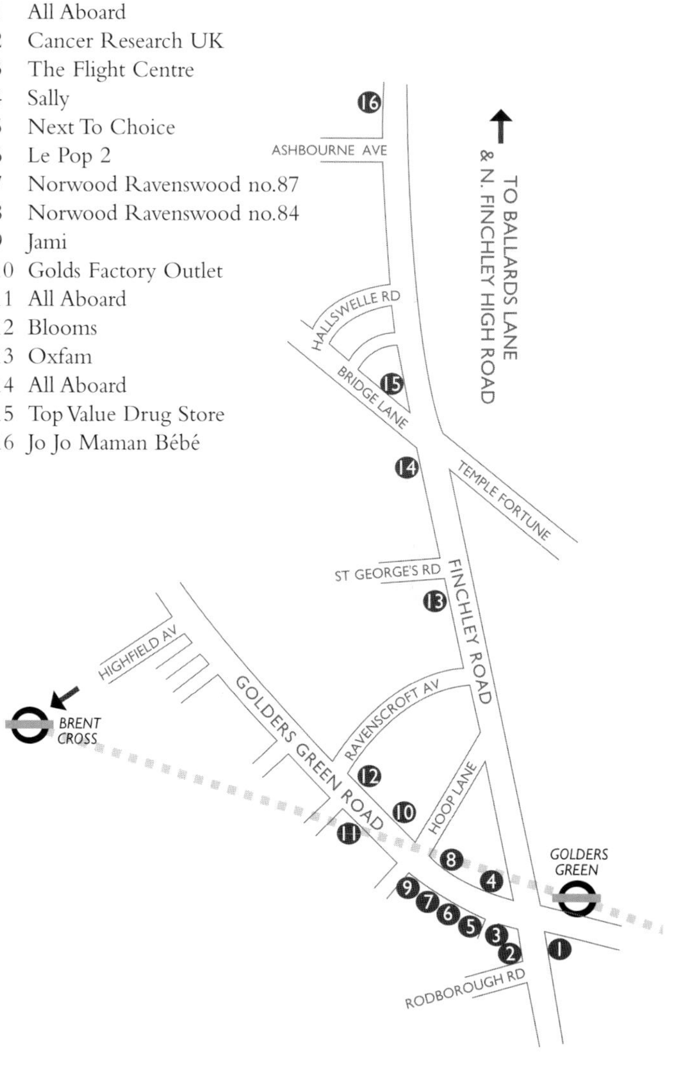

10. KILBURN

1 Traid
2 Benny Dee
3 Scope
4 Oxfam
5 Atlantic Clothing
6 Pdsa
7 Cancer Research UK
8 Relief Fund for Romania
9 M. P. Moran
10 Cash Xchange
11 Taurus Pine
12 Computer Repair Centre
13 Pandoras Box
14 TV4U
15 Bosnia Herzegovina Community Charity Shop
16 D. A. Thomson
17 Emporium Gallery
18 The Community Charity Shop
19 JBTV
20 Capital Appliances
21 Scope
22 All Aboard
23 Cancer Research UK
24 Oxfam
(a) Kilburn Market

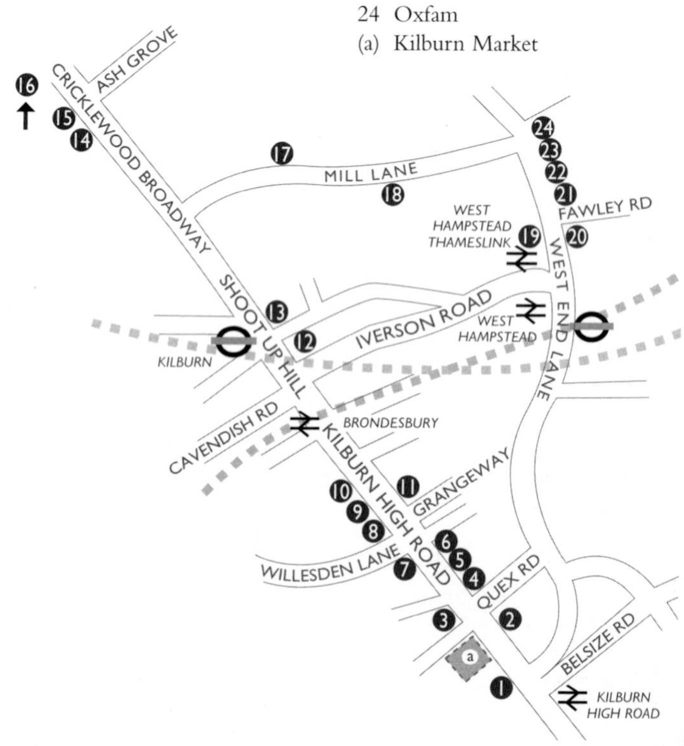

11. Brick Lane

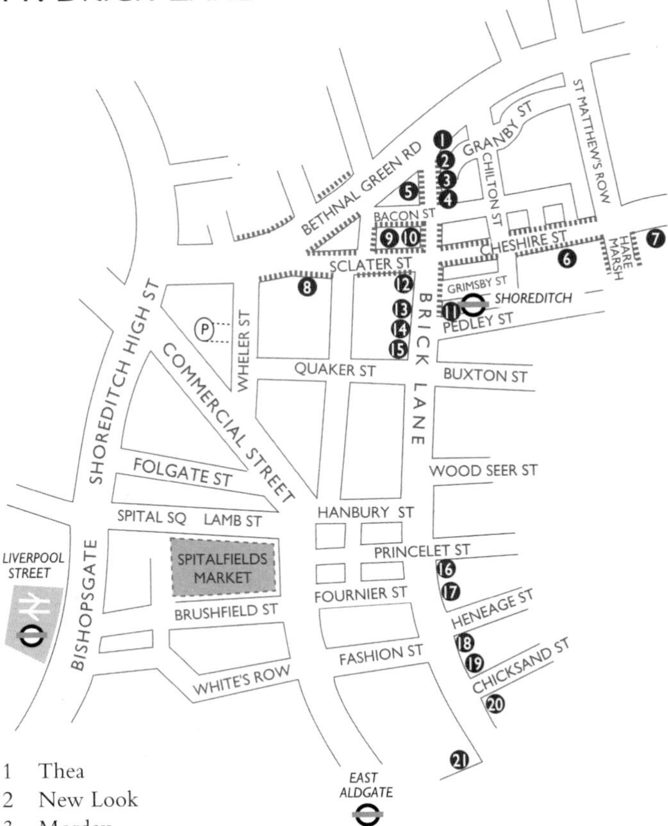

1 Thea
2 New Look
3 Mordex
4 Muslim Care Charity Shop
5 Truth Trading
6 Performance
7 Beyond Retro
8 Dublin Jim
9 Kitchen Warehouse
10 Bacon Street Junk Shop
11 Evil Cathedral
12 Junk Shop
13 Rokit
14 Laden Showroon
15 Rokit
16 Bhopal Fabrics
17 Ideal Fashions
18 Epra Fabrics
19 Empee Silk and Fabrics
20 Z. Butt Textiles
21 KVJ
III Sunday Market

INDEX

C

D

T

U

V

W

X

Y

1, 2, 3, ...

SUBJECT INDEX

Kids' Clothing & Equipment p.136-41

Kitchenware & Cutlery p.132-35

Leatherware

Office Furniture

Photography p.163-70

Picture Frames

The London Theatre Guide
Author: Richard Andrews
£7.99,ISBN 1 902910 08 7

Museums & Galleries of London
Author: Abigail Willis
£8.99, ISBN 1-9029-10-079

Book Lovers' London
Author: Lesley Reader
£8.99, ISBN: 1 902910 13 3

Food Lovers' London
Author: Jenny Linford
£7.99, ISBN 1-902910-12-5

English Experiences
Author: Susan Briggs
£6.99, ISBN 1-902910-16-8

Gay & Lesbian London
Author: Graham Parker
£7.99, ISBN 1-902910-09-5

London Market Guide
Author: Andrew Kershman
£6.99, ISBN:1-902910-14-1

If you would like to order any of these titles please send your order along with a cheque made payable to **Metro Publications** to the address below:

Metro Publications
PO Box 6336, London N1 6PY
E-mail: metro@dircon.co.uk
www.metropublications.com

Alternatively you can order our titles via our customer order line:
Tel: 020 8533 0922 (Visa/Mastercard/Switch)
Open: Mon-Fri 9am-6pm